Thinking And Talking

Collected Philosophical Essays

by

Giorgio Baruchello, PhD

NORTHWEST
PASSAGE
Books

Gatineau, Quebec, Canada

Thinking And Talking

Collected Philosophical Essays

by Giorgio Baruchello, PhD

Copyright © 2019 by Giorgio Baruchello. All rights reserved.

ISBN: 978-1-9991146-0-2

Published by
Northwest Passage Books
Gatineau, Quebec, Canada

To Severino Domenico Dolente and all my teachers

Contents

Preface vi
Acknowledgments vii
Introduction... ix
Original publication credits xii

PART I – Talking Knowledge 1

Chapter 1: The Disappearance of Buttons: A Philosopher's Look at Ergonomics 2
Chapter 2: The Socratic Method 4
Chapter 3: Reflections on Sergi Avaliani's Philosophical Investigations 14
Chapter 4: Reflections on Ian Hacking and the Science Wars....56
Chapter 5: Reflections on David Lewis' Australian Materialism 66
Chapter 6: A Phenomenological Reading of Donald Davidson's Philosophy 79

PART II – Thinking Rhetoric 101

Chapter 7: Reflections on Deleuze's Humour......................... 102
Chapter 8: Reflections on Gadamer's Hermeneutics and Vico's Thought 140
Chapter 9: Reflections on Pareto's Rhetoric 155
Chapter 10: Reflections on Moral Philosophy in Pascal's Thoughts 183
Chapter 11: Reflections on Richard Rorty's Hortative "We"....196
Chapter 12: Gestalt Psychology and the Tropes of Rhetoric 218

PART III – Talking Rhetoric 256

Chapter 13: Heideggerian Aphorisms 257
Chapter 14: What Is Value? A Meditation on Inflation and the Meaning of Life... 260
Chapter 15: A Letter from Iceland 262
Chapter 16: Explaining Life-value Onto-axiology to a Child...267
Chapter 17: On Modernism... 270

Chapter 18: On Catholicism, Abortion, and Social Democracy:
Lessons from Iceland 276
Chapter 19: The Inequality of Political Correctness 281

Endnotes **291**

Preface

Some choices are a matter of duty. Other choices are a matter of preference. Sometimes, the two kinds of choice intersect each other. The process, typically, is complicated. The result, more often than not, rewarding. Many years ago, I was a doctoral student in the ancient discipline of philosophy, which was back then and still is today my calling, in the most personal sense of the term. Given the prevailing research interests among my teachers, I was expected to investigate and, if possible, publish scholarly articles on matters concerning the nature of knowledge, being, thought, and human discourse. In the stately parlance of academia, I had to write about epistemology, ontology, philosophy of mind and philosophy of language. However, since their earliest inception, my own philosophical interests had been spurred by questions and issues of a different ilk, such as the meaning of life, the proper conduct for individual behaviour, the requirements of a just society and, above all, the nature and ultimate justification of goodness. Existentialism, ethics, politics, and value theory were my true cup of philosophical tea and, as my previous four volumes of collected essays for Northwest Passage Books demonstrate, they have remained such a peculiar cup throughout my career.

Having to try other cups of philosophical tea proved beneficial, though. First of all, I familiarised myself with thinkers and problems that I would have otherwise largely ignored. Secondly, I discovered an entire field of intellectual inquiry that was going to become significant both in my research and in my teaching, namely rhetoric. Thirdly, the standard prose in Anglophone epistemology, ontology and associated study areas is extraordinarily dry, mandatorily impersonal, economically concise, and it demands great precision, to the point of scholastic hair-splitting and logical explicitness akin to mathematical demonstration. By necessitating all this, such a prose trains the intellect into a severe self-imposed discipline and forces it to become as acute as it can, while exemplifying at the same time the sort of writing that any sensible person should avoid, if she wishes to instruct, enthral and/or gratify her readers. Technical jargon may serve as a convenient shorthand for the practitioners of a specific academic discipline, but it is not necessary in order to communicate and grasp its key-concepts. In his classic 1967 book, *The New Industrial State*, "Ken" Galbraith (1908–2006) stated: "there are few, if any, useful ideas in economics that cannot be expressed in clear English." I believe the same point to be true of philosophy too.

Acknowledgments

While thanking once more Dr Brendan Myers, chief consultant at Northwest Passage Books, for his professional esteem and his personal encouragement, I hereby assure him—and the reader of the following pages—that I did my best to follow Galbraith's advice and make the more technical essays republished in this collection less rhetorically challenged, and less rhetorically challenging, than they were in the original version. The outcomes are likely to vary, since the starting points did vary considerably to begin with, but a consistent effort was made in order to achieve a measure of technical simplification and to secure a mutually reinforcing internal organisation of the book's three parts and nineteen chapters.

I wish to extend a fond, grateful and mournful thought to the late leading member of the Georgian Institute of Philosophy, Prof Sergi Avaliani (1928–2016), with whom, over many blessed years, I had the honour of exchanging views and notes on a number of philosophical subjects. These exchanges led to the publication of a handful of works on epistemology, ontology and social thought that reappear in this volume, though creatively recombined into one chapter, whose main aim is to recall the free flow, the eclecticism and the broad strokes colouring the dialogues between Prof Avaliani and myself.

In addition, I express my warmest thanks to Dr Ralph Weber of the University of Basel, Switzerland, with whom I collaborated on a project about rhetoric that is itself reissued in this book, yet duly modified and seized by first-person personal pronoun. The Rector and senior management of the University of Akureyri should be thanked too, since they granted me a teaching discount in the Fall Term 2018, so as to let me complete the present book. My gratitude goes then to those editors and publishers who allowed me to reutilise in this volume my older articles, book chapters, memoirs, notes and other works: full bibliographic references are supplied in a dedicated section.

Equally, I must acknowledge all those readers who provided me with feedback on my previous four volumes for Northwest Passage Books, commendatory as well as critical, and always constructive. Their genuine interest in my work gave me the mental strength and the moral conviction that were needed in order to prepare one more volume of collected essays—indeed one calling for considerable revision of a good few of the original texts, which were sometimes painfully patchy, outdated, imprecise, or otherwise unsatisfactory in the eyes of today's more experienced me. Misspellings and formal imprecisions were therefore corrected, references amended and integrated, and odd turns of phrase—as far as possible—adjusted. Despite being truly tempted to rewrite entirely some of my older works, I decided not to do so, because such a dramatic change would have made this book no longer a collection of essays, but a totally new project altogether. In any case, a modicum of improvement should have taken place, at least linguistically.

Conceptually, I must simply and humbly accept the fact that some earlier works of mine were marred by the then-larger inadequacies of my intellect, my previous lack of professional experience, the lesser technical knowledge of my long-gone youth, my immature blunt arrogance, and whatever additional source of imperfection any honest thinking person should acknowledge whenever assessing her past actions in light of the wisdom developed long after their execution. Among the mixed blessings of maturity is also the one whereby a person becomes presently more competent, only to spot with greater ease the many tokens of her previous incompetence.

Introduction

Given the variety of original sources and the technical character of some of them, the present fifth volume of collected essays of mine called for much rewriting, rearranging and reconsidering. It opens with a first part ("Talking Knowledge") on human thinking, its nurturing through linguistic interaction, and its ability to grasp reality for what it is in order to engage with it, whether successfully or not. In this first part, the chapters are organised along a scale of growing complexity, starting with some extremely brief reflections on the science of functional design (or "ergonomics"; chapter 1) and Socratic dialogue (chapter 2), then stepping into a much broader set of thoughts about ontology and scientific realism (chapter 3), which is articulated further in connection with the work of three major contemporary Anglophone philosophers, namely Ian Hacking (b. 1936; chapter 4), David Lewis (1941–2001; chapter 5) and Donald Davidson (1917–2003; chapter 6).

The second part of the book ("Thinking Rhetoric") explores to different degrees the so-called "art of speaking well" in conjunction with a variety of specific topics and well-known thinkers, such as humour in the philosophy of Gilles Deleuze (1925–1995; chapter 7), common sense in Hans-Georg Gadamer's hermeneutics (1900–2002; chapter 8), correct reasoning in the sociology of Vilfredo Pareto (1848–1923; chapter 9), morality in the religious thought of Blaise Pascal (1623–1662; chapter 10), emancipation in the politics of Richard Rorty (1931–2007; chapter 11), and the general principles of cognition in the psychology of the *Gestalt* school (chapter 12).

A shorter third part ("Talking Rhetoric") concludes the book and delivers few brief tokens of rhetoric in action: existential aphorisms inspired by the philosophy of Martin Heidegger (1889–1976; chapter 13); economic musings on inflation and life's ultimate meaning (chapter 14); a concise history of philosophy in Iceland (chapter 15); the key-tenets of life-value onto-axiology presented to a child (chapter 16); a succinct account of the Catholic doctrine on modernism (chapter 17); and two religious controversies, one dealing with abortion (chapter 18) and another with male privilege (chapter 19). Albeit extremely different from one another, all these shorter works of mine were penned with the aim of edifying, engaging or entertaining the reader, to an extent that is uncommon and/or unneeded in regular academic writing. In this sense are they tokens of rhetoric in action.

In particular, the last two texts were written by me alone for a book about religion co-authored with Prof Garrett Barden. Eventually, Prof Barden and I decided to keep them out of our book because of their freer style and character, which is less theoretical and more inflammatory than the essays included in it. Indeed, the controversy about abortion proved excellent conference material and ended up being published in the proceedings of a recent meeting of the research group of the Nordic Summer University dealing with human rights. Overall, however, both concluding texts resemble the tongue-in-cheek literary-philosophical sketches with which I closed my fourth volume for Northwest Passage Books (i.e. chapter 10). The brief account of modernism that precedes them, itself a short piece about religion, is instead part of a much larger essay prepared for, and discussed at, a 2016 conference held in Sandbjerg, Denmark, organised by Dr Gorm Harste.

Albeit focussing upon religion and devoid of fastidious technicalities, these concluding three essays contain key remarks on the different modes of experience available to us and, relatedly, on the diverse forms of knowledge that we can muster as thinking human beings. As such, the last three chapters establish an ideal connection with the first part of the present book and wish to offer a closure of sorts. Moreover, by discussing also diverse forms of cruelty that can affect our lives and be lethal or horribly life-disabling, these concluding three essays reconnect with the themes that were explored in the previous four volumes of mine for Northwest Passage Books: death, cruelty, and life-value. The closure that they allow for, then, embraces the whole book series.

Broad, eclectic, if not even rhapsodic in its content, the present book shows implicitly that philosophy is an immense field of possible rational inquiries, which can accommodate different personal interests and diverse intellectual temperaments, and that *a fortiori* the sharp divisions between professional factions that are so perplexingly commonplace in contemporary academia—notably the one splitting so-called "analytic" philosophers from "Continental" ones—are also something that I do not intend to contribute to. Philosophy is one; still, *ex uno plures*.

Philosophy is so rich and assorted a discipline that it can embrace an almost endless set of constellations, which actually shine above and upon all kinds of intellectual pursuits, across and beyond the humanities or the social sciences alone. What truly matters is that such stars should enlighten us and show us viable, fruitful paths of thought and action in the many dark corners and grey areas of human life; not that some sun should be deemed brighter than another, higher, purer, or more pristine. Factionalism, turf wars and obsessing about disciplinary divisions and pecking orders do not help. If anything, they add to the dark corners and grey areas of our existence; to all that is morally shady, spiritually petty and intellectually opaque.

With any luck, whatever dubious or doubtful element the reader may find in this book can be ascribed to the far more prosaic capacity of its author for plain error and imprecision. Perfection, despite prolonged striving, continues to escape me. Imperfection, despite prolonged familiarity, continues to outfox me. As to my awareness of not being alone in this sorry condition, it is actually a source of further worry, not of consolation.

Original publication credits

As done already in three previous volumes of mine for Northwest Passage Books, all the bibliographic information included in the book is comprised in the endnotes; there is no separate bibliography.¹ Original publication dates, authors' full first names and edition numbers are stated when available or relevant. Translators' names were omitted. Equally, as done throughout the book series, no analytical indices are included. Cited thinkers' deaths of birth and death, when known, were kept and inserted as of the introductory sections, while bracketed translations of foreign phrases were dropped. This economy of information allows the present book to be much slenderer than it would otherwise be, considering in particular its target audience, which is not the same as the one of the original texts. Readers looking for a bulkier, more detailed bibliographic apparatus can refer to the original published texts, which are listed below. Again, the term "essay" is used very broadly in this volume and applies to a plethora of types of publications, which differ enormously in length, nature, aims and tone; "papers" could have been used as well, with the same ecumenical flexibility. Whenever the chapter titles of the present book differ significantly from those of the original texts, the difference signposts intentionally that substantial redrafting occurred (e.g. deleted sections, renamed and rearranged paragraphs, conspicuous bibliographic amendments, etc.). As done in my previous volumes for Northwest Passage Books, I use the female pronouns "she" and "her" to refer to the human person in general.

PART I – Talking Knowledge

Chapter 1
The Disappearance of Buttons: A Philosopher's Look at Ergonomics, *Wrong*, 1(2), 2006, 13–14.

Chapter 2
The Socratic Method and the Peculiarities of Dialogue, Opening Address at the conference "Qualitative Research", University of Akureyri, Iceland, 24th November 2005.

Chapter 3
Vertical and Horizontal Ontology, *Philosophical Investigations*, VI ("Scientific Debates"), 2002, 389–401; Scepticism, Science and Social Science, *Philosophical Investigations*, XI ("Gnoseology"), 2007, 35–45; Citizenship: A Practical Notion, *Philosophical Investigations*, V ("Social Philosophy"), 2001, 62–74; and On Globalisation, *Philosophical Investigations*, VII ("Social philosophy"), 2003, 83–94.

Chapter 4
Nominalism and Antirepresentationalism in Hacking's *Social Construction of What?*, *Appraisal*, 3(4), 2001, 151–156; and a review essay of Ian Hacking's *The Social Construction of What? Symposium*, 5(1), 2001, 103–114.

Chapter 5
Assessing Lewis' Materialism, *Sic et Non – Forum for Philosophy and Culture*, 6, 2002, <http://archiv.sicetnon.org/artikel/historie/materialism.htm>.

Chapter 6
Bridging Between Mind and Language. A Phenomenological Reading of Davidson's Philosophy, *Philosophical Investigations*, IX ("Phenomenology"), 2005, 317–338.

PART II – Thinking Rhetoric

Chapter 7
Deleuze's Humor, *Existentia. An International Journal of Philosophy*, 12(3–4), 2002, 445–70.

Chapter 8
Pietist Prejudice in Gadamer's Reading of Vico, *Filosofia Oggi*, 26(3) ("Note critiche sulla filosofia contemporanea"), 2003, 291–306; and Vico, in J. Baggini and J. Stangroom (eds.), *Great Philosophers A–Z*, London: Continuum, 2004, 242–244.

Chapter 9
Pareto's Rhetoric, in J. Femia and A.J. Marshall (eds.), *Beyond Disciplinary Boundaries: Essays on Pareto*, London: Ashgate, 2012, 153–176.

Chapter 10
What is Morality? Pascal's Heartfelt Answer, *Nordicum-Mediterraneum*, 9(2), 2014, <https://skemman.is/handle/1946/18402> (proceedings from the colloquium "What is Morality?", in honour of Mikael M. Karlsson, University of Akureyri, Iceland, 19th April 2013).

Chapter 11
Who are "We"? An essay on Rorty, Rhetoric and Politics (with Dr Ralph Weber), *The European Legacy*, 19(2), 2014, 197–214.

Chapter 12
A Classification of Classics: *Gestalt* Psychology and the Tropes of Rhetoric, *New Ideas in Psychology*, 36, 2015, 10–24.

PART III – Talking Rhetoric

Chapter 13
Heideggerian Aphorisms, *Existentia. An International Journal of Philosophy*, 26(5–6), 2006, 471–472.

Chapter 14
A Meditation on Inflation and the Meaning of Life, *Existentia. An International Journal of Philosophy*, 28(3–4), 2008, 315–316.

Chapter 15
A Letter from... Iceland, *The Philosophers' Magazine*, 4, 2009, 43–46.

Chapter 16
Required Reading, *Our Schools / Our Selves*, 23(1), 2013, 30–32.

Chapter 17
Economic Rights from a Catholic Perspective, text prepared for, and discussed at, the conference "Constitutionalising Europe: After the Christian Heritages", Sandbjerg Manor, Denmark, 9th and 10th December 2016.

Chapter 18
Religious Belief, Human Rights, and Social Democracy: Catholic Reflections on Abortion in Iceland, *Nordicum-Mediterraneum*, 13(2), 2018, <https://nome.unak.is/wordpress/volume-13-no-2-2018/conference-proceeding-volume-13-no-2-2018/religious-belief-human-rights-and-social-democracy-catholic-reflections-on-abortion-in-iceland/> (originally an essay prepared by me for, but not included in, the book *Why Believe? Approaches to Religion*, written with Garrett Barden, Reykjavík: University of Akureyri Press, 2018).

Chapter 19
On Religion, Marxism, and Male Privilege (originally an essay prepared by me for, but not included in, the book *Why Believe? Approaches to Religion*, written with Garrett Barden, Reykjavík: University of Akureyri Press, 2018).

PART I – Talking Knowledge

Chapter 1: The Disappearance of Buttons: A Philosopher's Look at Ergonomics

In the 18th century, the Neapolitan philosopher and rhetorician Giambattista Vico (1668–1744) defined "common sense" as "the public ground of truth" whereby any given cultural community can "form judgments about needs and utilities".[2] Vico believed that all the adult members of such communities possess an almost immediate ability to judge aptly upon ends that are of fundamental importance to the community's members and to choose consistently the means appropriate to those ends. Whether he walked amongst the seamen of Capri or the farmers of Salento, Vico could observe numerous and most articulate ways of coping successfully with life's difficulties, which parents had received from their own parents and passed confidently onto their children without, literally, second thoughts.

In the 20th century, the cognitive scientist Donald A. "Don" Norman (b. 1935) devoted an entire book to the psychopathology of ordinary objects, for it appears that Vico's "common sense" is actually so scarce, that even objects as simple as doors, mugs and restaurant menus can prove frustratingly resilient to the user's attempts to handle them well.[3] Perhaps, the designers of tools and their users do not always belong to the same cultural community.

Another explanation for this apparent lack of "common sense" can be found in the ethological research of Konrad Lorenz (1903–1989). According to him, modern society is unique in the rapidity of its changes, to the point that no "common sense" is possible as such, for the knowledge required of its members is too volatile to survive for long periods of time and sediment into traditions or habits that may last across generations.[4] In the 1990s, for example, the expression "digital divide" became very popular in the Anglophone world. It indicated the cognitive gulf between those who could use the then-booming computer technologies and those who could not. This divide was economic, racial, occupational and, as Lorenz's studies predicted, generational. Younger people could do things with ease that older people could not even fathom to begin to understand.

However, the digital divide worked in reverse too. Younger people, who had been exposed and accustomed to computer technologies, could not do many of the things that their parents and grandparents regarded as banal. The need for learning how to typewrite, play an LP or adjust a pendulum had vanished and, together with that need, the ability to perform those actions had vanished as well. The vanishing of the ability to do certain things took away also other underlying abilities—a phenomenon that is most relevant to ergonomics i.e. the study of functional design.

Today's children, for example, are often incapable of perceiving thick, protruding, mechanical push buttons as buttons. It is not a matter of not knowing what a button is or how a button operates: they are perfectly at ease with flat, soft-touch buttons. Rather, when confronted with the former type of buttons, they are incapable of interpreting successfully the information available in the world—this, despite the mechanical buttons' endowment with feedback potential and visibility.

Experts in ergonomics expect well-designed objects—objects possessing so-called "affordance"—to have feedback potential and visibility. Old-fashioned mechanical buttons possess both features, perhaps even to a greater degree than later, flat, soft-touch buttons. Still, children cannot 'see' them. Most likely, the children's functional blindness reveals the fundamental role played by cultural factors in determining an object's "affordance" and, to a deeper level, the truth of Immanuel Kant's (1724–1804) aptly named "Copernican Revolution": it is the human being that, through the application of her conceptual apparatus, constitutes the world of experience, whose potential stimuli upon the same being can go otherwise unheeded.

Chapter 2: The Socratic Method

As a philosopher working among non-philosophers, I am often asked: "what is philosophy, exactly?". As a philosopher working as a philosopher, I have more than just one answer to this question. This polyvalence is something that, not unfrequently, puzzles my colleagues, especially those working in the hard sciences. Let us look at a few possible descriptions of philosophy, then.

Philosophy is police work. As logicians and well-meaning rhetoricians, for instance, we determine whether an argument is valid or not. Hence, we can tell you that when George W. Bush (b. 1946) stated on the 6th of November 2001, "either you are with us or you are against us", he was committing a logical fallacy, called "false dichotomy".

Philosophy is missionary work. As ethicists and axiologists, we argue on what the good may be like and, if we are confident enough in our results, we even tell people that they ought to be good—just like my mother used to do with me when I was young. Immanuel Kant, for example, in the late 18th century, tried to convince us never to use oneself or another merely as a means to an end, no matter how noble or desirable the end may be.

Philosophy is archaeological work. As intellectual historians and trained readers of foreign, sometimes dead languages, we dig and polish up old notions from the sediment of past cultural ages. This brief chapter is just an instance of it, as I am going to excavate out of ancient history the origins of the Socratic dialogue *qua* method, i.e. as a conscious tool for intellectual inquiry—and then look at some of its peculiarities. This topic was chosen because Socratic dialogue represents the first known intended method in the history of Western intellectual inquiry.

On Dialogue

The etymology of the term "dialogue" is of Greek origin and can be rendered in English as "through [*dia*-] the use of words [*logos*]".

As such, dialogue has existed for as long as the human being has been able to communicate by symbolic language. Language is symbolic because words and sentences stand for other things, i.e. they symbolise them. As symbols, words and sentences have to be interpreted, so as to be used and understood. Interpretations may differ and, consequently, there arise competing claims to what a word or a sentence may actually stand for or, in other terms, to what their actual meaning may be. Engaging in dialogue is a way in which one can clarify the meaning of words and sentences, thus facilitating their interpretation and making sense of how this interpreting is or should be performed (i.e. the province of so-called "hermeneutics").

Incidentally, allow me to specify that we should probably talk of sentences alone, for words can have meaning only within, or in relation to, sentences. Symbols never stand in the void: they are always surrounded by a web of other symbols conferring meaning to it by means of interpretation. Interpretation is no easy business either. For instance, I once asked my wife if it was fine with her that I went to the pub with a friend of mine. She answered: "do as you please". I was not sure if her reply symbolised permission or prohibition; hence I asked her: "will *you* be pleased if I go?" Her answer to that second question revealed that her first answer symbolised ground for divorce.

On Socrates

Dialogue as a conscious method for intellectual inquiry has existed at least since the 5th century BC, i.e. since Socrates (470–399 BC) made use of it for philosophical ends. That is why we often speak of the "Dialogical Method" as the "Socratic Method".

The philosophical end that Socrates had in mind was to determine whether the people who claimed to possess knowledge did in fact possess it. Politicians claimed to know what the common good was; priests claimed to know what virtue was; businessmen claimed to know what success was; lawyers claimed to know what justice was; artists claimed to know what beauty was. Did they really know what they said they knew?

Socrates was after the truth concerning their claims of knowledge. Socrates, whom the Oracle of Delphi had declared to be the wisest of men, started to *verify* their knowledge, i.e. to determine whether it was true or not. Thus, Socrates started inquiring politicians, priests, businessmen, lawyers and artists about their special competences. He started asking questions that have become the typical philosophical questions: 'What is the common good'? 'What is virtue?' 'What is success?' 'What is justice?' As aptly put by Canadian philosopher Christopher DiCarlo, Socrates became a major "pain in the ass".[5]

As rude as it may sound, DiCarlo's definition strikes the right note: Socrates was perceived as a dangerous troublemaker; moreover, he did portray himself as a gadfly buzzing around a lazy horse, i.e. Athens' citizenry.[6] As a result of this line of inquiry, Socrates was eventually condemned by a jury of fellow Athenians to drink the hemlock, whose flavour I do not personally know, but whose properties I am aware of. He died.

Dialogue as a method can bear unpleasant outcomes. But it can also do the opposite. Inspired by the martyrdom of Socrates, possibly the first champion of free speech and the pursuit of truth, Christopher DiCarlo even wrote a book about it. It is entitled *How to Become a Really Good Pain in the Ass*. So, if you need any help in becoming one, you know what book to read.

On Method

Professional dangers aside, let us look more closely at the Socratic Method: how did it work?

We know that Socrates went around Athens asking questions; but that is not enough. Questions can be uttered randomly. Socrates did not do it. There was a pattern, an organisation, a structure in the way Socrates asked questions. That is why we talk of his dialogues, reported to us by his pupil Plato (424–347 BC), as examples of a method.

The Socratic Method comprises two chief aspects. First of all, there is a negative aspect, or *pars destruens*, called "elenchos" or "irony". Then, there is a positive aspect, or *pars construens*, called "*maieutics*" or "obstetrics". The two aspects are often used together, but for the sake of explanation I look at them as two distinct, chronologically organised parts.

Irony, the first part, is negative, for the questions asked are aimed at eliminating those beliefs that are not supported by adequate reasons. For instance, Socrates would test the lawyer's belief about justice. He would ask the lawyer "what is justice?" and, in this manner, force the lawyer to produce a definition of "justice"— something like "justice is to punish irresponsible behaviour and reward responsible behaviour". Now, once you have a definition of a term, you have a hypothesis concerning how to interpret that term— and, correspondingly, the world itself, i.e. the world as described by that term. By means of irony, Socrates specialised in asking questions that could invalidate hypotheses and lead the interlocutor to reconsider the initial definition. In fact, hypotheses can be valid or invalid, depending on whether they are backed by more basic beliefs that must be consistent with the ones that they are intended to justify.

On Invalidation

Fundamentally, there are two ways in which Socrates or, for that matter, anyone else, can invalidate a hypothesis. First of all, you can determine whether the hypothesis is consistent with other important beliefs that are held by the person that is being interrogated—or by anyone who would be accepted as a sane member of that person's community. For instance, let's say that by asking more questions, Socrates discovers that our lawyer believes not only that "justice" means "punishing irresponsible behaviour and rewarding responsible behaviour", but also that "human behaviour is determined by one's own character and social circumstances". In that case, our lawyer believes that people are not responsible for their actions, which contradicts his or her initial definition of justice, insofar as that definition implies that people are responsible for their actions, and their misdeeds in particular.

Secondly, you can determine whether the hypothesis at issue leads to paradoxical consequences, which the questioned person or the person's social peers would never seriously endorse. For instance, let us say that, by asking more questions, Socrates leads our lawyer to state that "justice" means as well that "we should incarcerate irresponsible people and give a medal to responsible people". That is what the interrogated person believes "punishing" and "rewarding" to be like. Would then that mean also that we should incarcerate 10-year-old Páll, who stole five candies, and give a medal to 9-year-old Ásta, who told the nanny? Unless the person interrogated is some kind of fanatic, it is likely that nobody among us would be so harsh with Páll and so commending of Ásta. For most of us, to reproach verbally Páll would be sufficient as a punishment and probably no one would like to educate children to act as informants and spies, except perhaps for some nostalgic admirers of Joseph Stalin (1878–1953). In short, the definition at issue seems to need correction. Something must be modified in order to avoid paradoxical consequences.

On God

Gilles Deleuze, one of the greatest French philosophers of the 20th century and a most innovative psychotherapist, described beautifully the two ways in which Socrates, or any of us, can reveal the invalidity of a hypothesis as "the way of Job" and "the way of Abraham".[7]

The way of Job is the way of questioning God directly, so as to force Him to change His mind. Like Job questioned God from the pit of utter misery that He had forced Job into, so does Socrates retrieve another belief of the questioned person that can be used to question the belief of the same person that is being investigated. Logical consistency is used here to challenge a belief with another belief held at the same level of importance—consistency, in other words, destructs. We are used to thinking of consistency as a constructive virtue of intelligent discourse and reliable theory. That much is true; but consistency can be equally a powerful weapon of destruction.

The way of Abraham is the way of following God's command to the point of making God ashamed of Himself. Like Abraham showed willingness to follow God's command and sacrifice to God his own and only son Isaac, committing *ipso facto* an outrageous sin which God could not allow, so does Socrates unpack all sorts of unseen and embarrassing implications from the investigated belief, to the point of making that belief untenable. Consistency is used here to challenge a belief with its ridiculous or abhorring outcomes—consistency, in other words, self-destructs.

On Birthing

Let us now move to the second part of the Socratic Method: *maieutics* or obstetrics. This second part is positive. It is positive because, by challenging old beliefs, it can produce new definitions and new hypotheses, of which the holder was either unaware or only tacitly aware. As soon as Socrates starts asking questions about what virtue or justice may be like, he starts helping the questioned person to come forth with new ideas, which were kept, until then, inside her head, hidden from sight. By discovering what lies behind our beliefs and by forcing people to think about them and, if necessary, modify them, dialogue can often bring to life new knowledge and new understanding. In this process, Socrates is the midwife; his interlocutor, instead, the mother.

When the Brazilian educational theorist Paulo Freire (1921–1997) characterised his Liberation Pedagogy as dialogical, he was referring to this life-enhancing ability of dialogue. Dialogue creates new spaces of thought, hence of possible action, hence of possible life. Dialogue can generate new thoughts and new thoughts, in turn, can open perspectives on the world that were previously unavailable. New perspectives on the world mean several new worlds altogether, insofar as that which is already known is transformed into a novel reality. Thus, for example, while involved in a dialogue with a colleague of mine on what "being grumpy" may mean, I came to realise that grumpiness is a form of self-protective shyness. I informed my wife about my discovery and, since then, she has been able to think of me no longer as a grumpy old bore, but as a tender, self-protecting, timid man—well, maybe.

On Peculiarities

After sketching the Socratic use of dialogue as a method, we can now look at some of its peculiarities.

First of all, not all forms of questioning are dialogues. When we are asking for directions, whether as tourists or as supplicants, we are not questioning anyone's beliefs. When I am asking my wife for her opinion, I am not always trying to question her views: frequently, I am requesting orders to comply with. A Socratic dialogue, then, is a form of questioning, which aims at putting to the test someone else's beliefs. Plato's work *Parmenides* is a splendid example of how this can be done, for it portrays Socrates questioning and defying the philosophical beliefs that Plato himself cherished the most.

Secondly, not all forms of debate or discussion are dialogues. In political debates, all parties involved try to sound more competent and more capable than the others, even if they are neither more competent nor more capable than the others. A Socratic dialogue, then, is a form of debate or discussion, which does not aim at winning at all costs. Victory is not the goal, but a possible, incidental feature of Socratic dialogue. Many of Plato's works portray Socrates concluding his dialogues with empty hands, as no-one, not even Socrates, seems to know all the answers. Irony outweighs obstetrics, sometimes, if not even more frequently. Not all pregnancies, unfortunately, end up with living births.

Thirdly, we are capable of having conversations, in which no-one is trying to win. When I am talking about the weather with a stranger or about football with a friend, I am not really interested in the content of our verbal exchange, but in the pleasure of being together with that person. And when I am talking to my wife, I am well aware of the fact that anything I say is never going to make any difference at all; still, I talk to her, since I am expected to do so—and because I secretly like her a lot. Furthermore, much of contemporary self-proclaimed dialogical methods in several different fields are not aimed at discovering the truth or even attempt to discover the truth.

Post-modern clinical psychotherapy, for instance, denies that any inter-subjective truth can be found to restore the patient's (aka client's aka customer's) mental health. In that context, if we want to use the term "truth" at all, then we must speak of subjective truth that the patient (or customer) tries to retrieve *via* the dialogical therapy in order to create an alternative account of her own life. Similarly, in today's inter-faith panels and organisations, it is denied *a priori* that dialogue amongst theologians and believers in general may produce any truth capable of resolving once and for all whatever fundamental disagreements and differences of dogma that there may be among them. Socrates may not have been able to attain the truth some, if not most, of the times that he engaged in a dialogical exchange of views. However, that hope, or ideal goal, did animate nonetheless his intellectual efforts, his entire life, and his horrible death.

Fourthly, dialogues, when aimed at testing beliefs, hence definitions, hence hypotheses, are examples of qualitative research. The validity or invalidity of a hypothesis, in fact, depends on the quality of the answers provided to the inquirer. It is not a matter of measurable quantities of words or repeated observations, although such matters may sometimes enter the picture. The ability to test the validity or invalidity of a hypothesis depends on the quality of the questions asked. The Socratic Method is an art: the art of asking comprehensible, relevant, effective questions. It is a practical skill to which certain individuals may be naturally inclined, but which requires recurrent exercise and serious training. Like all human arts, the Socratic Method belongs to that sphere of hidden competence that the brilliant Hungarian scientist and philosopher Michael Polanyi (1891–1976) called "the tacit dimension".[8]

Without doubt whatsoever, there is an explicit and communicable face to the Socratic Method too. It can be found in all textbooks of elementary logic and in all lists of logical fallacies. Yet, that is not all of it—it is not even most of it. Ramon Llull (1232–1315), in the Middle Ages, and Gottfried Wilhelm von Leibniz (1646–1716), in the late 17th century, attempted to produce a formal language that could allow us to decide whether a hypothesis was valid or not by sheer application of rules of deduction. Today's computers are the children of their computational dream, which many AI experts share, often without any awareness of such earlier fellow dreamers.

Still, even computer programmers and mathematicians need to master the art of their own disciplines, namely the art of knowing, say, how to start, which insights to rely upon, which segments of technical information to work on, how much demonstration is enough demonstration, which goal to set from the start, and when enough is enough, i.e. when exactly to conclude and move on to something else, how to focus their attention, interpret the perceptions they accumulate, direct the will, etc.

Fifthly, dialogues are not rare at all in our life. All those who have children know far too well that a little Socrates hides inside every family. As human beings acquire a language, their perception, knowledge and understanding of the world is fashioned by their many mentors (e.g. parents, relatives, the TV), for they are trained to 'see' certain things and call them by certain names. It is a practice or exercise, and if they do not perform it well, our mentors are to say: "no, this is not like that", "this is like that", "that is A", "this is B", "that is mistaken", and so on. On their part, children will ask continuously "what is that?" or "is that X?", i.e. they will look for newer and better definitions. They will also ask continuously "why is that so?", i.e. they themselves will test the hypotheses and modify beliefs about themselves and the world surrounding them—beliefs that they are helped to generate from their own minds. Learning a language, in brief, consists in engaging into Socratic dialogues too.

A Concluding Remark

The next time that we find ourselves with our sons and daughters, and they do not stop asking difficult questions, it may be wise to recall that they are just behaving like Socrates: they are little pains in the ass, as my Canadian colleague Christopher DiCarlo would say— himself being a father of two. We were blessed with one or more tiny wee Socrates roaming in our living rooms. Not everyone can boast such an amazing domestic reality. Cherish this thought, which I hope may bring some comfort to any reader who happens to be a parent.

Chapter 3: Reflections on Sergi Avaliani's Philosophical Investigations

Sergi Avaliani's "Philosophy of the Pseudoabsolute" presents a concise, sharp, and intriguing exploration of the notion of the pseudoabsolute, both in epistemological and ontological terms, i.e. as regards our knowledge as well as the ways in which there can be existence that our knowledge bears upon.[9] Through a thorough elucidation of the many technical aspects of this concept, Avaliani offers a comprehensive account of how our cognitive structures require what is "relative" to be "absolutized" in order to overcome the threat of "relativism" and to make "knowledge, thinking, and speech" possible (e.g. assuming the objective validity of measurement units and methods, the existence of an external reality, etc.).[10] Avaliani's works on this issue extend over forty years of scholarly research, primarily in Georgian and Russian, and the aforementioned article may be regarded as a synthetic "distillate" of it—as Giambattista Vico would have described it, its *"succum et sanguinem"* [juice and blood].

On Epistemology

With regard to the epistemological sphere, Avaliani depicts human knowledge as bound to be always and ultimately "relative" to something else, for the objects of our inquiries are usually "ambiguous, multimeaning" (e.g. the many possible descriptions of any given object or event).[11] Such is the case, for instance, of empirical phenomena, known "by means of sensation, perception, and notion".[12] The same applies to the explanatory terms employed in the sciences, which proceed from these very same phenomena and gather them under broader generalisations, or "concepts", often by way of formalised symbolic systems, thus achieving a "higher level of community".[13]

"[R]elative" is our knowledge, according to Avaliani, also when the object of inquiry is "absolute", i.e. "unambiguous", mono-meaning, univocal.[14] Such is the case of "philosophical knowledge", which deals with the "highest general features of the being" *sub specie aeternitatis* and nevertheless remains "relative", insofar as the "cognitive faculty of [each and every] philosopher is limited".[15] As Michael Polanyi had already argued long ago, all knowledge is ultimately personal knowledge.[16]

On Ontology

With regard to the ontological sphere, Avaliani provides the reader with a "hierarchical" representation of the real, which follows step-by-step the epistemological "ascension" from the level of particular phenomena to the comprehensive universal abstractions of philosophy, which attain the "highest level of community" (e.g. from the particular toad observed in a particular pond at a particular time in a particular place, to the notion of evolutionary law in the life sciences).[17] "Relative", in this context, comes to mean "conditional", whereas "absolute", on the other hand, comes to mean "unconditional", in accordance with the Latin etymology of the word itself.[18]

Employing a geological lexicon, Avaliani defines reality's being, i.e. its ontology, as a series of "layers" or "strata", which are differentiated by degree of "profundity and community".[19] "The most superficial" one, rather unsurprisingly, is that of observable "phenomena", which stem out of a deeper substratum, namely that of "special essences", which are not the ultimate texture of the universe, though.[20] Throughout them all, in fact, lies a principle of "unity" and interconnection, namely the "substantial essence or, simply, substance".[21] All of them, despite their differences, are something and, to an even deeper level of scrutiny, they all *are* as such. Were it not for this commonality in their being, their differences could not be grasped.

Though abstract and, at least to some readers, possibly abstruse, the parallel development of epistemological and ontological considerations in Avaliani's work sounds, from a logical point of view, sensible and linear. Nevertheless, this is so *prima facie*. The equation between thinking and being thereby presupposed is, in fact, difficult to accept as an immediate given, especially when Avaliani himself reminds the reader that our cognitive capacities are limited, imperfect, and doomed to be "relative".[22]

On Phenomenology

It may be easy, at least in principle, to accommodate together the "world of phenomena" with our "prescientific knowledge", or even the "world of special essences" with our "scientific knowledge", because of the assumption of their being equivalent or otherwise homogenous.[23] It is not at all clear how, though, we can harmonise *any* absolute or ultimate being with our radically defective intellectual skills. After all, it is Avaliani's own view that even the most comprehensive philosophical devices are "relative", and so are they irremediably.[24]

Avaliani's pairing of ontology—i.e. being; the world 'out there'— with epistemology—i.e. our knowledge of it, including the phenomenal representation of the world 'inside us'—cannot but face a challenge similar to the one famously encountered by pure reason in Kant's first *Critique*.[25] Our cognitive structures are regarded therein as dramatically unable to attain "absolute knowledge" of the sort required to back the claim that we are dealing with an "absolute object", as Avaliani calls it.[26] All that we can do in such a situation, according to Kant, is to postulate this sort of being, yet avoiding any stronger ontological commitment, lest we revert to old-fashioned metaphysics, which kept stating that reality was being discovered and discussed, but also kept producing different representations of it.

Kant and many, if not most, philosophers after him, have argued that we may hypothesise, suppose, postulate or decide, for our convenience's sake, that there is an absolute 'thing' of this sort, but we are not allowed to claim a full, uncontroversial knowledge of it, for we do not possess it for sure. All that we can fully and indubitably know, rather, are the "phenomena" and the "special essences" that we study and contemplate; while the unifying, interlinking "substance" lurking behind them might simply be projected or deduced, or (religiously) believed to be there.

Despite its success in modern times, some thinkers have challenged this Kantian sceptical note, which clearly weakens the powers of philosophical investigation *ab ovo* and leaves us in the midst of a notorious gap between *phenomena* (i.e. things as they appear to us) and *noumena* (i.e. things in themselves). The celebrated German thinker Georg Wilhelm Friedrich Hegel (1770–1831) was among those who did so by claiming boldly that rationality and reality were, though not identical, effectively equivalent.[27] He thought Kant's understanding of human reason to be too timid and pessimistic. Reason could do the job, in his view: reason could grasp the dialectical *logos* determining the flux of reality in its many and often puzzling manifestations, by way of as well as beyond the achievements of modern science itself. Asserting that all aspects of reality arise from overcoming previous limitations and generating new conditions (e.g. organic from inorganic, thinking from numb, liberty from necessity), he claimed thought capable of surpassing the daunting distinctions inherited from Kant (e.g. knowledge *versus* speculation, free will *versus* strict causality, phenomena *versus* noumena). In his confidence, Hegel followed a long line of metaphysicians, from classical Greece to modern Germany, *via* the great systematic thinkers of the Middle Ages.

After him, the boldest members of scientific positivism followed Hegel's lead, sometimes without being aware of it, and they are today the most numerous proponents of an optimistic interpretation of human knowledge, and specifically of scientific knowledge, which is believed to carve Nature at Her joints and, by so doing, spell out the laws written by God in mathematical language, as the Christian scientist Galileo Galilei (1564–1642) had famously quipped in the early 17th century.[28] We may be studying phenomena, all these optimists would argue, but we can dig deeper and get to the noumena, i.e. the things in themselves, such as the fundamental laws of physics or evolution, for example.

If Avaliani is correct, however, and if our faculties are indeed limited, then how can he himself justify his claim that philosophical knowledge deals with the ultimate features of being? How can he state with confidence that there is such a thing in the first place? One thing is our need, logical or psychological, for such a thing, another is leaping from an epistemological "requirement" to an ontological certainty.[29] Couldn't this "absolute" be nothing but an ulterior attempt by our notoriously poor intellect at making sense of what surrounds us? Couldn't it be that the "absolute" about which Avaliani is talking is just another instance of the "pseudoabsolute"? Given the "relative" character of human knowledge that he endorses, it would seem far more plausible for the sphere of the "absolute" to be a postulate of reason, rather than an ontological *datum*. How can we humans, *qua* humble "relative" beings, have any access to any "absolute" whatsoever?

On Geology

With his theory of "strata" of being, Avaliani provides no definitive answer to these questions. Rather, he offers us an example of what I would call a "geological ontology". The science of being is directed, in his view, to the determination of the "layers" of which reality is composed and of the dynamic (or static) relationships existing among them. According to Avaliani, "the ontological structure of reality (being) consists of three strata or levels: the world of phenomena, the world of special essences, and the substantial essence or substance", which is "infinite in the sense of unconditionality, i.e. independence" and "unites the infinite variety of things and phenomena of the world".[30]

There is another author who, fairly recently, made use of an analogous geological ontology, namely the French philosopher Gilles Deleuze. According to him, the totality of being can be seen synchronically as indeterminate matter or, in accordance with modern physics, as a flux of intensities of energy.[31] This "planomenon" (also called "plane of consistency" or "body-without-organs") is thus "permeated by unformed, unstable matters, by flows in all directions, by free intensities or nomadic singularities, by mad or transitory particles".[32]

Seen diachronically, Deleuze's manifold intensities "solidify" temporarily into formed unities, which can be conceptually better grasped as couples of "coding and territorialization", namely as precise linguistic descriptions ("codes") of states of affairs ("territories").[33] The unending wave of existence moves through the "body-without-organs" and determines contingent conditions for definable entities—definitions coming themselves into being *via* human communication alone.[34]

The elucidation of the modes of being is the perhaps perplexing but characteristic task of ontology, which approaches the totality of being as a divisible complex of structures and substructures. In Deleuze's evocative terminology, being can be described as the "ecumenon" and its substructures, which are described as the "layers" resulting from an articulate process of "stratification" akin to geological layers:[35]

> *At least... pairs, one serving as substratum for the other. [Yet,] The surface of stratification is a machinic assemblage distinct from the strata. The assemblage is between two layers, two strata; on one side it faces the strata (in this direction, the assemblage is an* interstratum*), but the other side faces something else, the body without organs or plane of consistency (here it is a* metastratum*). In effect, the body without organs is itself the plane of consistency, which becomes compact or thickens at the level of strata.*[36]

All divisions into "strata", in this sense, are expressions of the undifferentiated "body without organs", but they can be linguistically determined, that is, understood through ontological categories or "decoded", yet only as couples of "layers" resting (or building) one upon the other. The "stratum" of ethology, for instance, rests upon that of biology, while that of geology upon that of chemistry, and this one upon that of physics. As Deleuze adds, such pairs of "strata" are also and actually lying upon several others at the same time: ethology upon biology, chemistry, and physics; chemistry upon biology, physics, and linguistics; and so on.

Considering just a pair of them in a given hierarchical relationship, albeit convenient, is merely a starting point, a possibility among many. In his ontology, Deleuze describes the reality of the complex articulation of being at large in a far less well-ordered manner too. Any chosen "stratum" implies a "substratum", but the "substratum" can be scrutinised as a "stratum" itself, thus involving the determination of its own "substratum", and so on and on, for as long as human ingenuity can concoct codes of description.[37]

Following the example of geology, ontology can thus talk about a hierarchical organisation of "strata" or, in Deleuze's intentionally unique terms, "epistrata", these being distinguished from "parastrata", namely "strata" considered as parallel manifestations of the "planomenon", which is then conceived of horizontally rather than vertically.[38]

By suggesting the possibility of a non-hierarchical organisation of our codes describing reality, Deleuze wants to avoid confusing ontology's hierarchical determination of "layers", as manifested as well in the canonical organisation of the realms for disciplinary study, and the reality of being, particularly when the latter is seen as inclusive of our own ontological representations; namely when it is seen as a totality that is all-encompassing, all-comprehensive and all-embracing, which we break up nonetheless into distinct strata for the sake of our own understanding and agency. As Deleuze affirms: "Above all, there is no lesser, no higher or lower... The plane of consistency is the abolition of all metaphor: all that consists is Real"—horizontal is the horizon of God's mind.[39]

There are, then, at least two interpretations of the geological ontology hereby outlined. The former is that of a *vertical* ontology, which connects with an equally vertical epistemology, and which sees the hierarchical human categorisation of reality as a reflection paralleling the hierarchy of being itself. The latter is that of a *horizontal* ontology, which does not contradict the possibility, or not even the plausibility, of a vertical epistemology, but which distinguishes nonetheless between the human hierarchical models for our own representation of the real, and the notion of a deeper, non-hierarchical organisation of the same.

Whereas the vertical interpretation follows a Platonic pattern of steps or degrees of being and corresponding knowledge, the horizontal interpretation entails a more Spinozistic insight, which calls for hierarchy as a mere matter of human cognition but denies that any such thing is actually the case in concrete reality: being is *in se* univocal and all-encompassing; it is the infinite totality of what is in all forms, conceivable and inconceivable.

Deleuze's account is ultimately horizontal; Avaliani's, instead, vertical: the use that the latter thinker makes of notions such as "superficial", "profound", "internal", "deep", "foundation of foundations" and "last instance", as well as his insistence on "three strata or levels" in both ontology and epistemology, does point fairly patently towards a vertical ontology.[40] Which of these two interpretations may be the correct one is, however, difficult to determine. In truth, it would appear to be an academic question, given that the only way in which we are assumed to be capable of making sense of reality is by way of verticality. Our mental horizon, unlike God's, is vertical.

On Scepticism

Philosophy, despite giving birth to nearly all the scientific disciplines that are known to us, is notorious for having spent at least twenty-five centuries debating again and again the same few fundamental issues, without ever finding any conclusive answer. Literature and poetry, which so much share with philosophy in terms of stylistic devices, dwell in the domain of personal idiosyncrasies; fiction, not reality, is the place for such a dwelling.

Even mathematics, although few people are aware of it, has failed to produce a conclusive foundation for its most basic conceptual tools, thus placing radical doubt beneath its whole edifice. Physics, the icon of modern science, has itself undergone so many ground-shaking re-conceptualisations of its most fundamental aspects that physicists can sometimes outdo philosophers in the art of scepticism

—except perhaps for when they apply to governmental grants. When it comes to the most fundamental aspects of physical reality, none less than Richard P. Feynman (1918–1988) told his audiences: "What I am going to tell you about is what we teach our physics students in the third or fourth year of graduate school... It is my task to convince you *not* to turn away because you don't understand it. You see my physics students don't understand it... That is because *I* don't understand it. Nobody does."[41]

This lack of certainty is not a big problem for most academics, scientists and researchers. For one, the fact that we may not really know what we are talking about does not prevent us from talking and doing things. Academics, scientists, researchers and engineers keep writing books, designing bridges, curing diseases, creating computers capable of crunching enormous amounts of data, and, all things considered, we are still alive. Only philosophers such as Kant or Deleuze, and a few other theory-driven intellectuals, seem to take the lack of epistemic certainty seriously, and wonder occasionally whether we have really advanced in our knowledge of reality from the times of Julius Caesar (100–44 BC), when, in fact, they were already building bridges and curing diseases; or from the times of Laurence Sterne (1713–1768), when, in fact, they were already creating thinking machines.

Sceptically inclined philosophers and theorists also wonder whether any theory or worldview is actually reliable. The history of human intellectual enterprises is full of bizarre hypotheses that have been taken most seriously. For instance, Edmund Halley (1656–1742), the famous astronomer, while studying the Earth's magnetic field, came eventually to believe that the Earth was hollow and that, within it, there were up to four spheres with their own magnetic field, atmosphere, ecosystems, including animal and human populations. His speculations on the subject led to major debates, involving important mathematicians and daring explorers, up to the early 20th century. Now little is said about his hollow-Earth hypotheses, and Halley's name is revered among the austere founders of respectable modern astronomy.

Similarly, the history of human intellectual enterprises is punctuated by cases of scientifically heretical speculations (e.g. asteroids in the 18th century, colliding celestial bodies in the 1950s) that, decades or centuries later (e.g. atomism), had to be recognised as correct or, at least, as temporarily correct. US physicist Albert Michelson's (1852–1931) may have stated in 1903 that "the most important fundamental laws and facts of physical science have all been discovered, and these are now so firmly established that the possibility of their ever being supplemented in consequence of new discoveries is exceedingly remote", but it did not take long for his colleagues to challenge radically his convictions.[42] Iconic scientists such as Charles Darwin (1809–1882) himself have uttered words of caution about taking scientific theories too seriously, at least rhetorically, including his own: "To suppose that the eye with all its inimitable contrivances for adjusting the focus to different distances, for admitting different amounts of light, and for the correction of spherical and chromatic aberration, could have been formed by natural selection, seems, I confess, absurd in the highest degree".[43]

Not to mention the knowledge that was lost in the centuries separating us from Julius Caesar, his own predecessors, or Laurence Sterne: where are Daedalus' flying machines? Where are the herbal remedies devised by the great doctors of Medieval Baghdad? And what happened to the sorceries of the heathen Celts, Scythes, and Finns? Were they just sorceries, whatever those may be, or did they form a body of science now inaccessible to us?

Again, such interrogatives are likely to be academic—in the disparaging sense of the term. But this is precisely the context where such questions can be asked, without risking ridicule, exclusion, or indifference. The great Austrian physicist Ludwig Boltzmann (1844–1906) wrote on this point: "The most ordinary things are to philosophy a source of insoluble puzzles. With infinite ingenuity it constructs a concept of space or time and then finds it absolutely impossible that there be objects in this space or that processes occur during this time... the source of this kind of logic lies in excessive confidence in the so-called laws of thought".[44]

On Fideism

As to whether there can be any truth or certainty whatsoever, a most representative contemporary philosopher, the American neo-pragmatist Richard Rorty, claims that the commonplace notion of truth is fraudulent: "We need to make a distinction between the claim that the world is out there and the claim that truth is out there... Truth cannot be out there – cannot exist independently of the human mind – because sentences cannot so exist, or be out there... The world does not speak. Only we do."[45]

According to Rorty, the problem with the habitual notion of truth is that we think that there are two distinct blocks of being that we can compare with each other: reality as such on the one side, and our representations of reality on the other side. Given these two blocks, we can claim that certain instances of the latter are accurate portrayals of the former. On this basis, we can then praise Galileo and ridicule the Aristotelians who opposed him: Galileo's telescope could carve Nature at Her joints; much more so than Aristotle's (384–322 BC) science would have ever been capable of doing. The portrayal of reality given by Galileo was accurate; Aristotle's was not: the former was true, the latter false.

Yet, as Rorty muses, the sceptical mind has room aplenty in order to wonder: how can we know that such portrayals are accurate? How reliable is the paintbrush, the camera, or even the telescope, that we have used to produce such portrayals? How do we know that these paintbrushes and cameras were properly designed? And how do we know, in effect, that we have really isolated reality *per se*, so that we have "insights into the intrinsic nature of nature", rather than our own conceptual constructs?[46]

No matter how amazing the achievements of the human species may look, the sceptic will always be able to ask such disturbing questions, for she operates from within the crack separating reality and our representations of reality. As long as we think of knowledge as the mirror of reality, a matter of mutual fitting between distinct and opposed blocks, the sceptic will thrive, for she is allowed to question the accuracy of the image appearing in the mirror. If we conceive of truth as "adequacy" or "correspondence", as the technical jargon would dub it, then we can never be certain of the truths that we claim to possess.

A corollary of Rorty's position is that our commonplace confidence in the findings of neurology, chemistry or, until few decades ago, racial anthropology and historical materialism, becomes somewhat irrational. If we trust in them, it is not because we have some ultimate demonstration of their certainty, but because we want to believe in them and we want to endorse the non-ultimate criteria for justification available as pseudo-ultimate, to the point of believing it ultimate *tout court*. Whether and what truth ultimately exists is a matter of faith, as exemplified by centuries of religious culture—a point made repeatedly by Michael Polanyi in the 20th century.[47]

It may be therefore inspiring to quote a point on this matter made by the former Pope of the Catholic Church, John Paul II (1920–2005), who, well versed in matters of religion, stated: "Science can purify religion from error and superstition. Religion can purify science from idolatry and false absolutes".[48]

On Ethnocentrism

There is an alternative way to interpret truth, according to Rorty. As we seek it, we shape and re-shape concepts about the world, and devise methods through which such concepts can be confirmed by other concepts, so that, in the end, we can claim to have reached true and sound conclusions. Truth, under this perspective, is not a matter of correspondence to reality, but of coherence internal to specific conceptual (or "metaphorical") sub-systems, which are designed to produce specific results according to specific methods.[49]

A different way to explain the same point is to say that there is nothing like objective, immediate, direct knowledge of the world. Man does not live of bread alone. Man lives of concepts, such as that of bread. We are linguistic-conceptual creatures, and we cannot but read the world through the concepts that we possess, namely concepts that we have inherited from our culture, our ethnos. Reality is always that which we interpret to be real given the conceptual framework that we adhere to.

Speaking of truth as a discovery about the intrinsic nature of the world is, for Rorty, a form of preposterous self-deception:

> *To say that we should drop the idea of truth as out there waiting to be discovered is not to say that we have discovered that, out there, there is no truth. It is to say that our purposes would be served best by ceasing to see truth as a deep matter, as a topic of philosophical interest, or "true" as a term which repays "analysis".*[50]

If we privilege certain forms of inquiry, such as physics or medicine instead of astrology or parapsychology, it is because that is what our culture, and the evaluative structures embedded thereby, has taught us to do—and that we have decided to take seriously, Polanyi would add. For Rorty, the very fact that we may find certain cognitive approaches more effective, rational, or even intuitive, is nothing but the result of centuries of conditioning into certain conceptions of effectiveness, rationality and intuitiveness. This is how intuitions and deep convictions get established, from the lofty realm of theoretical physics to that of daily human agency. As Rorty writes: "Morality [itself] is a matter of... 'we-intentions,' [i.e.] the core-meaning of 'immoral action' is 'the sort of things *we* don't do'."[51]

On Pragmatism

Conceptual changes may take place, but not because we have discovered where the truth lies. Rather, we decide to shift to another theory or worldview because the old ones have "become a nuisance", whereas "a half-formed new vocabulary... promises great things".[52] For Rorty, a self-declared heir of traditional American pragmatism, the reasons for conceptual change are not theoretical, but practical. They have to do to with will and hope, not just with good arguments and convincing demonstrations. In his view, practical are also the distinctions internal to knowledge (e.g. opinion vs. knowledge, disciplinary divisions and subdivisions).

Rorty invites us to stop regarding knowledge as a mirror of something else. Knowledge is better understood, in his view, as a collection of adaptive practices, namely structured modes of experience by means of which we cope with the environment surrounding us. For Rorty, each domain of knowledge responds to different goals, and that is what separates poetry from architecture, physics from ethnography, tarot reading from history, and musicology from entomology. No deeper principle of individuation is needed. Looking for it means falling back into the trap of scepticism or, at least, setting the stage for it to resurge.

Rorty does not conceive of the human intellectual endeavour as a collection of theoretically and cognitively differentiated disciplines, but as a vast ongoing conversation of humankind in which priests, haematologists and anthropologists participate, *inter alia*, with equal rights. All of them, in fact, do nothing but interpret reality from a certain pragmatic angle, in yet another feat of practical adaptation. Knowledge is, under this perspective, a matter of collective hermeneutics involving all sorts of variously possible and plausible inquirers, for "there are no constraints on inquiry save conversational ones – no wholesale constraints derived from the nature of objects, or of mind, or of language, but only those retail constraints provided by the remarks of our fellow-inquirers."[53]

On Conversation

Which constraints may be in place is, however, something that Rorty does not explore. On my part, I believe that there are at least two major types of interpretation of reality.

First of all, there are *one-level* readings of the world of which we can have experience. Natural sciences and Freudian psychoanalysis are good examples of this type of hermeneutics. Their mode of understanding proceeds by subsuming phenomena, which are determined by appealing to discipline-specific defining predicates, under abstract umbrella-terms, which are meant to embrace as many phenomena as possible (e.g. "force", "species", "neurosis"). Whether they study the reactions occurring between two chemical substances, or the reactions of university teachers to the behaviour of their students, the final product is the re-description of the events at issue as instances of a larger pattern of causal interaction. The level of meaning admitted in the picture is one alone: the only interpretation that matters is that of the inquirer, who applies the concepts proper to her science onto the world.

There are as well *two-level* readings of the world of which we can have experience. I believe the human sciences, and history in particular, to be representative of this kind of hermeneutics. Their mode of understanding refers to events in their specificity and to subjective accounts for the interpretive perspectives internal to them. Analogies with other phenomena can be and are often drawn, so as to produce generalisations. Still, the deeper is the understanding of a particular social, political, legal, or historical event, the more case-specific its analysis must become. This implies that the levels of meaning admitted in the picture are two. On the one hand, there is the interpretation given by the scholar; on the other hand, there are the interpretations given by the human beings involved in the event, of which the sociologist, psychologist, lawyer, political scientist or historian may take more or less detailed and attentive account.

Rorty is probably correct in stating that the world's intellectuals are "keeping a conversation going", but this conversation is not to be thought of as a homogenous process of interpretation.[54] A double hermeneutics—a two-level interpretation—is not the same as single hermeneutics—a one-level interpretation—and this is a point that Rorty neglects. Additionally, there are different forms that a conversation may take, which is something else that Rorty neglects.

There can be a *chat*, in which no final convergence of opinion is actually expected to take place. The two chatting interlocutors are merely expressing ideas, without even needing to back them with reasons. In the arena of human interactions, this is a kind of exchange that is allowed mostly in trivial situations, such as many a conversation in pubs and barbers' parlours, and it is not considered to be conducive to significant knowledge by any recognised conversational standard.

There can be a *dialogue*, which we have met in the preceding chapter, namely a conversation between two or more interlocutors who are aiming at some kind of final convergence, and who need to construct compelling arguments in order to discharge invalid hypotheses and foster each other's understanding of the matter at stake. Ideally, all scholarly conversations should belong to this genre, which has as its main goal the development of the best hypothesis for which the agreed structures of scientific conceptualisation allow.

There can be a *dispute*, in which two or more interlocutors are trying to disqualify each other by appealing to accepted criteria of validity for the ideas that are being expressed. Logical validity aside, these criteria are not grounded in eternal, certain, unshakeable foundations, but refer to provisory standards of acceptability that are held valid by the interlocutors and their audiences. Most scholarly conversations seem to degenerate, at some point, into this third type of exchange.

On Practical Reason

That which is implied by the distinction among forms of conversation, is that it is still possible to separate and rank disciplines on theoretical grounds, and specifically on the basis of how deep they go in terms of probing for the justification of their conclusions. Such grounds for justification may not be the divine ones of Plato or Hegel, and they may not be the mirrors of reality itself, but they are there as the mirror of the three most valuable sources of belief upon which humans can rely intra- and inter-culturally: tradition, intuition, and reason.

Discriminating between forms of conversation, whilst being aware of the ethnocentric nature of knowledge, is likely to become extremely important when we switch from theoretical subjects to practical ones. The ingenious mathematical rendition of the fundamental physical forces of the universe may be truly fascinating and highly demanding of the human intellect, but it is also largely irrelevant *vis-à-vis* the truly pressing needs of human life: food, hydration, shelter, rest, socialisation, or care when ill. Without satisfying them, besides, no great intellectual endeavour could be pursued. How to preserve one's own life, rights and dignity is something that cannot be put on hold for long, even if it escapes the complex beauty of formal expression and, at best, can aspire to the more level of juridical formulation alone (e.g. constitutional provisions on social and economic rights), rather than mathematical formula.

On Citizenship

Let us consider, for example, the concept of citizenship, as this notion is understood in Western countries—our ethnos. It is a concept that I regard as both intriguing and poignant, especially if we think of the plight of African and Asian migrants that have been drowning by the thousands in the Mediterranean since the beginning of the so-called "War on Terror" in the Middle East.[55] Citizenship is a fundamentally debatable topic, not unlike most of our chief political notions. Justice, freedom, fairness, equality and liberty, just to mention a few, have been continually disputed and variously imagined since Plato's first utopian Republic. There may be a concept for each of them, but the conceptions are many and diverse.

Under a sceptical perspective, the controversial nature of these notions can be traced back to their origin: political and moral concepts are human products for human societies. Moral and political concepts must, in some way, be necessarily human, even for the fanatic, the realist, or the idealist, i.e. even for those who believe that there is a transcendental or transcendent source and/or univocal definition of them. The necessity of their human aspect can be easily explained: unlike quarks or bosons, moral and political concepts are to be embodied in, interpreted within, and intentionally transferred into human social practices, into personal understanding, and into individual behaviour.

Social practices have frequently changed, personal understanding differs between individuals, and the behaviour of individuals exhibits numerous contradictions. Nonetheless, Western civilisation has often been seen retrospectively as moving gradually towards better conditions of social life, centred upon some or all of the nominally "civilised", "advanced" or "timeless" notions that we think of as characteristically Western. However, this sort of coherent view can be reached only by drastically simplifying and harmonising the chaotic collection of our past experiences. In order for it to come into focus and hold its grip on the collective conscience, it must ignore many numerous alternatives which have appeared along the way and the attendant hard choices that had to be made. The alleged virtues of Western societies are neither fixed nor timeless.

Political and ethical notions have changed significantly in the course of time, although their names may have remained the same. "Honour", for instance, has been completely transformed in the last hundred years (e.g. the importance of premarital virginity). Furthermore, even if both political and moral values were actually objective and discoverable realities, they have seldom been interpreted or applied in the same way.

Citizenship itself has been variously conceived through the ages: Pericles' (495–429 BC) Athens, Augustus' (63 BC–14 AD) Rome, Jefferson's (1743–1826) US, Andropov's (1914–1984) USSR all recognised a status referred to as "citizenship". The mechanisms for acquiring this status, or for being recognised as a citizen, may have even been quite similar in these various contexts: *ius sanguinis*, based on the citizenship of one's parents; and *ius soli*, based on one's birthplace, are still by far the most common criteria on these matters. But the sets of rights and duties connected with this condition have been sharply dissimilar, not to mention whom the rights and duties could be conferred to or denied (e.g. slaves, men, women, patricians, plebeians, aristocrats, commoners, bourgeois, proletarians, etc.).

It might be thought that a coherent, comprehensive evolution of a few basic features of citizenship has moved progressively through a number of historical steps—but toward what final target? The wider acquisition of political rights for all of the members of society? A higher awareness of the need for the effective distribution of wealth? A mindful definition of the powers that citizens are allowed to exercise? Which virtues, more or less "Western", are to be preferred? Which political, ethical, legal notions comprise the essential features of citizenship, its natural context and its conceptual background?

On Membership

"Citizenship" seems to denote a kind of membership. In the most general sense, a citizen is a member of a citizenry, i.e. a certain community in a certain place, where all of the members have certain common characteristics accounting for their membership. If citizenship is political membership, then it implies certain forms of legal, moral and behavioural equality, not necessarily included in the more global idea of membership. As Jürgen Habermas (b. 1929) puts it: "the citizen's status is constituted by a web of egalitarian relations of mutual recognition".[56]

In contemporary liberal states, citizens are said to share determined sets of equal rights. A deeper inquiry may furnish a sharper view of these rights (civil, political, social, economic, cultural rights) and also the duties deriving from subjection to the State and its laws (e.g. military conscription, electoral participation, strict requirements for gun ownership, etc.). Going still further, a manifold distribution of rights and duties becomes apparent too, according to provenance, age, sex, profession, income, and the like. If we compare citizen status in different political communities, though, or even in the same community at different times, we seem to find that a precisely defined list of the rights and duties consequent upon citizenship cannot be drawn up, and that there are indeed "deep questions about what binds citizens together into a shared political community".[57]

Admittedly, certain groups of states characterise citizens' rights in a similar way. Such a characterisation is what allows us to talk about "liberal" states, setting them apart from dictatorships, sultanates or totalitarian states. "For a long time, however, *Staatsbuergerschaft*, *citoyenneté* or *citizenship* meant only, in the language of law, political membership ... it is only recently that the concept has been expanded to cover the status of citizens defined in terms of civil rights".[58] Western political literature is replete with examples of this kind: declarations of rights, bills of rights, international charters, constitutions, etc. But are persons living under a dictatorship not also citizens? Are they not citizens of a tyrannical state?

Those progressives who reply that they are not, tend to argue that such persons do not enjoy their civil, political, or social rights. Mostly, these persons have duties. Their rights, the progressives would say, are excessively restricted, systematically neglected; these people can do nothing lawful to change their condition, and they are not allowed to express their opinion about it. In short, their status is considerably closer to that of a mere subject, or of a slave, than to that of a citizen. Neither subjects nor slaves are real citizens. But what are real citizens, then?

On Progress

As long as we think of citizenship in terms of certain rights (civil rights in particular, as Habermas stresses), we seem actually to be telling a story about North America and the Old Continent; that is, a progressive story about liberalism, "a philosophy concerned with upholding the dignity and inherent rights of individuals, understood as instantiations of a universal humanity."[59] This is a story that may well be our preferred history; a collective history that is dignifying and important for our well-being and our self-comprehension. This story may even constitute a historical and theoretical pillar of our social self-conception, whose primacy gives us the "right to criticize the idea of a localizing and pluralizing citizenship", because "we ought to be disturbed by the claim made by post-modern social theory that all social reality is local, plural, fragmentary, episodic, and infinitely rearrangeable."[60]

Nevertheless, it is possible and legitimate to say, as Habermas does, that: "Citizenship as membership in a state only assigns a particular person to a particular nation whose existence is recognized in terms of international law".[61] Under this perspective, 'mere' subjects, slaves, or members of an autocratic state may be considered citizens: if they meet the requirements for citizenship in their state (e.g. they were born by members of that state, or they were born inside its borders, or they have engaged in certain activities inside it, etc.), then they are citizens.

'Real' citizens—as put by the progressive defender of civil rights here hypothesised—would mean only the citizens of those states in which she would like to live; but personal preferences or political engagement ground no valid argument for the essence of citizenship. Talking in a progressive way may sound persuasive to liberal ears, but it carries neither absolute logical nor strict legal weight. The use of "real" in this sense does not distinguish two actual logical counterparts, but two or more moral/political perspectives. It is an intelligent, informed and plausible rhetorical device, aimed at emphasising our position within the frame of an ongoing ethical or social conflict, and yet providing no conclusive logical or legal license for the application of "citizen".

Linking together citizenship and certain rights may be seen as a consequence of having been born and raised in Western countries, or in any country where the word "citizen" is an umbrella-concept recalling terms like "democracy", "private property", "freedom of speech", "liberty", "equal opportunity" and the like; places where "citizen" is a word belonging to a modern liberal lexicon, perfused with democratic spirit; or, in any case, belonging to a lexicon whereby citizens are expected to have an important role to play within the State either as autonomous agents, or as protected subjects, or both—a political vocabulary which stresses the elements of popular sovereignty and human rights.

Nonetheless, there are and there have been "citizens" all over the world, with valid passports and even sets of shared equalities, living in popular democracies (e.g. East Germany, Viet Nam) and sultanates (e.g. Brunei), where few of the 'real' citizens' rights had or have had legal recognition, or where their role was or has been merely passive.

On Form

There have been liberal states with slaves or with different classes of citizens having different sets of (internally equal) rights (e.g. men and women in most of Europe). And the more deeply one investigates history—even that of the Western countries alone—the more discrepancies of this sort one uncovers. A formal or legalistic notion of citizenship like Habermas' one—free, as such, from contexts and contents—may sound exceedingly broad and empty. But the law itself, in liberal states, is supposed to be abstract and formal, in order to be applicable to the largest number of possible cases. Even if grounded in individual cases that the legislator wishes to address, the law must nevertheless be abstracted from those cases and raised to a higher level of generality to become a rule.

Citizenship as membership implies only the "satisfaction of criteria" and "shared equalities", saying nothing about content; that is, about how to connect the concept up with these rights or those duties. Providing substantial connotations for the formal-legal concept of citizenship is a subsequent step. "Citizenship", understood in the formal-legalistic Habermasian way that I am here outlining, can thus be a ground-level concept useful to any human group bound together by some plan, conception, event or concern.

Taking this formalistic approach, one will not end up over-loading "citizenship" with too many prejudicial assumptions. We assume only what is needed to capture the idea that we are surrounded by other human beings, with whom we share certain simple basic features (e.g. places, needs, instincts) as well as more complex forms of life (e.g. patterns of behaviour, psychological scripts, communicational devices). Our social membership may be stretched further, wider and wider, by connecting it with broader basic needs and abilities (e.g. nutritional necessities, aptitudes for locomotion), or may be rendered narrower and narrower—i.e. more and more aristocratic—by connecting it with rare or strictly specific features (e.g. common ancestors, physical appearance, etc.). The choice between the two horizons is moral, political, and important; but it is not something that can be fished out of the concept of citizenship as such.

On Theory

Whenever we go to the theatre, support a football team, work together with other people, meet in a temple to attend a religious service, or apply for a degree program, we 'cut' the people around us into a manifold of sub-collections, communities, legacies. We are members of hundreds different groups that we cannot avoid belonging to; we take part in thousands "different forms of life which coexist in ... [any] society".[62] We could even be said to belong to thousands of different cities without ever leaving our hometown. Citizenship is one of these memberships.

Theoretically speaking, it is always possible to specify a larger category within which any two (or more) distinct memberships may be included. An endless number of such classes is easily definable, and the level may be pushed upward to include mankind in general, or even to include all sentient beings. But what has this to do with "citizenship"?

The answer is that this line of reasoning suggests again that "citizenship", like "membership", is to be considered logically as a formal condition, a stipulative legal term, a status for people fulfilling certain requirements, in compliance with chosen requirements. More than this, unengaged philosophical analysis—especially if informed by sceptical doubt—cannot provide. A candid, neutral, logico-philosophical approach leaves us only with a thin conceptual 'bag' for some further conceptual 'shopping'—nothing more. History provides the shelves and the goods that we can put into the bag, but this requires engagement, taking a stand, abandoning neutrality, and leaving sceptical suspension of judgment behind us.

All the discussions about who should be recognised as a citizen, what 'real' citizenship consists in, which states deny 'true' citizenship and so on, are actually debates over normative attitudes towards "citizenship". What is normatively or politically relevant is a product of moral and political choice, not of logical and linguistic analysis. And in this case, it is a choice as to where we want to draw the line (or lines) between "us" and "them". It is in this sense that "citizenship" differs radically from the logical notion of "membership" (i.e. being an element of a set).

Moreover, "citizenship" implies the presence of a state or public authority of sort, which "is unlike all other associations. It both frames civil society and occupies space within it. It fixes the boundary conditions and the basic rules of all associational activity (including political activity). It compels association members to think about a common good, beyond their own conception of the good life."[63] But such a notion of "citizenship" is a term already loaded with all of the political heritage of our 'preferred' history.

On Practice

For the sake of attaining practical ends, it would therefore be better to speak openly of the kind of membership that we would like our politicians to give shape to, what community we would like to be members of, how we might improve and reshape our State through the recognition of certain persons (and not others) as citizens, rather than pretending that a candid philosophical account is being carried out.

Honest self-assertions of this kind happen all too rarely among philosophers, despite declarations such as the following one, penned by J.L. Hudson:

> *[M]ore and more philosophers have been writing extended treatments of specific public issues and offering recommendations as to how, morally speaking, these issues should be resolved... Most applied philosophy is applied moral philosophy, in which ethical theory is brought to bear on a specific moral issue, usually one of a public nature. But the applied philosopher is embarrassed by the lack of a generally accepted ethical theory. The obvious way to back up his recommendation as to what should be done would be to combine*

a statement of the facts of the case with a statement of general ethical principles, from which his recommendation would follow. But if his ethical theory is controversial among his colleagues, and will appear novel and dubious to his nonphilosophical readers, then it would seem that the philosopher has misplaced his efforts. He should have been thinking and writing about ethical theory rather than about a practical issue. His primary aim should have been to prove the correctness of his theory, which must be more important than any one specific application. On the other hand, the existence of a comprehensive and noncontroversial ethical theory would make the philosopher largely superfluous in debates over public issues. Once the ethical theory is grasped, the only remaining questions are empirical; once we know what in general is right, the only doubt is about the facts of the situation confronting us. In this area the philosopher qua *philosopher has nothing to offer and must defer to social scientists, historians, journalists, etc. The philosopher must become an amateur social scientist in order to deal intelligently with public policy questions, yet he cannot become more than an amateur without abandoning his primary vocation.*[64]

"Citizenship" as a legal term is, like any legal term, a public instrument. As instruments, laws require interpreters, users, exploiters, and interpretative assistance such as constitutions, judicial opinions, procedural codes, etc. Once again, our characterisation depends upon the selection that we operate on the data available to us. It is therefore a matter of historical accounts, and of preferences, aims, prejudices, commitments. Revealingly, despite the supposed neutrality of many philosophical works, in just the few articles that I have already mentioned in this chapter, there appear seven different conceptions of "citizenship".[65]

On Instruments

In all likelihood, we should take seriously Ludwig Wittgenstein's (1889–1951) idea that the meaning of a term is its use.[66] Then, "citizenship" becomes nothing more—and nothing less—than an instrument; and instruments say nothing final about their own use. In looking for content, as Hudson hints, philosophy should open its disciplinary borders to other fields and abandon the technical, ascetic virginity which supposedly makes philosophy higher and more ultimate than other disciplines—what Hudson calls the "primary vocation" of philosophy. And if one thinks in this way, "philosophy" becomes a generic term indicating, among other things, both a literary tradition and a stylistic attitude, which may be useful for the purposes of what we are used to calling "politics".

The primacy of politics over philosophy makes sense also because —more plainly yet more dramatically—problems related to citizenship are practical, legal, political problems. Which criteria are chosen for conferring the status of citizenship, which rights we want to hang upon this status, and whom we want to include and exclude, are the topics for a political discussion, not just and not even primarily for a philosophical one. It is in such a context that unforeseen uses of "citizenship" occur, whose outcomes may be abuses—but not abuses of the term itself, as it might be thought to appear in an abstract theoretical inquiry, but rather abuses of those who, through our choices, instantiate this term.

The concept of citizenship is more comprehensible (i.e. less ambiguous) if considered as a formal legal condition, term, or instrument. What is to be done with such an instrument cannot be discovered through conceptual analysis; this is something that we, human societies and their institutions, decide, on practical grounds. In keeping with Hudson's suggestion, then, we should tackle the notion of citizenship as amateur social scientists, or journalists, or applied philosophers. We should put politics first "and derive all of the rest out of it", as Rorty himself claims against the keen theorists, the conceptual analysts, and all of those who believe that the philosophical scrutiny of a term may yield instructions for using it correctly.[67] Analysis, even when keen and cunning, can give us only suggestions, at best.

On Distinctions

Within the social and political sphere of contemporary Western societies, for instance, we can discern three contexts where "citizenship" has a troubling sound, i.e. contexts that show a puzzling, and negative connotation of citizenship. They are: when you are not a citizen; when you do not want to be a citizen; and when you are obliged to change citizenship. These are three critical moments in human existence, and they may occur in very different situations:

1a) you are not a citizen and other people are not;
1b1) you are not a citizen, but other people are;
1b2) you are not as much of a citizen as other people are;
1c) you are not a citizen and other people do not want you to be;

2a) you do not want to be a citizen, but you should;
2b) you do not want to be a citizen, but you must;
2c) you do not want to be a citizen, but you cannot but be one;

3a) many citizens decide to change everybody's citizenship;
3b) few citizens decide to change everybody's citizenship;
3c) foreign citizens decide to make you take their citizenship.

1a) refers to some of the most tragic moments of social life, i.e. when social life disappears and humans fall back into a Hobbesian condition where, as the Latin proverb goes, *homo homini lupus*. Such is the case of civil wars, as the conflicts in the Balkans showed to the rest of allegedly 'civil' and united Europe. Citizenship becomes far less relevant than some other form of membership, such as one's belonging to an ethnic group.
1b1) suggests something much more common but nevertheless very puzzling: the situation of the illegal alien, the refugee, the

stateless person and the immigrant in general, i.e. all those who do not fit the requirements for citizenship in a state into which they have moved or into which they were forced to move. Despite the many international agreements, their position before the law has to be defined through complex adjustments of existing legal frameworks. Cooperative treaties and humanitarian support have broken through the resistance of individual states and communities and have worked to enlarge the cultural perception of "us", thus causing changes in the interconnection between citizenship requirements and attendant rights and duties. Closure and rejection are nonetheless possible, however, especially in times of perceived or real insecurity of the recipient communities.

1b2) reminds us of the madman, the child and the prisoner, who are peculiar examples of citizens. They may fulfil the requirements for being considered citizens of a state, but they do not share fully in the rights and duties of typical citizens. In some cases, they may even be denied their basic fundamental rights, i.e. the so-called "civil rights". Women have often represented a distinct category of citizens too, whereby they had not the same rights, or the same duties, as men. Often, in not too distant a past of our civilisation, women were second-rate citizens enjoying fewer or lesser rights.

1c) reflects some of the mental dispositions that may be implicated in 1b1) and 1b2). The contraposition between "us" and "them"; "you are not one of us" in its many shapes: racism, xenophobia, paternalism and intolerance in general.

2a) describes a grey zone inside a community's life. There may be persons who are actual citizens, but who do not take this status very seriously. They place themselves in different sorts of aggregations or make unusual personal life-choices. As far as such peculiarities and peculiar organisations do not threaten the stability of the State, they are normally tolerated. But whenever there is a conflict between the interests of such associations and those of the citizenry at large, they can become a source of serious trouble. There may be superficial conflicts that are easier to tolerate—e.g. the personal eccentricities of punk or hippie communities—but others are far more difficult— religious sects, subversive political groups, violent localism, etc.

2b) reflects the general tendency of thinking about one's own citizenship as a collection of rights, rather than as a collection of duties; a fact explainable both for the historical development of the notion of citizenship as a defence of individual freedoms against State authority, and for a more general egotistic spirit of self-interest. It is today quite rare to listen to somebody who is happy because she has to join the army, or go to school, or pay taxes, which Benjamin Franklin (1706–1790) thought of as painful and unavoidable as death itself. The terms which are used to describe our duties as citizens have often a negative connotation: "compulsory", "obligatory", "mandatory", etc. And if we want to promote, enforce or introduce some commitment, we exploit the lexicon of the highest moral examples (e.g. saints, heroes, patriots, men of good will): "responsibility", "awareness", "duty", "altruism", "solidarity", etc.

2c) refers to an unpleasant and extreme kind of "citizenship", but one that is useful to see how much our being is legally, socially and inter-subjectively determined. Luigi Pirandello's (1867–1936) plays and novels have shown how much and how deeply we are labelled by people around us, and how tough it may be to overcome, if ever possible, the masks that society puts onto our faces, whether we like it or not, in order to render us easily recognisable and predictable, within both the private and the public sphere.

3a) recalls one of the hidden, often forgotten, risks of any democratic liberal state. Despite written constitutions, law courts and representative assemblies, the spectre of totalitarianism is nevertheless present on the scene. Constitutions can be modified, courts' injunctions ignored, assemblies disregarded. The 20th century provides many clear examples of how far institutional guidelines and monitoring bodies may be disrupted: the constitution of the Weimar Republic was ignored by the national-socialists whom the German voters had elected into power; and corrupted politicians have often sat in the Italian parliament even when condemned for bribery and extortion. Citizens can even vote in support of a dictatorship, or welcome a *Putsch*, as a consequence of widespread dismay, especially after the ruin of the national economy caused by a handful of wealthy investors and their trusted financial wizards.

3b) alludes to less dramatic scenarios than 3a), but to similarly great changes in the citizens' public life. You do not need a revolution or a mass resolution to get rid of the existing legal framework: both its pre-conditions and its consequences may be radically changed, even by minorities. It has often happened in European history that few select individuals decided for the great many, on the grounds of both economic status and gender. The most ancient form of democracy worked this way, namely the Greek *polis*, in which our concept of citizenship is partly rooted. Aristotle even argued for the natural rationality of such a discrimination, Greeks being better suited than foreigners; free citizens than slaves; and men than women. In contemporary world politics, phenomena representative of 3b) may be the foreign investors' tight control of national economies, technocratic diktats to national governments, or media monopolists' control of and influence upon political consensus.

3c) furnishes the collective parallel to 2c), that is, when you cannot but accept what other people have decided for you. If in connection with 2c) we spoke of Pirandello's works, here we may mention Václav Havel's (1936–2011) plays. Foreign soldiers can change the shape and meaning of your citizenship, plus the borders and the name of your country. Invasions, annexations, and also many forms of settlement and colonisation, oblige the previous citizens (or merely owners or inhabitants of a certain land) to become something that they did not expect or ever want to become.

On Application

The scheme sketched here is just an outline and might be reformulated under alternative perspectives. It shows merely how far and how variously citizenship can be denied in practice (by non-citizens, by citizens themselves, by outside citizens), as well as the ways in which it can become troublesome.

Generally, citizens of Western countries do not worry much about citizenship, unless it starts creating problems. Most of them are born as citizens; this is as natural as anything can be: a reminder of our social dimension, a sort of automatic confirmation of our unavoidable membership to a group or *polis*. But when we would reject such membership, or when we are denied it, then citizenship becomes relevant and is no longer automatic, simple, or obvious. It may even become something worth fighting for.

Some of the cases mentioned under 1a) and 3c) show precisely how such a shift in relevance can happen. Some of these cases may even overlap (e.g. 1b) and 1c)), while others show very different ranges of possible social menace (e.g. 2a) and2c)); but all of them presume some sort of negation of citizenship.

The examples used here are all contestable, but the aim of this chapter is only to provide a token of applied philosophy; or better, a token of how citizenship may be scrutinised in applied philosophy. It is an explanatory sketch or brief methodological demonstration, giving an indication as to what would cause our commonsensical notion of citizenship to cease to be considered such, along with some additional suggestions.

First of all, 1a)–3c) represent various possible losses of equilibrium within an ideal liberal polity. Most citizens of a liberal democracy would probably admit that 1a)–3c) embody different kinds of difficulties: difficulties for peace, wealth, social welfare, self-realisation, freedom, etc. More generally, they all exemplify troubles for those equalities mentioned earlier in this chapter; equalities which may be divided into formal and substantial, whether it is the former or the latter that should be more relevant. This is not a theoretical subject, again, but a political one. Assumptions, ends and solutions are to be found in actual political contexts, for which philosophy may furnish methods, arguments and helpful hints.

Politics being primary, philosophy has a subsidiary role; but in this role it does participate in all of the disciplines and human activities affecting crucial political issues, such as the separation of powers, the charisma of leaders, the economic interests and irrational preferences of the individuals, etc. Philosophy may be *ancilla politicae*, but she is certainly kept busy in this ancillary function. In making a mostly formal contribution to the political debate on citizenship, philosophy plays a limited role in the political game.

Applied political philosophy can help us, for instance, to appreciate the fact that 1a)–3c) represent different conditions that threaten people's equality under the law, their chances for controlling their own lives, their freedoms, their desire for moderate conformism, and so on.

On Equality

The history of Western thought provides many examples and reference to it is important for the achievement of a value hierarchy among the various equalities which are sought after and, if enjoyed, defended. Again, this history reveals the extent to which Western countries have been required to tolerate a high degree of compromise, both because there is little unanimous agreement on such matters (e.g. private and public ownership of key resources) and because not all equalities are coherent and mutually compatible.

In addition, equalities are not shared at the same time by all citizens. For instance, individuals are not considered full citizens for a long period of their lives, and other people, such as parents or tutors, must decide for them. Furthermore, not all equalities are joyfully accepted (e.g. the citizens of most countries have to pay taxes and many try to avoid it by all sorts of schemes), and there are various cases of civil disobedience as well as patent law-breaking showing this. There are equalities of duties as much as of rights, since it cannot be rights alone that support citizenship in the face of other citizens, but they are often suffered rather than celebrated.

The difference between equality in rights and duties may be a further useful reminder provided by applied political philosophy: we often forget about duties when characterising the constitutions, and social development, of Western countries. Duties may sometimes be utterly unwelcome, especially insofar as they imply limitations upon individual freedom. Our forgetfulness with respect to duties is not rare, strange or incomprehensible, because contemporary liberal democracies are the outcome of a long struggle for rights, and so the emphasis is placed thereupon. Historically, the achievement of new notions of "citizenship" has often been part and parcel of the struggle for democracy, freedom, self-assertion, etc. Europe's and, to a lesser extent, the world's *citoyens* consider themselves the authors of one of the most radical shifts from ancient absolutism in the direction of the modern liberal state: France celebrates it solemnly in July every year.

Something of the spirit of the revolutionary citizens of the 18th century is still alive in contemporary polities, at least in public rhetoric, through which the existing states praise themselves for being beacons of freedom, egalitarian communities and tolerant peoples. Such are at least some of the values on which social ends, legal procedures, the relations between State and citizen, and the public relations between citizen and citizen, are based.

Still, it would be dishonest not to admit that there have been contradictions and struggles that we commonly forget when we observe our communities retrospectively and tell edifying stories about ourselves. Historically, "citizenship" has been as highly dynamic as the historical "cities" inhabited by their "citizens", where many people, many interests and many voices produced countless alternative ways of thinking about social welfare and social ends. Today's liberal states arose from movements which, in their time, were radical, revolutionary, outlawed, and allegedly illiberal. Their establishment was frequently the outcome of repeated acts of civic discord, violence and forcible dispossession (e.g. the sorry fate of clergymen and Church properties in revolutionary France).

On Change

Towns and their squares have often been chaotic and dynamic. By contrast, rural civilisation has typically exemplified constancy and continuity. Unlike agrarian communities, we are unlikely to find a static set of values for urban civilisation or even static descriptions of the equalities hereby proposed as the basis of our understanding of the term "citizenship".

The awareness of historical change in primarily urban political entities reflects in a specific area of collective human agency Richard Rorty's broader understanding of the social justification of human knowledge and beliefs at large. In his neo-pragmatist, sceptical philosophy, Rorty argues that, at the very bottom of things, we endorse some issues, and some values, because we were born within an ethnos with its own tradition, rhetoric, literature and economic standards.

Changes may always come about; but these will accord with new and distracting arrivals on the scene: a climatic change, a religious prophet, an economic collapse, etc. New hierarchies, new accounts, new goals, new preferences. Given enough time, all change. Such vast cultural shifts may take more than a generation to occur, hence we do not always feel involved in an endless value-dance, although periods of rapid technological innovation or great economic cataclysms can cause occasionally extreme discomfort and swift transformations.

Immobility is pretty uncommon in an *agora* where people come and go, chat, and buy and sell goods almost unceasingly, e.g. a liberal ethnos. Observing which values survive and which decline is thus a dialectical game, and even if we may state that there is a hard nucleus of values withstanding all of the changes; in fact, it is very likely that their relevance, i.e. their position within the axiological hierarchy of the community, is in constant flux.

On Value

In recent years, however, despite the predominantly sceptical and relativistic culture of our age epitomised by popular thinkers like Richard Rorty, a significant effort in determining a nucleus of values that varies little and, above all, ought not to vary ever, has been made by Canadian value theorist John McMurtry (b. 1939), whose book *The Cancer Stage of Capitalism* serves here as an introduction to life-value onto-axiology, namely the theory of value according to which life is the fundamental ground for all evaluations (i.e. determinations of what is good, better, bad, or worse).[68]

McMurtry's book is aimed at revealing and analysing both the inner logic and the structural consequences of contemporary market theory, i.e. a historical bastion of modern liberalism, which is seen instead as the utmost expression of the economic degeneration of today's actual markets, commonly named "globalisation", the development of which is portrayed as the correlative of a carcinogenic pathology.[69]

Globalisation's process of worldwide affirmation is criticised by McMurtry as destructive at various levels: medical, environmental, social, and cultural. Its allegedly necessary conquest of the planet in the name of measurable economic growth is explained as the avoidable result of the uncritical institutionalisation of an essentially ethical, not just economic, paradigm, which is characteristic of modern Western history but is not recognised as such by most economists, philosophers and intellectuals.[70]

In its shortest formulation, McMurtry claims that contemporary market theory entails a fundamental conflict between the requirements of the dominating economic forces and those of planetary life, akin to the ways in which a cancer disrupts and destroys its life-host. McMurtry's critical exploration starts with the essential features of the traditional Marxian critique of the capitalist economy. As Karl Marx (1818–1883) described the inner logic of capitalism, money is invested in the production of commodities to raise more money (i.e. the economy of profit; $\$ \rightarrow C \rightarrow \$^1$): the bourgeois "money-sequence economy" that revolved the pre-capitalist feudal conception of money as a means of exchange of commodities for other commodities ($C \rightarrow \$ \rightarrow C^1$).[71]

Stepping beyond Marx, McMurtry analyses commodities in terms of relevance for life. In this way, he describes the first sequence of the "money-sequence economy", i.e. money invested into commodities *qua* means of life (MoL) in order to make more money at the end of the economic transaction ($\$ \rightarrow MoL \rightarrow \$^1$). Many of the commodities produced in the market do not fall into this category, for they do not improve or merely sustain life-forms, but are actually harmful under both respects (e.g. junk food and cigarettes).

In the second sequence or variation of the same economy, some of the commodities are revealed to be explicitly designed to destroy life (e.g. weapons, carcinogenic pesticides). They are means of destruction aimed at making more money, i.e. life-destructive commodities ($\$ \rightarrow DC \rightarrow \$^1$).

The third sequence or variation of the "money-sequence economy" is not mediated by any commodity that is not money itself. It is decoupled from any sort of materially productive activity. In contemporary parlance, it is the so-called "virtual economy" or "paper economy" (e.g. speculative investments in stocks, bonds and currencies), as opposed to the "real economy" (i.e. the previous two sequences). Its algebraic expression is $\$ \rightarrow \$^1 \rightarrow \$^2$, i.e. money invested into more money for the sake of accruing more money, potentially *ad infinitum*, and without any consideration whatsoever of whether life is damaged or destroyed in the process (e.g. profitable investments in the shares of arms manufacturers, polluting industries, pathogenic service providers).[72]

Once characterised in light of life requirements, these three variations of the money-sequence economy show the root of McMurtry's preoccupation. None of the life-distinctions that these sequences embody are or can be recognised by the money-sequence economy. All that can be recognised by it is, on the contrary, money; i.e. the services and the so-called "goods" understood as money-equivalents, that which alone can be computed by accounting standards and that, as a matter of investment practice, makes a firm attractive. In this way, the whole of today's capitalist economy can be said to be detached *in principle* from any life-based goal, which may be served at times, yet accidentally and not inherently.

McMurtry focuses his attention on the case of the virtual economy, since this third variation has become the leading force within today's market economy. In today's global context, the first two variations have largely turned into appendixes of the third, and the financial market has become the arbiter of the real economy.[73]

What also propels McMurtry's alarm at the widespread success of the paper economy is that the life-protecting powers of the public institutions, i.e. the sole seats of collective rationality directly engaged in the promotion of the common good as such, are being weakened or even annihilated by the same economy. This crippling happens because of the progressive financial subjugation of the public sector to the private, which can blackmail the former by withholding investments and can direct it as well by financing politicians, media outlets and educational institutions promoting private interests over public ones.

In all these dealings, which shape the fate of the real economy, universal life requirements do not normally matter *qua* parameters of computation and, even when they do (e.g. triple bottom-line accounting), they are treated as marginal, expendable and inessential. A firm may lie on the carcinogenic gaseous emissions of its products and yet survive a media storm tarnishing its reputation; being unprofitable for several consecutive fiscal years, instead, would never shield it from bankruptcy or takeover.

Additionally, the virtual economy is super-national in nature, whereas public institutions operate mainly at a national level. Because of this gap between the market and the institutions that could protect the general welfare, the money-sequence economy has become in effect a trans-national sovereign, overriding life-protecting control of national and regional goods.

The pathogenic relationship between globalisation and systemic damages to life-hosts is, however, not discerned as a decisive problem from the market view, and this is therefore not adequately revised, both because the existing economic structures are often considered as necessary as physical laws, and because the same market forces have a role in determining the social consciousness of these phenomena, in spite of ongoing mass extinctions, cancerous pathologies, massive pollution and countless additional life damages over generational time. With the hidden insidious pervasiveness typical of a disease agent, the money-sequence economy is not recognised as responsible for the life-damages it causes, so that the "immune defences" embodied by the public authorities do not arrest its development but, on the contrary, operate inadequate regulation or even serve the advance of its life-decoupled sequences as a requirement of "competing in the global market".[74]

On Hope

The "cancer stage of capitalism" of the book's title is not a metaphor, but an explanatory model for understanding the modalities whereby the so-called "virtual economy" has been taking over the "real economy", damaging in the process the life-support systems of the planet by imposition of a pecuniary cost-reducing and revenue-increasing regime, which at the same time reduces any genuinely life-protecting public institution as "unaffordable" or a deplorable source of "interference" in the presupposed positive workings of the market.[75]

Hope is not lost, though, according to McMurtry. Once the previously invisible contradiction between global market demands and life requirements is unconcealed, a responsive solution becomes possible. McMurtry's formulation of a cure involves two distinct moments: the identification of the theoretical criteria for a paradigm shift; and the determination of operative criteria to guide the paradigm shift.

The first moment—providing theoretical criteria for a paradigm shift—requires the introduction of life within the life-blind Newtonian-engineering model of dominant market theory. This is possible, argues McMurtry, if and only if one recognises that the dominating economic paradigm is also and fundamentally an ethical paradigm, i.e. a "value program" about what is good and what is bad that can be changed as a matter of collective choice, so as to progress from a "money-sequence economy" into a "life-sequence economy".[76] This "life-sequence economy" substitutes the priority of the "money-sequence economy", that is, "more money" at the end of each transaction ($\$^1$, $\$^2$), with a new one: "more life" at the end of each transaction (L^1).[77] "More life" means satisfying genuine needs, a need being defined as all that whose regular deprivation "results in an absolute reduction of its owner's life-range capabilities".[78]

Economic transactions would then become truly profitable and accrue to "real capital", i.e. "life capital": profits would not to be finally judged by corporate incomes, but by fulfilment of life-hosts' requirements.[79] According to the logic of the "life-sequence economy", life ranges are increased, or at least maintained at the same level, at the end of each economic transaction, which may not need to be unprofitable in the myopic pecuniary sense either, as the extended formula of the "life-sequence economy" exemplifies: $L \rightarrow \$ \rightarrow MoL \rightarrow \$^1 \rightarrow L^1$.

Increases or decreases in terms of life, argues McMurtry, are measurable by the degrees or ranges of biological movement, felt being and thought they enable or disable. Conceptual and material instruments required for these measurements are amply available and supplied by, for example, medical science, statistical demographics, biology, and many other disciplines and codified criteria (e.g. measurements of functionality for organs, surveys on the level of literacy, comparative records on infant mortality or life-expectancy rates, etc.).

The synthetic, combined efforts of these discipline reveals in fact the existence of an infra-structural, reactive "life-ground", whose exigencies cannot be damaged by "the cancer stage of capitalism" without some form of life-protective response.[80] Just as the combination of the information derived from different branches of medical science has made it possible to discover and understand the mechanisms used by the human body to react against diseases, so the synergy of all these sciences can individuate how a collective of living organisms can defend themselves from attacks to its integrity.

Consistently with this insight, the second moment of the cure, i.e. the determination of the operative criteria for the shift, articulates the nature of this life-ground upon which we stand. Unlike Marx, who bases his resolving principles of social revolution as productive force development and the political movement of the working class towards the "creation of society anew", McMurtry works from the basis of life-value as such, namely the evolved "civil commons" that are already in place, and which require the recognition and response of societies across class divisions.[81]

On Commons

The "civil commons" are not the same as the standard "commons" addressed by economists and ethicists in their textbooks. The mere "commons" of ordinary scholarship are, in fact, a "nature-given land or resource which is not regulated by human agency to serve life", whereas the "civil commons" imply co-operative social agency whereby, *inter alia*, "such natural or human-made goods of life... are regulated".[82] Specifically: "[T]he civil commons is human agency in personal, collective or institutional form which protects and enables the access of all members of a community to basic life goods".[83]

McMurtry cites many examples of the civil commons, ranging from the pre-agribusiness village commons in England, or the Turkwei's woods of acacia in Kenya, to widespread funeral customs (intended as practices to avoid epidemics caused by rotting corpses) and children's primary education (i.e. the ABC to be able to interact with the other members of the community). Other examples reach beyond the evident regulated "commons" of a community, such as the internet, indigenous music, sidewalks and footpaths, or, interestingly, vernacular language itself.[84] The civil commons are not an idealistic principle of good will, or a declaration of universalistic intent, but something that is already present in the world as its own life-protecting institutions. Such is the case, for example, of phenomena as different as the welfare state, the Nuremberg Charter, the Ozone Protocol, public gardens and city plans.

As McMurtry argues, if we want to respond to the pathogenic privatisation of the global market, we need to turn our gaze towards the life-ground of the civil commons, which operates in its primary moment as a social immune system. On this basis, further life-protecting operative criteria can be implemented on the already-existing life-protective human structures.

In the first place, McMurtry articulates principles to select among public offices, for "whatever is required for the civil commons to serve life is a legitimate function for public financing and support".[85] These offices would have then to respect their constitutional ends, i.e. those life-enabling ends that qualify as genuine civil commons.

In the second place, McMurtry describes the sort of constitutional and legal framework to be applied in order to respond. The Universal Declaration of Human Rights, the International Covenant on Civil and Political Rights, the International Covenant on Economic, Social and Cultural Rights, represent preeminent constitutional and legal instruments that express precisely the defining principle of the "civil commons" in codified form and articulate it in justiciable and policy-guiding applications. The crucial point becomes therefore the full recognition of this unifying life-protective *telos* and its concrete enforcement as "the rule of law".[86]

In contrast with all this stand the existing regimes of international trade, which regularly override the enforcement of the legal principles stated in these life-protective official Charters and Covenants as a trend of dreadful metastases. International trade, McMurtry demonstrates by its exclusions, permits any sort of crime against humanity because no recognition prior law against these crimes is included in their thousands of articles. Application of already instituted international charters on a level with, say, international copyright conventions, would achieve most important advances.

Analogously, argues McMurtry, control over the prime source of the carcinogenic pathology, i.e. the proliferating "money-sequence economy", is the complementary ground of resolution to society's war against itself. Thus, McMurtry offers many policy proposals on money issuance and circulation, such as an outright ban on speculation over national currencies and the introduction of an international system of taxation on financial transactions. In an economy where liquid capital overrides all other forms of capital, controlling and steering money for the sake of accruing to real capital, i.e. life capital, becomes paramount.[87]

A Concluding Remark

Academic speculation can lead the inquiring mind from one end of the conceptual spectrum, such as scepticism, to the opposite end, such as McMurtry's utter realism with regard to the paramount character of life, and yet leave the same mind free to choose between them, upon the strength of the related arguments, insights and perspectives for individual and/or collective agency. In the meantime, academic speculation will have mapped a vast territory occupied by diverse interpretative frameworks, divergent assumptions of value, alternative logical articulations thereof, competing rhetorical advocacies, and inevitable gaps or errors to be identified and, if possible, resolved. As such, academic speculation can be as frustrating as it is capable of being fascinating. In it, dialogues do not always reach a conclusion, but are pursued nonetheless; if not for the final result, at least for the wealth of thought that engaging in them can pour out. Hopefully, this third chapter offers a token of the latter sort of activity, letting frustration exceed not its counterpart, fascination.

Chapter 4: Reflections on Ian Hacking and the Science Wars

Ian Hacking's 1999 book *The Social Construction of What?* addresses the two ends of the conceptual spectrum involved in the so-called "science wars" between "constructionists" and "inevitabilists", whereby the former term refers to those who believe that the entities with which natural and human sciences deal are in some way "socially constructed" (i.e. they "need not have existed, or need to be at all as [they are]"), while the latter term refers to those who claim that such entities are actually as they are described by science or, in other terms, that scientific knowledge is capable of representing the "inherent structure" of the world.[88] According to the latter stance, any genuinely truthful science of the future would discover "inevitably" the same "universal truths" that the present one has attained, insofar as it would be committed to outline the very same "inherent structure".[89]

Each chapter of the book contains an essay investigating a distinct area, or a specific set of cases, inside which the "science wars" have allegedly taken place: gender, numbers, quarks, schizophrenia, child abuse, intelligence quotients, dolomite and deification. With such a variety of instances on display, Hacking's work constitutes an unusual path to approach the debated issue of "scientific realism" and, as Richard Rorty's sceptical stance is concerned, the equally disputed issue of "antirepresentationalism", whereby:

> *[An] account that does not view knowledge as a matter of getting reality right, but rather as a matter of acquiring habits of action for coping with reality... [In] the attempt to eschew discussion of realism by denying that the notion of "representation", or that of "fact of the matter", has any useful role in philosophy... Antirepresentationalists need to insist that "determinacy" is not what is in question – that neither does thought determine reality nor, in the sense intended by the realist, does reality determine thought. Both of them are pseudo-explanations.*[90]

The scope of Hacking's critical analysis is wide, indeed much wider than most philosophical studies on the issue of "scientific realism", orbiting normally around physics, mathematics and, to a lesser extent, linguistics. Hacking stretches the borders of the discussion to geology, psychology, psychiatry, endocrinology and several other fields of research. And parallel to the width of his interests is the spirit with which he approaches them. Hacking has no *a priori* preclusion to any contribution or direction, for he is trying to find grounds favourable to both "constructionism" and "inevitabilism" (aka "inherent-structurism").[91]

Sticking Points

Declaredly, Hacking does not want to either chastise or exalt anybody.[92] Rather, he claims that he wants to understand. He states that he wishes to see through and behind the various issues of contention, the deeper causes of the "science wars" themselves, and the reasons for and against the two antagonistic sides. He argues that he aims to investigate the margins of their relevance, highlight the insights that they can provide, and detect the key-elements of their mutual opposition, which recalls the problem highlighted by Kant in his first *Critique*, i.e. that our best science may be confined to the realm of phenomena and therefore incapable of grasping the noumena, or things-in-themselves.

In defence of "constructionism", Hacking argues in favour of the idea that we do choose and create our own categories of understanding, in both natural and human sciences. According to him, it is undeniable that we make concepts, terms and jargons and that, through our creative "kind-making", we give shape to the world that we inhabit, i.e. the very universe of our scientific examinations, the hunting fields for our cognitive enterprises, the scope of "what is held thinkable... at some moment in time".[93] Importantly, through the same process, we shape also the universe of any present and, to a significant extent, future possible study, insofar as the concepts that we are going to employ are bound to delimit the logical space of the questions that can sensibly be asked by the researcher.[94]

In defence of "inevitabilism", Hacking stresses the point that whatever language or categories of understanding we choose, the world remains for the most part as it is. Quarks could have never been discovered, or a completely different science of the physical realm could have done without them. Nevertheless, quarks would have remained in either case the same as they are. One thing is the concept that we mould, another is the object that we intend to refer to by that concept.

Of course, the dividing line between the two things is not so easy to draw, above all when we are dealing with "interactive" kinds, namely kinds that are somehow affected by the selected categorisation.[95] Certain concepts, in fact, cut down to the deeper ontology of the objects themselves, causing them to react to such thorough super- and trans-determination. For instance, many a family found itself at a loss when "autistic children" were supposed to imply, *by definition*, "refrigerator mothers".[96]

The ecumenical spirit of Hacking does not nullify the divergences existing between the two factions. As a matter of fact, Hacking individuates three "sticking points" or "hot spots" where the unspecified metaphysical assumptions of the two parties rise to the surface, thus explaining their mutual theoretical misunderstandings and showing the irreconcilable contrast that is present between them: "contingency", "nominalism" and "(the explanation of) stability".[97]

Roughly summarised, the first point or spot deals with the idea that valid "scientific knowledge" could be different from the one we have *hic et nunc* and involve different concepts.[98] The second point or spot deals with the idea that the "facts" described by scientific knowledge are dependent upon the ways we represent the world.[99] The third point or spot deals with the idea that the uninterrupted belief in certain truths of scientific knowledge may depend on reasons that are external to mere scientific acceptability, as well as with the idea that mere scientific acceptability itself can be heavily influenced by factors of economic, cultural, religious, or sociological nature.[100]

In this chapter I focus on nominalism, albeit the analysis of any of the three sticking points involves indirect references to, and direct consequences for, the other two. I choose nominalism for it is the one that more evidently alludes to the issue of antirepresentationalism and, more broadly, the philosophy of Richard Rorty, whom the reader has already encountered in the present book. Additionally, it is the sticking point that more candidly manifests Hacking's own "sticking points", namely his own likely unspecified metaphysical assumptions and possible theoretical misgivings.

Nominalism

Hacking uses the word "nominalism" to mean that "the world does not come with a unique prepackaged structure" and that, by abandoning the commonplace reverence for scientific facts as the objective backbone of any sensible discussion, the "constructionist" party is committed to dismantling science's unspoken dogmas and science's far-reaching intellectual authority, sometimes in the name of a neo-Romantic "rage against reason".[101]

Hacking claims the constructionist party to be implying that scientific concepts do not convey anything more than their stipulated sense, whereas their opponents believe that such concepts are able to carve nature at the joints. The constructionist would then reply that the world has no such joints or that, even if it had joints, they could not be described once and for all, for scientific knowledge, namely the terms that we use in science, change trough time. Hacking believes that he himself could be judged to belong to the constructionist party in his willingness to be a "nominalist", whereby he signals that he should be regarded as a thinker aware of the deeper meaning of words, their philosophical history and their theoretical background.[102]

Though historically and philologically debatable, Hacking's use of the medieval label of "nominalism" for his chosen party aims at bringing forth the unspecified metaphysical stances underpinning the claims made by the two contenders in the ongoing "science wars".[103]

According to Hacking, the central and constant issue of their debates regards the problem of the ultimate relation between human concepts and the correspondent entities in the world, which is thought of as independent of us—a problem that metaphysicians have been wrestling with since the days of classical.

Contemporary scholars, especially outside philosophy departments, are however largely ignorant of the metaphysical debates of old. Metaphysics, which used to be the queen of all sciences, has long lost its status, not only as a science, but even as a scholarly discipline at all, taught at any level of the existing educational systems. From a metaphysical perspective, in any case, the constructionists claim that whatever we are referring to with words, these words are nothing but human-made tools, and so profoundly are they human-made that they cannot and will never assure any incontrovertible outcome *vis-à-vis* our knowledge of reality. Rorty's declared gulf between the opposed blocks of language and reality resurfaces here and, with it, the possibility itself of sceptical doubt.

The inevitabilists, on their part, reply that, even if the referential process may be socially and historically determined, the outcomes can be, at least sometimes, incontrovertible, necessary and true, for there must be a world limiting in a substantial manner the freedom and variability of the human inquiry and its attendant words. Hacking follows in part the inevitabilist stance, insofar as he argues that we can distinguish between "indifferent" and "interactive" kinds, namely that there are "natural" or "artificial" kinds which do not change when the related concepts are being revisited (e.g. crystals and pathology).[104]

Still, Hacking accepts the constructionist perspective in admitting that we do mould our cognitive pigeonholes in complex and variable socio-historical frames of research delimiting the horizon of what can be known and even hoped to be known (e.g. how the massive money spent on weapons research open certain avenues of research and close others).[105] Similarly, Hacking seems to appreciate the insights coming from his colleague Henry Nelson Goodman (1906–1998) concerning "irrealism" (i.e. the suspension of judgement over the realism vs. anti-realism debate) and "world-making" (i.e. that we determine the universe to be investigated by determining the concepts allowed to exist inside it).[106]

At the same time, Hacking discusses contemporary metaphysicians such as Hilary Putnam (1926–2016) and Saul Kripke (b. 1940) in order to retrieve a causal "theory of meaning" as a plausible explanation of why we hold certain beliefs and of how concepts may come into existence in the first place. Hacking endorses both the former's insights into the creative element that the concepts' genesis involve, namely the power that they have of instantiating a new universe through their mere application, and the latter's stress on the causal connection that characterises reference, which is not a matter of sheer and unconditioned human creativity.[107]

Hacking zigzags between the two camps in the ongoing science war and no eventual synthetic or resolving input is given. On the other hand, Hacking does make it repeatedly clear that he intends to decline the temptation of responding once and for all to the metaphysical issues at stake, adhering *ipso facto* to a specific metaphysical stance (i.e. Goodman's irrealism). All that Hacking wants to achieve, apparently, is to present clearly the likely uses and possible abuses of "elevator words" that both constructionists and inevitabilists employ, namely those words that convey metaphysical ideas about higher or deeper levels of understanding (e.g. "facts", "truth", "reality"), whether the person proffering them is aware of their metaphysical character or not.[108]

To put it lyrically, Hacking's journey between the Scylla and Charybdis of the so-called "science wars" ends up with a continuation of the same, no final port being reached. Hacking's own metaphysics shares Odysseus' fate.

Antirepresentationalism

The ultimate ground of the struggle between inevitabilists and constructionists is representationalist in character, for it focuses upon the issue of whether whatever lies beyond our linguistic and conceptual systems of reference operates some form of constraint on their by-products (e.g. scientific theories and laws) or not. It is not clear whether the same ground might be lying beneath Hacking's own approach, which now sides with irrealism, then speaks of "nominalism", and finally commends Kant's "transcendental idealism", while at the same time declaring recurrently that no conclusive metaphysical claim is being made.[109] Albeit highlighting elevator words as the focus of his own investigation, Hacking states that the same elevator words are used far too frequently and therefore cause detriment to the proper understanding of science, which would fare better without speaking much of "facts" or "reality".[110]

Hacking does not seem fully aware of this side of his personal intellectual odyssey, which is not irrelevant to the problems that he tackles in his book. In the end, his notion of nominalism comes across as being as troublesome as the alternatives, namely constructionism and inevitabilism, whilst also being dissected far less in its metaphysical implications than the other two options. It is quite clear that Hacking's nominalism is meant to reduce the room for metaphysical challenges when they are not required (i.e. the science wars), but it is not clear whether and why such a position and not some other should be taken, since he states to be avoiding grand metaphysical claims.

The only way in which I can see Hacking's nominalism to be able to reduce the room for metaphysical knots in his own interpretation of science and reality is by attributing him a form of antirepresentationalism *à la* Rorty. As already observed, Hacking's nominalism recognises the role that we play in formulating the terms through which we cope with the world. Repeatedly, Hacking stresses his belief in material entities as existing independently from our ideas about them, i.e. as being what they are. Yet, the gap between "interactive" and "indifferent" kinds is described as sharp and broad, and Hacking maintains that the categories of explanation formulated and employed in the sciences, the social ones in particular, are eminently practical, rather than "semantic", and historically "dynamic", rather than static.[111]

Hacking is torn between the two sides involved in the ongoing science wars. He recognises the good reasons of both sides and does not know how to solve their conflict, though he offers suggestions, namely the reduction of their metaphysical claims. Such a suggestion is coherent if and only if it is seen as the adoption of an antirepresentationalist view, which, on the one hand, discharges the gap between language and facts as a pseudoproblem that should be better abandoned and, on the other hand, allows for a primitive, ordinary rendering of terms such as "true", "real", "actual", etc. Under such an antirepresentationalist perspective, these terms, instead of being or implying metaphysical claims, would merely commend the social practices that we, in our ethnos, happen to find most useful.

Without this Rorty-esque step into "antirepresentationalism", I cannot see how Hacking's advice may be taken as non- or anti-metaphysical and, above all, how his analysis of the science wars may sound less ambiguous than the metaphysical options that he himself scrutinises. I say "less" because some ambiguity is going to be left on the scene, inevitably. Critical doubt can pierce any position.

What is more, Hacking's possible "antirepresentationalism" is not self-evident, but merely inferrable from his zigzagging remarks. Either he is not aware of it, or he does not like the idea of being grouped with post-analytic authors such as Donald Davidson and Richard Rorty. That much, I must admit, I do not know, though Hacking does describe himself in his book as an "analytic" philosopher, not a post-analytic one.[112] Also, in the book's footnotes, Hacking does express his preoccupation with regard to being lumped together with postmodernist, sceptical, or otherwise 'unscientific' thinkers such as Richard Rorty, who actually suffered from considerable ostracism in Anglophone philosophy departments. For instance, Hacking stresses the fact that he wants to "save" the notion of "truth" from becoming an old-fashioned term that is hopelessly relative to the conceptual scheme inside which it is applied, even if he knows that his "contingency thesis may be confused with multiculturalism... Truth", Hacking writes, cannot be put "in ironical shudder quotes".[113]

With respect to the notion of truth so defended from ironic disintegration, Hacking's solution does not differ much from Rorty's own post-analytic approach, in the sense that truth gets rescued merely as a primitive notion, which turns troublesome only when the expression itself is, in Hacking's terminology, "elevated". As he writes, notions that may sound even remotely like "epistemology and metaphysics" are actually to be regarded with suspicion, in spite of Hacking's own love for such disciplines.[114] Hence Hacking's own methodological "[m]axim: *if, in a philosophical discussion, you become tempted to engage in semantic ascent in order to make some point you think is important, stop, and try doing the thinking at ground level.*"[115]

Analogously to Rorty, Hacking wishes to deflate the problem of truth—as well as those of objective facts or being in touch with reality—which carry far too easily into the terrain of metaphysical dogmatism, but he is also terribly afraid of being confused with superficial "relativists", irresponsible "ironists" and, overall, all those 'isms' that "We analytic philosophers" disapprove of, i.e. the pariahs in Hacking's own professional ethnos or sub-ethnos.[116]

A Concluding Remark

By discussing metaphysics in order to learn and instruct to avoid it, Hacking's position can be justifiably read as not very different from Rorty's one. Avoiding elevation in favour of a plainer approach to widely accepted knowledge and current scientific praxes is pretty much what "antirepresentationalism" instructs us to do. Sharing an analogous levelling spirit, Rorty himself wants us to discharge "the idea of the intellectual as someone who is in touch with the nature of things, not by way of the opinion of his community" or, in Hacking's terms, by way of the various "kinds" that we make up and employ in dealing with reality.[117] A self-declared neo-pragmatist, Rorty too wants to get rid of those elevator words of which Hacking disapproves, if not of the process of elevation as such, which

Hacking too wishes to avoid *per* his cited operational maxim. A horizontal approach animates Hacking's work, which invites us to stay on the ground level and resist the temptation of leaping any higher, or lower, into the dream of the superior philosophical "depth" critiqued by Rorty.[118] A shared nominalist spirit pervades their enterprises, at least as far as I can make sense of Hacking's own version of nominalism. Without rejecting the practical use of terms such as "truth" and "facts", Rorty himself wants us to reject the ideal goal of a philosophy that "must lead to the truth, to correspondence to reality, to the intrinsic nature of things" and that actually sees "solidarity", i.e. our mutual responsibilities as human beings, as far more important than "objectivity".[119]

Chapter 5: Reflections on David Lewis' Australian Materialism

Most of David Kellog Lewis' works in philosophy were republished in 1999 by Cambridge University Press in a three-volume collection belonging to the book series called "Cambridge Studies in Philosophy". The second volume of this set is devoted to Lewis' papers in metaphysics, ontology and epistemology from 1983 to 1999 and is the central source for the present chapter.[120] The other two volumes reissue, respectively, Lewis' papers in philosophical logic and ethics.

It is interesting to have a chance of approaching Lewis' thought through an extensive collection of philosophical papers, namely his favourite means of scholarly expression, which allows the reader to get a better grasp of its more general distinctive traits and motives. Each paper, taken individually, tends in fact to be too specific and too technical to permit such an overall grasp, whereas having so many of his works grouped together and on such diverse topics as intrinsic properties, holes, truth-makers and *qualia*, constitutes the perfect occasion to acquire a sense of the *fil rouge* linking them all together as the product of a single mind, driven by certain dominant scholarly interests, personal commitments and intellectual passions.[121]

In particular, I comment here on a single aspect of such an underpinning 'red thread' that I believe to be both relevant and controversial. It is relevant in the sense that it plays an important role in Lewis' overall approach to philosophy. It is controversial in the sense that it highlights tensions that are either inherent to Lewis' own thinking or to Lewis' overall approach *vis-à-vis* some of his famous colleagues' in contemporary Anglophone academe. The aspect that I have in mind is Lewis' self-declared project for the formulation of a fundamental, comprehensive, materialist ontology, which can take into serious account the data furnished by contemporary natural sciences, and by physics in particular.

Materialism

As Lewis himself sketches it, his ontology can be placed under the label of "Materialism", namely: "[T]he thesis that physics – something not too different from present-day physics, though presumably somewhat improved – is a comprehensive theory of the world, complete as well as correct. The world is as physics says it is, and there's no more to say. World history written in physical language is all of world history."[122]

This is as clear as it is a strong, though certainly not uncommon, philosophical statement. To which Lewis promptly adds: "that is rough speaking indeed"; his own "goal will be to give a better formulation", namely "to formulate Materialism as a supervenience thesis: no difference without physical difference."[123] Thus, in a more refined way, Lewis restates "materialism" as follows: "Among worlds where no natural properties alien to our world are instantiated, no two differ without differing physically; any two such worlds that are exactly alike physically are duplicates."[124]

Seen from a different angle, Lewis' position could be even defined as a contemporary version of "physicalism", insofar as it is up to physics to determine the natural properties around which his ontology orbits: "[P]hysicalists take physics – as it is now, or as it will be – at face value. And physics profess to discover the elite properties" through which we can determine "objective sameness and difference, joints in the world, discriminatory classifications not of our own making".[125] Physics, and no other science, is the instrument to be used to undermine anti-realist and phenomenological hypotheses, the claims of which irritate Lewis' openly declared "*a priori* reductionism about everything".[126]

Materialism and reductionism do not imply each other logically, but in the case of David Lewis they stem out together of his alleged faith in the natural sciences, and physics in particular, *qua* comprehensive theory of the world. As stated, this element of Lewis' philosophising is relevant. It is meant to justify his aspirations to the reduction of the number and of the kinds of beings to be admitted in his fundamental ontology, which is however controversial too, since:

[A] It implies the presence of a conflict with those who are not committed to the materialist, physicalist, and, up to a relevant extent, reductionist program as David Lewis claims to be himself; and

[B] Lewis' reductionism is so "minimal", as he himself observes,[127] that it becomes difficult to believe that he is defending a materialist position at all, at least in the critical sense that this term has acquired in Western philosophy through the centuries—sometimes simplistically or even unfairly but nonetheless most firmly—from Democritus (ca. 460–ca. 370 BC) and Epicurus (341–270 BC) to Etienne Bonnot de Condillac (1715–1780) and Karl Marx, *via* Roscelin de Compiègne (ca. 1050–ca. 1125) and Thomas Hobbes (1588–1679), namely a nominalist and polemical position according to which *all that exists is matter*. As I am going to show, Lewis seems to be stating something along the lines of: *all that matters exists*.

With respect to [A], Lewis states: "I am an 'Australian materialist:' I have long held that mental states are states, presumably physical states of the brain, definable as occupants of certain folk-psychological causal roles."[128] Beyond the mere area of psychophysics, the hope is that "[t]heoretical advances make it possible to simplify total science by positing bridge laws identifying some of the entities discussed in one theory with entities discussed in another theory." Instances of this kind are "the identification of water with H_2O, of light with electromagnetic radiation, and so on"; these correspondences being "not merely... posit[ed]... for the sake of parsimony" but implied by the theory at stake.[129]

With respect to [B], Lewis admits that:

(1) Materialism is not a thesis of finite translatability of all our language into the language of physics. (2) Materialism is not to be identified with any one Materialist theory of mind. It is a

thesis that motivates a variety of theories of mind: versions of Behaviourism, Functionalism, the mind-body identity theory, even the theory that mind is all a mistake. (3) Materialism is not just the theory that there are no things except those recognised by physics... (4) That suggests that Materialism is, at least in part, the thesis that there are no natural properties instantiated at our world except those recognised by physics... [Although] a Materialist ought not to hold that all natural properties instantiated in our world are physical properties.[130]

Two Critical Remarks

To a closer scrutiny, the faith professed by Lewis in materialism grows softer and softer as one reads over the whole collection, dwindling his reductionism *via* interposition of sophisticated qualifications and fastidious provisos. Though more precise, Lewis' materialism becomes less and less convincing as an ideal goal, or as a school of thought, because of its being multivalent and profoundly differentiated. Physics too becomes less and less manifestly the only and absolute ruler inside his project for an ultimate ontology. As marginally but importantly noted by Lewis, not all natural properties might be physical; therefore, it would not be the task of physics alone "to provide an inventory of all the fundamental properties and relations that occur in the world".[131] Materialism itself, at the end of the day, "is meant to be a contingent thesis, a merit of our world that not all other worlds share".[132]

Lewis' subtle, marginal, but numerous and recurrent self-restraining corrections make his position so blandly materialistic, that referring to it as "materialist" becomes, from a polemical point of view, irrelevant. Firstly, to a close scrutiny, his materialism is very generous towards hardly material entities such as "gods and spooks".[133] Secondly, the "scientific worldview" that he espouses is not very distant from the "commonsensical worldview" of the average Western reader, to whom his works are directed.[134]

As regards the generosity of his ontology, it is not difficult to find passages where Lewis proves to be open to many realms of legitimate existence that many a materialist would probably discharge:

> *Among "things" I mean to include all the gerrymandered wholes and undermarcated parts admitted by the most permissive mereology. Further, I include such physical objects as spatiotemporal regions and force fields, unless an eliminative reduction of them should prove desirable. Further, I include such nonphysical objects as gods and spooks though not – I hope – as parts of the same world as us. Worlds themselves need no special treatment. They are things – big ones, for the most part.*[135]

All these 'things' can be admitted because Lewis defends an "ontology [that], though Nominalistic, is in other respects generous. It consists of *possibilia* – particular, individual things, some of which comprise our actual world and others of which are unactualised – together with the iterative hierarchy built up from them."[136]

Arguably, Lewis' position can be defended by stressing its technical acuity and, with it, the distinction between *possibilia* and actuality; but this is eminently and firstly an epistemological distinction, not solely and uniquely an ontological one. What we assume as being possible at one stage is something that we could discover to pertain to our actual world at another stage. Experiments are set in physics to prove that the entities postulated by our mathematical models are actually there. *Gestalt* effects are employed in psychology laboratories to demonstrate that perceptual experience actually involves more than the mere physical stimuli entailed by it. Mystical visions or divine illuminations are granted by the Divine Will to some subjects, as blessed or hallucinated as these may be, so as to bestow upon them at least the certainty that what they believed possible is actually there.

This distinction between possible and actual being is blurred in Lewis' own accounts, leaving more than enough room to the Pandora's box of the determining the 'right' interpretation of what is merely possible and what is actually there:

In the broadest sense, all possible individuals without exception, even the poached eggs, are possibilities for me... But some possibilities are accessible to me in various ways, others are not. My counterparts by description are metaphysically accessible to me; or better, each counterpart-by-description relation is a relation of metaphysical accessibility. My alternatives are visually, perceptually, doxastically, epistemically... accessible to me. Metaphysical and (for instance) epistemic possibilities for me are not things of two different sorts. They are possibilia *out of the same logical space. The difference is in the accessibility.*[137]

Accessibility is not determined once and for all, through a verification principle or an axiom of observability of some sort. As Lewis pens: "if the subject has two alternatives in a single world, we need not wonder which is the right one. That is a question to settle by stipulation."[138] Even more permissive sounds Lewis when asserting: "[W]e cannot limit ourselves to 'real' possibilities that conform to the actual the laws of nature, and maybe also to actual past history. For propositions about laws and history are contingent, and may or may not be known."[139]

Lewis has no sharp preclusion to existing alternatives, for ontology is a work in progress, sensitive to the changes taking place in the mutable and perfectible system of human knowledge. Some of the alternatives that are not available right now, for they cannot be defined as credible members of the materialist family of beings, might become feasible in the future. When discussing the issue of necessity, Lewis magnanimously writes:

Perhaps God's existence may be supposed to be necessary in some sense. Yet in a second sense, it still might be contingent. (We could expect disagreement about which sense is straightforward and which sense is artificial.) A conviction that the property of being divinely created is not intrinsic would then be evidence, for those of us who are prepared to take the supposition of God's necessary existence seriously, that it is the second sense and not the first that should be used in defining 'intrinsic.'[140]

En passant, while discussing the distinction between "extrinsic" (i.e. external, disjunctive) and "intrinsic" (i.e. internal, conjunctive) properties, Lewis leaves the door open to God himself —or Zeus, if one prefers, albeit Lewis seems unaware in his works of the philosophical discussions occurred among his Greek colleagues twenty-three centuries before him.

Rather than the divine, the only clear case of strict, philosophically commonplace materialism in Lewis' account seems to be the one regarding the phenomenological data of experience. In such a circumstance, in fact, Lewis defends a thorough supervenience thesis. While discussing the notion of the "reduction of mind", he writes:[141]

It is a task of physics to provide an inventory of all the fundamental properties and relations that occur in the world... If materialism is true, as I believe it is, then the a priori supervenience of everything upon the pattern of coinstantiation of fundamental properties and relations yields an a posteriori supervenience of everything upon the pattern of coinstantiation of fundamental physical properties and relations.[142]

Given his own professions of allegiance, one would be tempted to take this passage as the heart of Lewis' thinking. Probably, he himself would like to do so. Unfortunately, as the previous quotes show, such a move is largely dubious, if not illegitimate. The truer expressions of thorough materialism appear almost entirely in his essays on phenomenological entities alone and are not paired with equally powerful claims in the others.[143] Why is Lewis so straightforward when it becomes an issue of phenomena?

Professional turf might be the answer. As already observed with regard to Hacking's self-characterisation in the small realm of philosophical academe, knowing where one stands in the analytical-*versus*-Continental divide seems to matter much, at least in the

Anglophone world; and insofar as phenomenological entities are a crucial differentiator between analytical ontologies and several Continental ones, Lewis is very keen not to be perceived as ambiguous at all on such a subject.[144] Nonetheless, there are two dissonant voices audible behind the lines: that of a 'strict' David Lewis, the devotee of the well-established, materialist, Australian *credo*; and that of a 'munificent' David Lewis, who could embrace a far more ecumenical and sophisticated ontology.

As regards the curious harmony between the scientific worldview and the commonsensical one, it can be said that Lewis' accounts on the reality of *physis*, i.e. the realm to the description of which natural sciences are destined, do not give us a very different picture of the world as the one that common sense offers, to which I refer as *nomos*, in order to indicate the openly social or human-made character that is often attributed to it.

A good example of the peaceful co-existence of the two worldviews can be drawn from Lewis' discussion on the issue of persistence of objects through time, whereby Lewis rejects with great subtlety the claims that "properties are relations to times", or that there is only one real time, namely the present, despite our ordinary references to the past and the future. Logic and epistemology, in his view, must cohere with our ordinary insights, rather than disturb them and ask for a top-down reconstruction of our normal categories of thought.[145]

A further instance can be envisaged in Lewis' theory of colours, which he wants it to be "both materialistic and commonsensical".[146] No radical physicalist approach is justified. According to Lewis, "it is a Moorean fact"—namely a fact that we know better than any premise of an argument to the contrary—"that there are colours rightly so-called. Deny it, and the most credible explanation of your denial is that you are in the grip of some philosophical (or scientific) error".[147] Rather than relying on hard-wired sense-based accounts, Lewis prefers working on the ordinary use of linguistic expressions concerning colours, as well as on "folk psychophysics", which "is a Moorean fact", and therefore "is close to true".[148]

Lewis is ready to dismiss any aspiration to precision, if it is necessary to preserve the integrity of the "commonsensical view", for if one asks whether my 'red' and 'yours' are the same red, "a straight answer would be unwise".[149] Similarly, we read that "folk psychology" and not science, "sets presumptive limits on what our contents of belief and desire can be... In short, folk psychology says that we make sense. It credits us with a modicum of rationality".[150]

Not too distant from the overall cautious and ecumenical approach just outlined is also Lewis' response to the paradox of 1001 cats, namely that Tibbles-the-cat gradually sheds in the Springtime, hence it has up to, say, 1000 parts that cannot be said to be fully his, and therefore that there are actually many cats, and not just one, depending on whether we attribute some of those hairs to be still Tibbles' or not. Now, even if Lewis' arguments leave the semantic decision open, and entail just a limited, "partial... almost-identity" thesis, he still concludes that "context will settle the matter", and that our linguistic habits still "give us some good sense in which there is just one cat".[151]

Even more representative of this merry wedding of *physis* and *nomos* is Lewis' treatment of individual substances. Instead of breaking them down into bundles of force fields, sub-atomic particles, or *quanta* of energy, he assumes that we can distinguish:

> *[Between] Bruce [and] the cat-shaped chunk of miscellaneous and everchanging matter that follows him around, always a few steps behind... Bruce, unlike the cat-shaped chunk, has a boundary well demarcated by differences in highly natural properties. Where Bruce ends, there the density of matter, the relative abundance of the chemical elements... abruptly change. Not so for the chunk.*[152]

This account may be eminently sensible, at least *prima facie*, but it sounds less so to a closer scrutiny. It is hardly applicable, for one, to many real Bruces hanging around in the real world. Lewis' boundary-criterion is highly dependent on context and, above all, very limited in the information it can give us. For instance, should

Bruce be mounting Lily, or should Bruce be piled on a stake with a bunch of other cats to be burnt as diabolic animals, then boundaries would be far more complicated to delineate, especially for physics. Biology could help us, but biology clearly relies on categories drawn from common sense. It is, in other words, parasitic upon the commonsensical worldview, from which it borrows fundamental notions such as 'cat' and 'life', for instance.

Furthermore, whether the poor cat is dead or alive, possible or actual, is not something that can be easily determined through Lewis' criterion. *Nomos* would tell us something (e.g. Bruce is sleeping), *physis* would tell us something else (e.g. biology could tell us that Bruce is in a coma; physics could tell us nothing, for life is not its business).

Concluding Remarks

Lewis' acceptance of a wide, complex ontology is not something against which I want to argue. On the contrary, I do believe that the world itself is wide and complex, and that, therefore, it deserves an ontology that is wide and complex. I am surprised, though, to find an allied in Lewis, especially after considering the way he likes to depict himself, namely an "Australian", i.e. hard-core, *a-priori* reductionist "materialist".

If I had to determine a point of reference with regard to the inclinations that I tend to favour in matters of fundamental ontology, then I would elect the Italian philosopher Michele Marsonet (b. 1950) as exemplar. A devoted follower of classical US pragmatist John Dewey (1859–1952) and a full-blooded critic of US neo-pragmatist Richard Rorty, Marsonet is profoundly dubious about any reductionist program that aims at simplifying the manifold scenery of the universe into a neat collection of scientific propositions.

Marsonet is a keen believer in scientific objectivity, but he is an even more devoted believer in the pragmatists' aspiration towards the unity of all sciences—in fact, of all culture. This explains why neither logic nor physics can be the exclusive guides to the accomplishment of a fundamental ontology, according to him. These two practices are too fond of 'mutilations' and cold-blooded disciplinary 'cleansing', according to him. In essence, Marsonet does not take Ockham's (ca. 1287–1347) razor as an absolute, all-purpose regulative ideal.

To begin with, a razor is not a Swiss-army-knife and it must therefore be used only when it is convenient; i.e. when a razor is needed, rather than some other tool. Secondly, while dealing with Willard van Orman Quine's (1908–2000) "ontological reductionism", which is pretty much a standard token of translation of 'complex' commonsensical beings (e.g. love) into 'simpler' scientific ones (e.g. biochemistry), Marsonet writes that Ockham's razor:

> *[I]s not such a good ontological criterion: why should we decide to simplify, following our personal taste and opinions, a reality which is itself complex? The fact of the matter is, in my view, that we must make out our ontological decisions on empirical bases, and not on logical and linguistic ones.*[153]

The results of Marsonet's own empirical observations, which I find most plausible, are that:

> *There are O_1 objects like dreams. Their existence, however, is strictly dependent on human minds, in the sense that, should mankind disappear, there would no longer be dreams.*
>
> *There are O_2 objects like books. Their existence is still tied to human minds as far as we consider both their contents (ideas and theories contained in the books, etc.) and their shapes (their book-like appearance), but not when we take into account their ultimate material ingredients which belong to an external and mind-independent reality.*
>
> *There are O_3 objects like trees from which the cellulose we use to make paper (and thus books) ultimately comes. Their existence is not dependent on human minds.*[154]

Such an apparently overcrowded ontology should not be shaved with Ockham's razor, which would like to nullify or reduce O_1 and O_2 to O_3. Yet, each in its own way, all these levels partake of the predicate of existence, which is real for both cases of mind-related and mind-independent entities. Naturalism, in Marsonet's view, does not imply either materialism or reductionism. The world is big enough for all sorts of things. It is rather a matter of accepting O_1 and O_2 as legitimate parts of the natural world, insofar as the human mind and what derives from it are seen as "the terminal (by now) point of an evolutionary (natural) process which is still under way. Our world (i.e. nature-as-we-conceive-it) would not even exist without mind's capacity of conceptualizing and, as a matter of fact, we cannot even imagine a different way for getting in touch with reality itself."[155]

One thing is to find a good example of ontological pluralism coming from a (neo)pragmatist, another is an analogous example coming from a self-incensed physicalist. One should expect Lewis to be fond of chopping off branches and leaves of the tree of existing beings. On the contrary, his fundamental ontology resembles a sumptuous tropical garden. Moreover, non-material entities such as spatio-temporal regions and force fields are placed among other more ordinary beings, rather than being located underneath such beings. Normally, materialists and, even more so, physicalists, see such realities as the ultimate 'stuff' of which the universe is made, and to which any scientific fundamental ontology would grant a position of honour. The rest would not be merely supervenient, but even fictitious. Such reductionists are not so difficult to find, today, in areas of inquiry as diverse as genetics, socio-biology, neurophysiology, biophysics, and sub-atomic physics.

From what I can read behind Lewis' lines, his materialist option is such that either science is just a part of the commonsensical worldview, or the common sense is too intertwined with science to make the distinction feasible. In either case, *physis* and *nomos* go hand in hand: they are not opposed to each other, but complementary and interpenetrating each other. In Lewis' fundamental ontology there is no room for scandal. Or, if any scandal is permitted, it is more likely to be on the side of those Icelandic engineers, who would change the planned route of a new highway in order not to disturb the elves living on the hill to be bulldozed.

Chapter 6: A Phenomenological Reading of Donald Davidson's Philosophy

Much of Donald Davidson's philosophy can be regarded as a case of unaware phenomenology or, more precisely, a linguistic variant of the phenomenological enterprise in its standard Husserlian form. This, I believe, can be inferred from comparing Davidson's *Essays on Actions and Events*[156] and *Truth and Interpretation*[157] with Edmund Husserl's (1859–1938) canonical essay "Phenomenology", in which the father of this line of philosophical studies outlines the distinctive features of his approach.[158] This comparison follows here two main lines of analysis, one being more synthetic and formal, the other more analytical and related to specific contents of Davidson's theories. The former line concerns the method used by Donald Davidson, while the latter concerns the concepts adopted by him.

As to the former, I illustrate in this chapter how Davidson follows a descriptive method based upon reflection and inherent human cognitive experience, which is extremely close to, and consistent with, the one portrayed by Husserl in his "Phenomenology", especially as regards the role played by intentionality. Besides, I demonstrate how Davidson makes a systematic use of re-descriptions of the sentence-object, if not even of linguistic analysis in general, in a way that echoes Husserl's variations of the object of experience.

As to the latter, I refer to Davidson's reflections on notions such as holism, logical form and external reality, whose meaning and function are analogous to Husserl's ones, and specifically to the phenomenological terms "synthesis", "noema" and "epoche". In the end, I comment on Davidson's unaware phenomenology and its broader meaning within a Husserlian philosophical perspective.

The aim of such a comparison is not only to capture an original and strong analogy between Davidson's late-20th-century linguistic approach and Husserl's early-20th-century mental one, but also to support the notion that the phenomenological approach is unavoidable in order to answer major epistemological questions that the analytic method, when too strictly externalist and empirical in character, cannot adequately satisfy. Additionally, my comparison is intended to highlight the contributions that a phenomenological-like conceptual frame—i.e. even a non-explicitly phenomenological one—can provide to different fields of study such as philosophy of language, ontology and psychology.

My comparison of Davidson and Husserl rests on the hermeneutical strategy of reformulating the former's logical and linguistic philosophical idiom into the latter's phenomenological and mentalist one, thus crossing the boundary between a proudly declared inter-subjective philosophy and one that is distinctively placed within the inevitably subjective mind of the human person. Such a strategy may indeed look hazardous. I am well aware of the fact that Donald Davidson is not a member of the phenomenological school at any level, and that Davidson's sharing a relevant theoretical background with Edmund Husserl is very far from being an uncontroversial platitude. However, the value of my critical operation lies precisely in this hazard and in the novel interpretation hereby delineated, insofar as I explore Davidson's philosophical investigations and let what is therein presupposed, implied, or simply echoed, become manifest.

Methodology

According to Husserl, "[t]he term 'phenomenology' designates two things: a new kind of descriptive method which made a breakthrough in philosophy at the turn of the century, and an a priori science derived from it."[159] Focusing the attention on the former definition, what distinguishes phenomenology as a descriptive method is said to be:

> *[R]eflection, as a turning about of a glance which had previously been directed elsewhere. Every experience can be subject to such reflection, as can indeed every manner in which we occupy ourselves with any real or ideal objects – for instance, thinking, or in the modes of feeling and will, valuing and striving. So when*

we are fully engaged in conscious activity, we focus exclusively on the specific thing, thoughts, values, goals, or means involved, but not on the psychical experience as such, in which these things are known as such. Only reflection reveals this to us.[160]

Husserl's phenomenology can thus be understood as a descriptive method centred upon reflection, possibly inspired by the introspective study of the mind that, in the late 19th century, Wilhelm Wundt (1832–1920) had been experimenting with under the name of a novel science of the soul called "psychology", yet devoid of the latter's then-fashionable positivist overtones.[161]

One of the main goals of phenomenology is in fact the scrupulous reconsideration of the objects of our everyday experience and of the scientific enterprise, both of which share in Husserl's view the same uncritical, natural attitude towards the world, which is taken as an immediate field of apprehension and investigation. This attitude is discharged by the phenomenologist, for whom the obvious things of the world become far less obvious objects of a peculiar sort, that is, objects whose experience is made possible only in connection with the subject's consciousness. Phenomenology moves one step backwards from our usual accounts of the world, discovering (or recovering) the awareness that any allegedly simple, obvious, natural, given object lying out there, is not simple, obvious, natural, given, or 'out there'. The object of experience takes form within our consciousness as an intentional object, i.e. it is not the object as it is, *per se* or as such, but the object as it is in our experience: in our consciousness.

Along a very Kantian line of understanding, Husserl's main premise is that the object of experience is truly a phenomenon, i.e. the fruit of a dialectical inter-play between the subject and the object.[162] Minds are not *tabulae rasae*, waiting for the object to impress them as the press of a print would do on a white page or a virgin thin slab; minds play an active role, and the features of an object of experience can arise only in the context of the activity of consciousness. An important further shift takes place through the acquisition of this epistemological awareness: the reconsideration of the object as an intentional object allows us to become aware of our own consciousness. Its new understanding allows us to get the experience of our own consciousness, to achieve full "self-experience".[163]

Though never quoting either thinker directly, Davidson's philosophy operates along this basic phenomenological Kantian-Husserlian line of understanding. Let us take the case of his *Essays*. In these, Davidson constantly obliges the reader to reconsider the meaning of the most common linguistic expressions of ours, such as: "I did it because..." (i.e. the explanation of an agent's action on the basis of the agent's reasons for action or "rationalisation");[164] "it happened because..." and "this shows that..." (i.e. explanation and evidence; comparing our ordinary linguistic utilisation of certain terms and the scientific one);[165] "there is something such-and-such" (i.e. the ontology lurking behind our ordinary language).[166]

Davidson moves always one step backwards from ordinary linguistic usages and deeper into the presuppositions of our language, in order to scrutinise what is considered obvious, self-evident, given. The result is that what is taken for obvious, self-evident, given, is not like that. In *Truth and Interpretation*, Davidson stresses further the point that our statements about the world are not mere representations of things as they come about, for they impress themselves onto our senses, or because they are just observed. Even if we are causally exposed to what goes on in the surrounding environment, causal interactions are to be interpreted. Some sort of a mediation of our causal interactions with the world is anyhow required.[167]

As pieces of linguistic analysis, Davidson's works take always their moves from the way in which we speak and, in the case of his *Essays*, the way we speak of reasons, actions and events. The starting points are always and only descriptions of an event or a state of affairs, i.e. assertive sentences that we employ when talking about what happens in the world, what befalls upon us, and what we think we ourselves cause to happen. When trying to give an account of human "rationalisation", Davidson writes: "R is a primary reason why an agent performed the action A under the description d only if R consists of a pro attitude of the agent towards actions with a certain property, and a belief of the agent that A, under the description d, has that property."[168] And more generally: "[W]hen we explain an action, by giving the reason, we do redescribe the action; redescribing the action gives the action a place in a pattern, and in this way the action is explained".[169]

Any explanatory attempt can take place only after we consider the way in which things are, under a description. After all, if an explanation is a re-description, as Davidson's quoted passage suggests, then a simple observation about how things are must be already a description; namely, one description amongst the many that our language allows for. Davidson's linguistic analyses, which deal exclusively with assertive sentences of this kind, can be legitimately said to be, or to make use of to a significant extent, a descriptive method centred upon reflection. In other words, Davidson's linguistic analyses equate the workings of phenomenology as a discipline representing and investigating the way in which human beings can understand experience as an act of conscious reflection, i.e. looking backwards at the conditions that make the achievement of experience itself possible. In Husserl's case, it is the mind (the philosopher's or the psychologist's mind) which turns onto itself and looks at the way it works. In Davidson's case, it is the speaker (the philosopher of language or the linguist) who turns onto herself and analyses the way we speak.

Intentionality

Husserl's "being as consciousness" (see quote below) is intentionality: consciousness is always consciousness *of* something, namely the object of experience. Our knowledge, our perception, or any other cognitive condition implying consciousness, is essentially intentional, i.e. 'stretching' or 'in tension' towards the object of experience, which cannot but be given within an act of consciousness. Experience is always and inevitably internal experience, as far as we consider the fundamental role played by our own structuring of the object that engages us:

> *The terminological expression, deriving from Scholasticism, for designating the basic character of being as consciousness, as consciousness of something, is intentionality. In unreflective holding of some object or other in consciousness, we are turned or directed towards it: our "intention" goes towards it. The phenomenological reversal of our gaze shows that this "being directed" [Gerichtetsein] is really an immanent essential feature of the respective experiences involved; they are "intentional" experiences.*[170]

Husserl's phenomenology represents a 'stepping back' into the way that experience is given, i.e. as an intentional event. On its part, Donald Davidson's linguistic analyses respect this distinctive phenomenological trait, for experience is taken into account, or more simply given, as a linguistic event, that is, as a reflective state of consciousness, which is intentional in character: "[T]he distinguishing feature of the mental is not that it is private, subjective, or immaterial, but that it exhibits what Brentano called intentionality. Thus intentional actions are clearly included in the realm of the mental along with thoughts, hopes, and regrets (or the events tied to these)."[171]

However, all that is referred to consciousness in Husserl becomes referred to language in Davidson. When dealing with mental states such as belief, intention, desire, hope, and so on, Davidson speaks of "mental verbs":

> *We may call those verbs mental that express propositional attitudes like believing, intending, desiring, hoping, knowing, perceiving, noticing, remembering, and so on... Let us call a description of the form "the event that is M" or an open sentence of the form "event x is M" a mental description or a mental open sentence if and only if the expression that replaces "M" contains at least one mental verb... Now we may say that an event is mental if and only if it has a mental description.*[172]

Nevertheless, the starting point remains the same under both accounts. Experience is quintessentially intentional experience, insofar as human beings have to interpret the object with which they are engaged in a causal interaction.[173]

Re-description and Variation

In Husserl's "Phenomenology", reflection leads to a decomposition of the experience into the many ways in which we are related to the object of experience. Similarly, in Davidson's philosophy, the act of reflection leads to a decomposition of the experience into the many ways in which we talk about the object of experience. This decomposition, or divisibility, is described by Husserl as "varying differences in the modes of appearing of objects", i.e. the ways in which the subject de-structures and reviews the object in a multitude of alternative perspectives, inasmuch as the object is never given to the subject's consciousness once and for all, but only through a manifold complex of possibilities of experience, which may only arise in an intentional relation between subject and object:

> *There are continually varying differences in the modes of appearing of objects, which are caused by the changing of "orientation" – of right and left, nearness and farness, with the consequent differences in perspective involved. There are further differences in appearance between the "'actually seen front" and the "unseeable" ["*unanschaulichen"*] and relatively "undetermined" reverse side, which is nevertheless "meant along with it".*[174]

In Donald Davidson, the very idea of re-description recalls Husserl's "varying differences in the modes of appearing of objects, which are caused by the changing of orientation" by direction of the will. While in Husserl this idea of "variation" refers to the subject's objects of experience (e.g. Husserl's famous example of looking at a die), in Davidson the same idea deals with their linguistic counterpart (e.g. the use of singular terms denoting individual objects).[175] In his *Essays*, for instance, the way in which Donald Davidson analyses the object of experience called "human action" is a constant, stubborn, methodical activity of re-description of the event that we initially baptised as such.[176]

Throughout his work, Davidson takes events as considered under commonsensical descriptions, which justify our calling them "actions". He subsequently presents what is supposed to be the same event in alternative manners, stressing determinate features of it, referring to different aims of our descriptions, dissecting out of its original shape implications, associations and connections.[177] Similarly, when searching for the "logical form" of "action sentences", or of sentences entailing events as particulars, Davidson proceeds through a veritable variation of the object of experience, by re-describing and de-structuring the original action sentence from which the analysis begins, as in the following examples:

> *"Cass walked to the store" can't be given as "Cass brought it about that Cass is at the store", since it drops the idea of walking. Nor it is clear that "Cass brought it about that Cass is at the store and is there through having walked" will serve.*[178]
> *[...]*
> *(1) "Sebastian strolled through the streets of Bologna at 2a.m." is said to be true must make clear why it entails (2) "Sebastian strolled through the streets of Bologna". If we analyse (1) as "There exists an x such that Sebastian strolled x, x took place in the streets of Bologna, and x was going on at 2a.m." then the entailment is explained as logically parallel with (many cases of) adjectival modification; but this requires events as particulars. Chisholm analyses (1) as (1*) "There exists an x such that x is identical with the strolling of Sebastian, x occurred in the streets of Bologna, and x occurred at 2a.m.". This does entail (2), but fails to entail "Sebastian strolled".*[179]

Comparable instances are provided in Davidson's analysis of action sentences, and generally sentences embedding mental verbs like "wanting", "willing" and "deciding", all of which may be re-described as other more elementary sentences describing the pro-attitude towards an action;[180] or as the pieces of practical reasoning preceding the expression of the relevant "pro-attitude";[181] or as the "evaluation" operated by the agent on the "pro-attitude";[182] or as the determination of a belief that the desired action is of the right sort.[183]

Holism and Synthesis

A further distinctive character of intentional experience, according to Husserl's phenomenology, is the synthetic aspect of consciousness. Even if we can deconstruct an intentional phenomenon into more elementary intentional ones, the experience is somehow always unified. The stream of consciousness constituted by "the flux of modes of appearing" of the object, never loses its unitary character; in order to de-structure and understand the object, we must interpret its many variations as the many exposures of the same entity to our mind's eye:

> *Observing the flux of modes of appearing and the manner of their "synthesis", one finds that every phase and portion [of the flux] is already in itself "consciousness of" – but in such a manner that there is formed within the constant emerging of new phases the synthetically unified awareness that this is one and the same object. The intentional structure of any process of perception has its fixed essential type [seine feste Wesenstypik], which must necessarily be realized in all its extraordinary complexity just in order for a physical body simply to be perceived as such.*[184]

Davidson's analysis of language operates in the same way with regard to actions, changes and events. Even if we can vary the descriptions of an event, even if we can have many ways in which our language reshapes and deconstructs it, each re-description must actually postulate a principle of unity of some sort.

The postulated principle of unity may be just an epistemological device, namely an explanatory postulate intended to make sense of why something happened (e.g. causal relations, as discussed in "Actions, Reasons, and Causes");[185] or an ontological fundamental assumption, namely the acceptance of the existence of certain beings (e.g. events being said to be actually existing entities, as discussed in "The Individuation of Events" and "Events as Particulars").[186] Nevertheless, there is always a principle of synthesis involved in the manifold descriptions of actions, changes, etc., that may take place within our language.

The relational nature of Husserl's object of experience is similar to a knot in a net, or an intersection in a force field. The same can be said of Davidson's accounts of experience and the holistic character of the language. Although re-descriptions are always possible, although language recalls and requires implications, associations, wider and wider spirals of semantic connection, a firm kernel remains that binds them together. In Husserl's phenomenology, this principle of synthesis is understood as a form (*eidos*) inherent to the various intentional experiences that can be had with regard to the same object; in Davidson's philosophy, the same role is covered by the relevant features of the referent.

We should not forget that Davidson takes into account potential referents such as blows, births and growths, i.e. relational entities whose referential character comes into being only within our linguistic descriptions of the world, for they clearly rest upon non-full-blooded empiricist beliefs on what there is 'out there'. Under this perspective, Davidson's own ontology is a phenomenological ontology, such that he can state:

> *Last week there was a catastrophe in the village. In the course of explaining why it happened, we need to redescribe it, perhaps an avalanche. There are rough statistical laws about avalanches: avalanches tend to occur when a heavy snow falls after a period of melting and freezing, so that the new snow does not bind to the old. But we could go further in explaining this avalanche – why it came just when it did, why it covered the area it did, and so forth*

– if we described it in still a different and more precise vocabulary. And when we mention, in one way or another, the cause of the avalanche, we apparently claim that though we may not know such a description or such a law, there must be descriptions of cause and avalanche such that those descriptions instantiate a true causal law. All this talk of descriptions and redescriptions makes sense, it would seem, only on the assumption that there are bona fide entities to be described and redescribed.[187]

If we operated our re-descriptions without any principle of synthesis, the holistic character of the language would project any linguistic expression towards a net of relations with other meanings, beliefs, propositions, yet deprived of any point of reference. Interpretations would be indefinitely open and emptied of objective grounds. And Davidson, like Husserl, knows that he is dealing with objects of experience, not with mere wordplays, even if his approach is eminently linguistic. This possible "groundless" position could be that of a genuine, hard-core relativist like Paul K. Feyerabend (1924–1994), and possibly Richard Rorty, as Donald Davidson himself suggests.[188] It is not his own, however.

Logical Form and Noema

The synthetic character of intentional experiences is explained by Husserl in terms of "form of intention", whereby it is argued that there is an essential structure in the intentional experience, which lets us vary and de-structure the object of experience without losing contact with it. Conversely, it is just the operation of de-structuring and undertaking alternative perspectives that makes it possible for the subject to grasp the essence of the intentional object: "[T]he judging, valuing, striving consciousness is not an empty having knowledge of the specific judgements, values, goals, and means. Rather, these constitute themselves, with fixed essential forms corresponding to each process, in a flowing intentionality."[189] Davidson's linguistic analyses of action sentences ensue from an analogous insight. There is an element in the structure of sentences that allows us to give different descriptions of an action, but without losing contact with the action itself.

Under certain circumstances, and here there might lie a contradiction with Husserl's quoted remark, we can actually let the action vanish by describing it in a way in which it does not look like an action any more (for instance, by re-describing my pouring of the wine as having been the quantity of wine t in the bottle at a moment m and having been y in the glass at the moment n). Still, if this were the case, it can be easily replied that we would not be talking of the same thing or, in phenomenological terms, that we would have shifted our attention onto another object, somehow related to the previous one, but not essentially. Were this the case, it could be also affirmed that we would have hidden the object of experience that we were describing before, and that there is a way to let it appear again, i.e. by introducing a new description expressing what is shared by the many sentences about a certain event, and which can elucidate what is implicit or hidden in all those propositions that only seemingly refer to something else.

Examples of this reply to the problem of a vanishing action are thus all those conceptual operations that clarify the features of our linguistic grammar. These operations, which include Davidson's own quest for "logical forms", are usually performed by translating our linguistic intuitions into formal logic, in order to make explicit all that lies behind (or beneath) our ordinary utterances. After all, this is the very meaning of the word *formalisation*: making explicit.[190]

Additionally, Husserl's notion of *noesis* refers to the way in which the object of experience appears as "inner experience", i.e. to consciousness, once consciousness is engaged in phenomenological reduction.[191] The conditions for grasping and understanding the *noema*, i.e. that which appears to consciousness after its careful dissection, are seen as a complex transcendental framework, which transcends the subject, and of which the subject discovers herself being the bearer amongst other subjects. The 'I' discovers that she is involved in a broader and ultimately transcendental "life-process" and that she is the carrier of shared fundamental "habitualities", like the other 'Is' that she recognises around herself; such habitualities constituting the cognitive frame that determines the subject's conditions of possibility of experience:

> *To every mind there belongs not only the unity of its multiple intentional life-process [*intentionalen Leben*] with all its inseparable unities of sense directed towards the "object". There is also, inseparable from this life-process, the experiencing I-subject as the identical I-pole giving a centre for all specific intentionalities, and as the carrier of all habitualities growing out of this life-process. Likewise, then, the reduced intersubjectivity, in pure form and concretely grasped, is a community of pure "persons" acting in the intersubjective realm of the pure life of consciousness.*[192]

Such habitualities, emerging from collective life-processes, play a crucial role in Davidson's philosophy, insofar as the former's linguistic practices can be seen as constituting the intersubjective *locus* of Husserl's habitualities. The subject can be seen as a speaker, i.e. as a member of a community of speakers. As such, the subject is the bearer of the community's standards (epistemological, behavioural, ethical, etc.), which are acquired, communicated, transformed, brought into existence, etc. at a linguistic level. Furthermore, the linguistic level is, by definition, inter-subjective i.e. transcending the subject.

Unlike Husserl, the standards to which Davidson refers are not claimed openly to be universal, necessary and compelling, for he is not directing his gaze towards a fundamental transcendental horizon, but rather a historical and evolutionary one. Inside Davidson's conceptual world, we are allowed to imagine private dominions which share only part of the whole complex of habitualities that are present within the linguistic practices (e.g. individuals' idiosyncratic beliefs, a poet's literary universe, a community's peculiar traditions in comparison to another, etc.) or even hardly any at all (e.g. a madman, an autistic individual, an infant).[193]

These cases notwithstanding, it is true that we cannot imagine a language and more generally a public dominion, which does not imply any at all. Quite obviously, the very notion of a public dominion implies by definition something that is shared by more than one individual; and if there is something to be shared by two or more subjects, then there must be standards regulating the access to that which is shared in order to make it shareable. In the particular case of language, individuals are endlessly exposed to their community's standards and must adopt them, at least as far as it is necessary to be able to communicate with other individuals, or to understand their behaviour. Nobody is born in total isolation, and inter-subjectivity could be even seen as a pre-requisite for the origination of subjectivity: individuality emerging from a collective life-process.

What is more, Davidson's theory of interpretation suggests that certain standards might be common to all human communities, for we must attribute a minimal shared consistent pattern of beliefs to any person or population whose behaviours we want to interpret.[194] Were this not the case, that is, if there were no universal standards regulating human linguistic practices, the similarity between Davidson's account and Husserl's life-process would persist nonetheless. Davidson's studies are about the linguistic dominion, which is inter-subjective by definition, and which therefore transcends the particular 'I', for it invests this 'I' with the rules, usages, requirements, expectations, etc. of at least one particular language.

External Reality and Epoche

Husserl's use of ancient Greek philosophical expressions is probably one of his more distinctive stylistic traits. Among the many expressions that he revives, there is a borrowing from the Pyrrhonian sceptics, namely *epoche*:

A consistent epoche of the phenomenologist is required, if he wishes to break through to his own consciousness as pure phenomenon or as totality of his purely mental processes. That is to say, in the accomplishment of phenomenological reflection he must inhibit every co-accomplishment of objective positing produced in unreflective consciousness, and therewith [inhibit] every judgement drawing-in of the world as it "exists" for him straightforwardly. The specific experience of this house, this body, of a world as such, is and remains, however, according to its own essential content and thus inseparably, experience "of this house", this body, this world; this is so for every mode of consciousness which is directed towards an object. It is, after all, quite impossible to describe an intentional experience – even if illusionary, an invalid judgement, or the like – without at the same time describing the object of that consciousness as such. The universal epoche of the world as it becomes known in consciousness (the "putting into brackets") shuts out from the phenomenological field the world as it exists for the subject in simple absoluteness; its place, however, is taken by the world as given in consciousness (perceived, remembered, judged, thought, valued, etc.) – the world as such, the "world in brackets", or in other words, the world, or rather individual things in the world as absolute, are replaced by the respective meaning of each in consciousness [Bewusstseinssinn] in its various modes (perceptual meaning, recollected meaning, and so on).[195]

Once the philosopher realises that experience is given as intentional experience, the world or "exterior" disappears inside the consciousness. The reflection of the consciousness on itself, once engaged with a world turned into phenomena—once it is lost in the "flux of consciousness" that seems to be the only certainty attainable, at least for the moment—must suspend judgement on the world; hence Husserl's use of the term "*epoche*".

This Pyrrhonian move of the inquiring mind does not mean that the world is definitively lost, but surely innocence is lost. The innocence of the natural attitude is gone, and now a new challenge awaits the philosopher: after bracketing the world as it was previously given, she must find the epistemological foundations of knowledge, and eventually regain the world of experience as something much more complex than the mere collection of objective data impressed by the external world upon our senses and cognitive apparatus.

Husserl imagines a Cartesian overcoming of scepticism and regards this project as the highest task of phenomenology *qua* pure *a priori* and rigorous science—*als strenge Wissenschaft*. According to him, phenomenological reduction is the long path within the subject's consciousness that may hopefully lead to the discharge of the brackets that are temporarily surrounding the world of experience.

Davidson's studies cover a relevant trait along the line of Husserl's phenomenological reduction. In the first place, Davidson is not concerned about the specific extensions of the terms that he discusses. His selected sentences are exemplary cases, mere hypotheses about the world. In the second place, innocence is gone for Davidson too. No natural attitude is conceded once our commonsensical descriptions, or our scientific protocols, are seen as linguistic descriptions rather than just what is 'out there'. In a dramatic way, the world in itself disappears, bracketed within the language that we use. We may know that the world is such-and-such, we may believe that the world is such-and-such, and yet whenever this use of mental verbs occurs the semantics of our language remind us of our epistemological limits, since the truth-conditions of the proposition become dependent upon the subject. Mental verbs create non-extensional contexts, and therefore limit drastically the relevance of external conditions for truth.[196]

Truth, unless it is taken as primitive, becomes for Davidson a merely formal notion; verification a purely logical exercise; and any "evidence for a belief is other beliefs".[197] Experience, and more broadly knowledge itself, turn into "what is held for true".[198] And this condition becomes particularly evident and dramatic when Davidson is dealing with the ontology of causes[199] and events[200]. Davidson's considerations lead towards scepticism or, at least, towards scepticism-related problems such as solipsism, radical internalism and linguistic idealism. Since what we know is determined within an unavoidable linguistic frame, is what we say is there actually there?

Davidson's theory of truth is an attempt at finding an answer to this question. Davidson is aware that his coherence theory of truth might justify scepticism, relativism or idealism, i.e. all those philosophical hypotheses that deny any possibility of attaining any ultimate valid empirical knowledge, because of the lack of any immediate self-imposing evidence of the "exterior" upon the "interior". Davidson is not fond of any of these alternatives, but he does not deny that his speculation may open the door to such troubling options. He may accuse these options of being unreasonable, but he has no other counterargument to give than an appeal to reasonability and, from a strictly philosophical point of view, he cannot but suspend judgement.[201]

Unaware Phenomenology

My comparison between Davidson and Husserl does not need to go further. Once the intentional character of experience, its relevance for a correct epistemology and a non-empiricist ontology, the composite and synthetic traits of intentionality, the inter-subjective element implicit in it are individuated, then the presence as well as the relevance of their common theoretical background become patent.

This common theoretical background does not mean that these two authors are patently interchangeable. Davidson does not follow Husserl into an idealist transcendental resolution of the subject-object relationship, for one. Although our linguistic practices somehow constitute the fundamental conditions of possibility of perceiving, thinking, acting and communicating, Davidson's presupposed realism comes forth: "My slogan is: correspondence without confrontation. Given a correct epistemology, we can be realists in all departments. We can accept objective truth conditions as the key to meaning, a realist view of the truth, and we can insist that knowledge is of an objective world independent of our thought or language."[202]

According to Davidson, we cannot but express our knowledge in the form of beliefs and we cannot but test their truth with a coherence test; after all, we are linguistic animals. And language plays the role of a sort of Kantian transcendental frame of interpretation of our causal interactions with the world, even if Davidson does not forget the physical and biological elements on the scene. Objective reality is not a postulate within his theory, like Husserl's "pure a priori of a physical world (and specifically the organic) Nature as such".[203] In Davidson's background lies the conviction that this reality is the place where all theories take place and of which any consistent theory speaks.

The kind of natural attitude regained by Davidson can be attained, in my view, by way of a *reasonable act of faith*. I write "of faith" because this is a point that cannot be demonstrated (or at least it is not demonstrated in Davidson's writings); because scepticism is always logically possible (and similarly anti-realism in general, as amply discussed with regard to Rorty's neo-pragmatism in the third chapter of the present book); and because this point can only be assumed on a reasonable basis. I write "reasonable" because the way in which we interpret any linguistic act implies the attribution of a consistent pattern of beliefs to the interpreted subject; because we have no good reason to doubt that our beliefs are all wrong; and/or because scepticism sounds less and less sensible due to the two previous considerations.[204]

The gap between a realist approach and an idealist leap appears to be a matter of background formation, personal esprit and/or overall goals. Husserl, perhaps because of his doctoral studies in mathematics, is subject-guided. Although phenomenology blurs the subject-object distinction, if there is a party to be privileged between them, then the subject is the chosen one. Davidson is, on the contrary, object-guided. A scientifically realist and evolutionary sensibility is evident in his overall approach. Furthermore, Davidson does not share Husserl's foundational aims. Somewhat pessimistically, Davidson rejects as vain any attempt to ground our knowledge in something more than our language and the ways in which language helps us to cope with the environment, thus echoing Rorty's neo-pragmatist stance.

The ambiguity of human psychology individuated by Edmund Husserl constitutes another dividing line between the two authors: What are we? Are we just contingent, natural beings, or the bearers of a transcendental cognitive framework, which is to be seen as the fundamental pre-requisite of any epistemology and, in ultimate analysis, of any ontology? "Are we supposed to be dual beings – psychologically, as human objectivities in the world, the subjects of psychic life, and at the same time transcendental, as the subjects of a transcendental, world-constituting life-process?"[205]

Husserl believes that this duality can be overcome in favour of a rigorous science of the transcendental world-constituting life-process that could outline the fundamental forms of the process, "out of which everything transcendent (and, with it, everything that belongs to the real world) obtains its existential sense".[206] The contingent 'I' is then seen as the bearer of fundamental patterns of comprehensive understanding belonging to a transcendental community of 'Is', to which she herself belongs, and whose relevance is not only cognitive, but ontological too. Without it, not only is knowledge impossible, but also the knower's existence *qua* knower. The transcendental framework of habitualities does not dictate only the rules for a correct epistemology but provides the guidelines for our ontology as well.

Davidson resolves the duality within the 'real' world itself. However, he is not a strict empiricist, since there is actually at least one transcendental world-constituting life-process that he acknowledges, i.e. language, which transcends the subject as an inter-subjective collection of meanings and allows us to speak about the world, and even contributes to the world's ontology (e.g. causes, events). Davidson's view of language, though, is such that this transcendental world-constituting life-process does not transcend the world in a way that can make language itself give the world its existential sense. It is, if anything, the exact contrary: language arises within the world and from the world receives its own existential sense.

Concluding Remarks

Donald Davidson's linguistic analysis possesses relevant phenomenological aspects, even if it does not follow entirely Husserl's approach (e.g. the aforementioned "ambiguity of psychology"). Now, imagining that Husserl should state what sort of phenomenology Davidson has been producing, I hypothesise that he would regard Davidson's work as a linguistic contribution to "the systematic construction of a phenomenological pure psychology". Let us consider Husserl's requirements for this task:

(1) The description of the peculiarities universally belonging to the essence of intentional mental process, which includes the most general law of synthesis: every connection of consciousness with consciousness gives rise to a consciousness.[207]

Through the analysis of specific linguistic usages and related issues, Davidson tries to identify and describe the more general and distinctive features of the mental processes with which he deals, whose intentional character, in a strictly phenomenological sense, is assured by their being mental, *per* his own explicit reference to Franz Brentano (1838–1917) on intentionality. Such are the cases, for instance, of rationalisations[208] and pure intending.[209] Besides, Davidson's characterisation of the mental sphere, as this is represented in our language, is holistic, and as long as we maintain the re-descriptions of an original mental expression under the scope of a mental verb, the element of intentionality does not get lost, so that the character of intentionality keeps being present among the various inter-related sentences, playing therein the equivalent of Husserl's law of synthesis.[210]

(2) The exploration of single forms of intentional mental process which in essential necessity generally must or can present themselves in the mind; in unity with this, also the exploration of the syntheses they are members of for a typology of their

*essences: both those that are discrete and those continuous with others, both the finitely closed and those continuing into open infinity.*²¹¹

Davidson's search for the logical forms of action sentences and of sentences about events is an intellectual exploration corresponding to the one to which Husserl is inviting the scholar. The distinguishing logical features of the mentioned sentences, in fact, cannot but be expressed linguistically and, according to Davidson, they cannot but refer to mental—*ergo* intentional in a phenomenological sense— notions such as intentionality, agency and pro-attitudes. In this linguistic version, Davidson is exploring forms that are generally or necessarily presenting themselves in the mind.²¹² Moreover, insofar as Davidson is drawing logical—hence universal—expressions of the specific forms individuated behind specific sentences, then he is also constructing typologies of logical forms common to different sets of sentences.

(3) The showing and eidetic description [Wesendeskription] *of the total structure* [Gesamtgestalt] *of mental life as such; in other words, a description of the essential character* [Wesensart] *of a universal "stream of consciousness".*²¹³

Davidson's holism of the human language and, indirectly, of the mental sphere as this is represented in such a language, can be connoted as a linguistic counterpart to Husserl's own stream of consciousness. Both thinkers attribute an essential character of totality and pervasive relational being to our mental life, as shown for instance in Davidson's analysis of the process of interpretation of human behaviour, or by his claims about the non-reducibility of the mental to the physical.²¹⁴

(4) The term "I" designates a new direction for investigation (still in abstraction from the social sense of this word) in reference to the essence-forms of "habituality"; in other words, the "I" as subject of lasting beliefs or thought-tendencies –

"persuasions" – (convictions about being, value-convictions, volitional decisions, and so on), as the personal subject of habits, of trained knowing, of certain character qualities.[215]

As repeatedly discussed in this chapter, Davidson is dealing with the dimension of habitualities in terms of linguistic practices. He does not abstract completely from the social sense of the 'I' out of which Husserl wants to depart. Still, insofar as the phenomenological 'I' can be seen as contingent and historical, and not only as transcendental, then these lasting beliefs or thought-tendencies can be regarded as Husserl's expression of the inter-subjectivity that is taken to be the most distinctive and almost obvious trait of language in Davidson's writings.

PART II – Thinking Rhetoric

Chapter 7: Reflections on Deleuze's Humour

A key-component of the rhetorical toolkit, humour finds a special treatment in the philosophy of Gilles Deleuze, who distinguishes it and contrasts it with irony, namely another standard rhetorical trope, insofar as the divergent features of these two related notions make their ontological implications more evident. By "ontological" I mean the study of the forms that being may or does take at the most abstract level of reflection, inasmuch as Deleuze's philosophy deals with humour in conjunctions with questions such as: What are the relations between Ideas, language, and bodies? What are the boundaries of language *vis-à-vis* existence? Are there any? What can language reveal about the structures of being? What is the status of virtual beings?

Consider the following, representative quote from Deleuze's 1969 book, *The Logic of Sense*:

> *It is not clear, however, by what miracle propositions would participate in the Ideas in a more assured manner than bodies which speak or bodies of which we speak, unless the Ideas were "names-in-themselves." And are bodies, at the other extreme, better able to ground language? When sounds fall back on (*se rebattent sur*) bodies and become the actions and passions of mixed bodies, they are no more than the bearers of agonizing nonsense. One after the other, the impossibility of a Platonic language and a pre-Socratic language, of an idealistic language and a physical language, of a manic language and a schizophrenic language are exposed.*[216]

In *The Logic of Sense*, Deleuze faces a recurrent series of interrogatives with regard to the nature and mutual connection of these three levels (or "series"): the *ideal*, the *linguistic* and the *material*. In what amounts to an original reformulation of the problem of scientific realism in contemporary philosophy, Deleuze tries to find satisfactory answers to the dialectical inter-definition of these three levels, which are related to one another in our cognitive experience, but which seem also distinguished from each other in the nature of their being, i.e. their ontology.

Deleuze tries to solve one of the best-known paradoxes uttered by Chrysippus the Stoic (ca. 279–ca. 206 BC), which expresses the troublesome relation of the material level with the linguistic one and recites: "if you say 'chariot', a chariot passes through your lips."[217] In order to disentangle this complex inter-play of different ontological levels, Deleuze traces the problem back to the origins of philosophical thought itself.

Series and Surfaces

On the one end of an ideal historico-philosophical spectrum on scientific realism, Deleuze places Plato, i.e. the archetypal case of "foundation" of language, for eternal and immutable essences (i.e. Plato's interpretation of the ideal level) can be drawn out of empirical instances (i.e. Plato's version of the material level) by means of dialectics or philosophy (i.e. Plato's science of the linguistic level).[218] According to the Platonic account, there exists a continuity between the ideal, which is the model of all beings, the material, which is structured (or informed) around (or by) the ideal, and the linguistic, which encompasses the other two levels by referring to the material and, at the same time, by creating the immaterial context where all material instances are gathered under the ideal.

On the opposite end of the same ideal spectrum, Deleuze places Diogenes the Cynic (ca. 412–323 BC) and Chrysippus the Stoic, i.e. the archetypal cases of ontological "fracture".[219] According to Deleuze's interpretation of their doctrines, whenever one is asked to define an idea or explain what a certain body is, all that can be achieved by our use of linguistic expressions are instances of exemplification ('for example...'), references to singularities ('x is a case of y') and ostensive acts ('that is x'). There is no fixed ontological track moving through bodies, words and ideas as though they were equivalent, but only a mechanism of codified signs and more or less agreed indications.

Diogenes' and Chrysippus' understanding of language does not manifest any belief in the possibility of "incorporation": no eternal and immutable essence can be derived from the material level by means of modern linguistic analysis or Plato's dialectical techniques.[220] Their view of the linguistic level, unlike Plato's, is that of a mere complex of nominal tools pointing towards something else, either ideal or material, in order to cope somehow with it. Language is, for them both, a pure collection of *"mots d'ordre"*[221] suggesting the presence of something different, but logically and ontologically limited within itself, i.e. a self-contained instrument that cannot move beyond its own boundaries.[222]

Deleuze endorses Diogenes' and Chrysippus' position, which he considers capable of attaining a plausible description of the how signifiers (i.e. the linguistic level) and meanings (i.e. the material and the ideal level) work in practice. Roughly summarising his reasons to reject Plato's position in favour of theirs, it must be underlined that Deleuze claims that Diogenes and Chrysippus succeeded in showing the fracture between language and reality. They managed to do so by stressing the fact that there is always a way to frustrate any Platonic attempt to give a definition that is valid in any and every time and under any and every circumstance. Paradoxes, errors, absurdities, doubts, unresolved questions, puns, best yet transient explanations, abstractions, even Kant's much-later distinction between concepts and ideas: there is a great number of cases in the history of Western thought that Deleuze recalls in order to show how bodies never match exactly what we mean, and how ideas are inherently more problematic and quite simply ungraspable *in toto* in comparison to what we may say.

Deleuze argues that our language is an artificial structure of signs, where some signs play the role of signifiers (i.e. our words), while others that of signified (i.e. our meanings). No sign transcends its artificial and nominalistic condition. This is evident whenever we try to grasp the meaning of a meaning, whereby we realise its nature *qua* artificial and nominalistic sign, because we will then have turned the previous meaning into a sign, for which a new meaning is now being provided. Were we to provide the meaning of this new meaning, then we would repeat the same operation—and so on *ad infinitum*, in an endless series of signs.[223]

Following Michel Foucault's (1926–1984) teaching, Deleuze reminds his readers that any linguistic expression is not a mirror of what things are—things being either ideal or material—but the selected component of a closed system of orders, intentionalities, pragmatic purposes and functional abstractions.[224] Pragmatics precedes semantics. Deleuze is also ready to accept the problematic aspects implied by the fracture hereby illustrated, i.e. "one cannot posit a primacy of expression over content, or content over expression".[225] Any expression (i.e. the linguistic level) and any supposed content (i.e. the material and the ideal ones) belong to two different ontological levels or, in Deleuze's words, two different "series" or "regimes", namely "the regime of bodies and the regime of signs".[226]

Deleuze does not imply that there are no forms of interaction between the various levels, series or regimes. Their relationship has in fact to be regarded as an "assemblage" where each of them is in reciprocal presupposition, intervening on each other through a non-linear mechanism of "resonance", "deterritorialization", "enantiomorphism", and other strangely baptized forms of isomorphism or presupposed functional equivalence.[227] In Deleuze's mind, neither the ideal nor the material series are reconciled with the linguistic one, either in the form of a deep ontological correspondence or in that of a point-to-point structural mimesis, even when limited to the case of sheer denotation. This happens because the ontology of identity initiated by Plato is based on a representational conception of language, namely the idea that words, singularly (e.g. nouns) or in combinations (e.g. propositions, theories) mirror bodies and ideas.

Deleuze, like Michel Foucault and Richard Rorty, claims that such an ontology does not mirror anything but other mirrors. Words call for other words. The ontology of identity makes exclusive use of its own internal terms, letting them play in turn the role of the representation and of the represented, of the signifier and the signified, of the *denotans* and the *denotatum*. Whichever role such terms play, they remain arbitrary terms, stipulated signs, which in their constitutive being have nothing to do with "the 'silent order' of things".[228]

Instead of revealing the presence of a cognisable universal principle that is given once and for all—hence harmonising Ideas, words and bodies—the result of Diogenes' and Chrysippus' nominalist descent is a renewed Heraclitean view of reality. The end of their journey is a proliferating plurality of unrepeatable singularities, a frantic chaotic flux of events that we vainly try to coerce within the categories of our understanding. This is particularly evident insofar as Deleuze's ontology does not take into account only "actual" events (i.e. state of affairs) in a diachronic perspective (i.e. in the "first synthesis of time", namely time seen from the standpoint of the present), but also "virtual" events (i.e. all that may befall repeats its befalling as a precondition for the possibility of actual befalling) in a synchronic perspective (i.e. in the "second synthesis of time", namely time seen from the standpoint of the past).[229]

Ideas cannot be reduced to words, for words will face always the problem of expressing the almost infinite and yet-to-discover properties of any idea: connotation is doomed. Bodies cannot be trapped within words, for words will be always incapable of portraying the almost infinite and changing properties of any individual body: denotation is doomed. Whichever way one pursues to its end, ineffability arises.

As the giant of 20th-century Romanian philosophy, Lucian Blaga (1895–1961), used to argue, even our most cherished metaphysical and scientific "revelations are just metaphors of mystery and their transcendence is limited by the censorship of abyssal categories" such as "substance", "space", "time" or "light is an undulation" that, when seriously entertained, deepen the mystery and reveal "that mystery can never be converted into non-mystery": "The Great Anonym imposes a censorship upon human knowledge, which prevents us... from knowing in an absolute manner".²³⁰ But where does such a seemingly dismal nominalist descent throw us?

As denotation is concerned, this nominalist descent hurls us into the ground of bodies and the groundlessness of their mixtures. Every denotation is prolonged in consumption, pulverisation and destruction, without there being any chance of arresting this movement, as if the prophet's staff shattered everything it singles out and proclaims.²³¹ In order to avoid any idealistic drift, Deleuze assumes as a fundamental premise of his philosophy that language is just one of the many series of reality, and not a privileged point of observation over the real.²³² This apparent loss of privilege is compensated by the achievement of a better awareness of the illusions of much philosophy, idealism included.

According to Deleuze, those knots that representation cannot handle, the frustration of a comprehensive understanding of reality, the experience of cognitive limits provided by the Cynic and the Stoic, the conflict between epistemology and ontology, the "fracture" between language, bodies and ideas, are nonetheless a precious source of insights, indications and evocations:

When significations hurl us into pure denotations, which replace and negate them, we are faced with the absurd as that which is without signification. But when denotations in turn precipitate us into the destructive and digestive ground, we are faced with the non-sense of the depths as sub-sense (sous-sens) *or* Untersinn. *Is there any way out? By the same movement with which language falls from the heights and then plunges below, we must be led back to the surface where there is no longer anything to denote or even to signify, but where pure sense is produced. It is produced in its essential relation to a third element, this time the nonsense of the surface. Once again, what matters here is to act quickly, what matters is speed. What does the wise man find at the surface? Pure events considered from the prospective of their eternal truth, that is, from the point of view of the substance which sub-tends them, independent of their spatio-temporal actualization in a state of affairs. Or, what amounts to the same thing, one finds pure singularities, an emission of singularities considered from the perspective of their aleatory element, independent of the individuals and persons which embody them or actualize them.*[233]

Here lies the prize provided by the puzzling nominalist descent described above: we realise that reality cannot be grasped as a consistent totality inscribed within the logical space of concepts, the comparative interplay with a model, or the overarching synthesis of a principle of identity. Reality is unstructured, hence it can give birth to several structures; reality is multiple, for it includes all the virtual and actual events as irreducible singularities; reality is proliferating, for it develops into uncountable unfolding of intensities.

Language is just one of the various structures that can be formed within this surface of events and, as a consequence, it cannot handle the whole of it. The static representational grids imposed upon it cannot master the dynamic flux of events that compose the real. Not even proper names can "hibernate" or stop the multifarious flux of being, for a subject itself is nothing more than a cluster of series intermingling into one another in a system of "monstrations"; as Deleuze writes: "a proper name is made to connote signs".[234]

Surfaces and Humour

It is important to stress the fact that, in Deleuze's view, the real is not concealed behind a linguistic veil. Deleuze is not an idealist. He takes his moves from the presupposition that humans take part in, and have experience of, several diverse series, fluxes of being, ontological realms, among which is the linguistic one. In this sense we can explain our use of conceptual, linguistic and representational practices without being necessarily imprisoned within them: because we are conceptual, linguistic, representational beings, though we are not merely that.[235] Deleuze is not ranking ontological levels or series together with their functions. He is depicting an immense ground of being where events arise as "concretions" of different series; as discussed in third chapter, his ontology is horizontal.[236]

It is only with reference to this Pangea of being that a form of communication among the different ontological levels can be individuated by Deleuze. This communication is not an easy thing to detect and understand, insofar as it crosses the exercise proper to the specific faculty related to each series, in whose specific vocabulary each series can exclusively be explicated (e.g. biological functions for the organic body, conceptual activity for the thinking mind). However, Deleuze depicts contexts in which our cognitive limits allow us to postulate such a crosscutting communication.

Such is the case of perception, for example, where the process of inter-linkage between physical reality and perceptual reality is described as a violent projection of one dimension of being onto another, a traumatic experience, whose taking place or relevance is always reconstructed and understood only *a posteriori*, i.e. in terms pertaining to the sphere of being which has been affected by the violent one. Although unavoidably partial and eventually mono-dimensional—insofar as the vocabulary at issue pertains to the series that underwent violence—a form of connection can be reasonably asserted, if we want to make sense of why perception arose.

The relation between two levels of being is thus said to be "cruel" and "asymmetrical".[237] It is "cruel" because one level forces the other to interrupt its state of tranquillity and respond to the interference. It is "asymmetrical" because the former level animates the latter and disappears in proportion to the development of the latter. For instance, light activates our vision in a violent way, by exciting the receptive structures of our body. The more the activated structures respond, the less light maintains its original features as light proper, in order to become a recognisable construction of the structures that it awoke, being therefore interpreted as a sensorial datum.

The circumstance in which this "cruel" and "asymmetrical" mechanism becomes extremely evident is called by Deleuze the "transcendental exercise" of a faculty, i.e. when a faculty is carried to its very limit, being incapable of structuring an object out of that "cruel" being which is striking it and awakening it.[238] It is the experience of the "loop" or "epiphany of the limit", namely the revelation of the radical "otherness" of that with which we vainly try to cope.[239] The event that we intend to label by means of a linguistic expression, for example, escapes the labelling. At the same time, it is itself the context in which the fundamental frustration of a faculty of ours shows how another level of being is the entity that makes the possibility of experience itself arise (e.g. the undetermined, the unfathomable, the ineffable).

Although we cannot assimilate the aggressing event within our representational structure, we are indeed experiencing it, and through this experience we are experiencing too the faculty at play, which shows itself by exerting itself unsuccessfully upon a non-objectifiable object. Our categories, our objectifying devices, our representational structures, show then their own limitations as well as the "surface" from which they originate by being called into play unsuccessfully in a case of "transcendental exercise", which can occur also with regard to our intellectual abilities:[240]

> *To paint without painting, non-thought, shooting which becomes non-shooting, to speak without speaking: this is not at all the ineffable up above or down below, but rather the frontier and the surface where language becomes possible and, by becoming possible, inspires only a silent and immediate communication, since it could only be spoken in the resuscitation of all the mediate and abolished significations or denotations.*[241]

Chrysippus' paradoxes are cases of "transcendental exercise" of the logical faculty, according to Deleuze. The inadequacy of our language to connote and/or denote fittingly, once and for all, manifests the otherness of what is pointed at by our words, hence the frustration of any comprehensive understanding attempting to gather all that can be experienced within the clear framework of our intersubjective categories.

By bringing Chrysippus' paradoxes into play, Deleuze wishes to show how the frustration of our linguistic means of expression can lead to fundamental insights on the otherness of the series that we wish to capture with our words, our inherent cognitive limits, the irreducible ontological proliferation of singularities, and the vastness of the surface of being whence our linguistic constructs emerge. Deleuze quotes Chrysippus again: "If you never lost something, you have it still; but you never lost horns, *ergo* you have horns."[242] Here lies the root of Deleuze's notion of humour: "This exercise, which consists in substituting designations, monstrations, consumptions, and pure destructions for significations, requires an odd inspiration – that one know how to 'descend'. What is required is humor."[243]

Prima facie, Deleuze's use of "humor" appears rather counterintuitive, for it lacks an obvious comical or hilarious element, which is at the heart of the commonsensical understanding of the term. Despite the attention paid to the comic side of several authors to whom he refers repeatedly in his books—notably Franz Kafka (1883–1924) and Søren Kierkegaard (1813–1855)—Deleuze does not seem interested in humour's amusing character but in its paradoxical one and, specifically, in the ways in which paradox can be described: as iconoclastic, i.e. capable of breaking any fixed boundary or established law; as a signpost of the surface of singular events which language tries, in vain, to accommodate within broader abstract terms; and as pragmatically co-extensive with non-sense or the absurd. These features become so crucial in his view, that Deleuze even neglects the point that they may have, sometimes, nothing funny about them whatsoever (e.g. the tragic interpretation of Kafka's works, whose humour can be so bleak and dismal as to be hardly amusing).

Moreover, with regard to the ontology of difference emerging out of the groundless proliferation of singularities into which humorous "monstration" precipitates us, Deleuze adds:

> *This adventure of humor, this twofold dismissal of height and depth to the advantage of the surface is, in the first instance, the adventure of the Stoic sage... [I]t will also be the adventure of Zen – against the Brahman depths and the Buddhist heights. The famous problems-tests, the questions-answers, the koans, demonstrate the absurdity of significations and show the nonsense of denotations... Returned to the surface, the sage*

> *discovers objects-events, all of them communicating in the void which constitutes their substance. [...] The event is the identity of form and void. It is not the object as denoted, but the object as expressed or expressible, never present, but always already in the past and yet to come.*[244]

The undifferentiated multiplicity of being—the surface of existence resting upon a void sub-tending substance—is the place where humour is supposed to lead us in its descent. Humour descends from the One to the multiple by breaking down the unity of sense, annihilating any umbrella-concept capable of circumscribing all the possible instances of a phenomenon that, once the unifying bound of that concept has disappeared, explodes into a myriad of independent scattered phenomena. Humour moves:

> *Across the abolished significations and the lost denotations, the void is the site of sense or of the event which harmonizes with its own nonsense, in the place where the place only takes place (là où on n'a plus lieu que lieu). The void is itself the paradoxical element, the surface nonsense, or the always displaced aleatory point whence the event bursts forth as sense.*[245]

Several works of Deleuze's contain passages stressing the Dionysian, destructive, revelatory nature of humour. For instance, in *Difference and Repetition*, we read about the role played by humour in frustrating the attempt of subsuming the existent under unbreakable laws:

> *[Humour] overturns the law by descending towards the consequences, to which one submits with a too-perfect attention to detail. By adopting the law, a falsely submissive soul manages to evade it and to taste pleasures it was supposed to forbid... [Humour] is an art of consequences and descents, of suspensions and falls... [I]t is by nature transgression or exception, always revealing a singularity opposed to the particulars subsumed under laws.*[246]

As a destroyer of concepts, as an experience of our cognitive limits, humour is the shifty opponent by which the ontology of identity is bound to be defeated. Every law has its exceptions, every model its aberrations, every conception its counterexamples. In Deleuze's words: "The art of the aesthetics is humour, a physical art of signals and signs determining the partial solutions or cases of solution."[247]

Nothing can be solved once and for all; nothing can be inscribed within the scope of a norm regulating all the possible cases, all the occurrences of an event. Any concept, any word, insofar as it states how things are, or have to be, and insofar as it plays the role of a command within our understanding, is such a norm. However, reality finds always a way to break down all *mots d'ordre*, all norms, all laws. Humour is the protagonist of logical and ontological discontinuity, crack, pulverisation, which can be psychological as well: "We can see this [humour] in demonstration by absurdity and working to rule, but also in some forms of masochistic behavior which mock by submission."[248]

Deleuze scrutinises masochistic pathological cases in "Coldness and Cruelty", where he provides a brilliant analysis of Leopold von Sacher-Masoch's (1836–1895) famous erotic novel, *Venus in Furs*. In this work, Deleuze characterises masochism as a form of deceptive self-affirmation of the ego of the masochist, who persuades, stipulates a contract and educates the master or mistress, who is to impose pain upon the masochist. What is an apparent act of submission, humiliation, painful constraint, is seen as a subterranean expedient that the masochist utilises in order to achieve what the law —the paternal superego of Freudian psychoanalysis—would forbid: sexual pleasure, that is, in Freudian terms, the sexual possession of the mother.

The masochist does not enjoy pain as such, but rather as a suspension, a prior expiation, an only apparent annihilation of the self, aimed at the consummation of the eventual sexual gratification, which should have been forbidden and unattainable. Deleuze reads the violence to which the masochist exposes himself or herself as a way in which the masochist attains the elimination of the binding force of the law, i.e. the castration imposed by the father figure. In a subtle and indirect fashion, the masochist expiates the guilt that s/he intends to reach at the end of the stipulated torture.

The masochist plays around the supposed outcome of the law in order to transgress the law itself, and to dissolve the father figure within herself. The ego of the masochist triumphs on the superego by twisting the prohibition and the punishment to its own favour. And this is the quintessence of humour for Deleuze:

> *[T]he very law which forbids the satisfaction of a desire under threat of subsequent punishment is converted into one which demands the punishment first and then orders that the satisfaction of the desire should necessary follow upon the punishment... [M]asochism is not pleasure in pain, nor even in punishment; at most, the masochist gets a preliminary pleasure from punishment or discomfort; his real pleasure is obtained subsequently, in that which is made possible by the punishment... What else but a demonstration of absurdity is aimed at, when the punishment for forbidden pleasure brings about the very same pleasure? [...] The masochist is insolent in his obsequiousness, rebellious in his submission; in short, he is a humorist, a logician of consequences.*[249]

Something similar happens in a very different context, according to Deleuze, i.e. Foucault's interpretation of Martin Heidegger's philosophy:

> *There is no doubt that Foucault found great theoretical inspiration in Heidegger and Merleau-Ponty for the theme that haunted him: the fold, or doubling. But he equally found a practical version of it in Raymond Roussel, for the latter raised an ontological Visibility, forever twisting itself into a 'self seeing' entity, on to a different dimension from that of the gaze or its objects. We could equally link Heidegger to Jarry, to the extent that pataphysics presents itself precisely as a*

surpassing of metaphysics that is explicitly founded on the Being of the phenomenon. But if we take Jarry or Roussel in this way to be the realization of Heidegger's philosophy, does this not mean that the fold is carried off and set up in a completely different landscape, and so takes on a different meaning? We must not refuse to take Heidegger seriously, but we must rediscover the imperturbably serious side to Roussel (or Jarry). The serious ontological aspect needs a diabolical or phenomenological sense of humor.[250]

This phenomenological sense of humour operates in the same fashion as the masochist's one, i.e. by exploiting the consequences of the principles in order to liberate the subject from the respect of those principles themselves. The result is that, "in fact... the fold as doubling in Foucault will take a completely new appearance while retaining its ontological import."[251]

Humour and Irony

An additional way to understand the nature and function of humour can be gathered by contrasting Deleuze's notion of humour with that of irony. Deleuze considers them complementary, insofar as they are the destructive instruments of philosophy *par excellence*:

> *There are two known ways to overturn moral law. One is by ascending towards the principles: challenging the law as secondary, derived, borrowed or "general"; denouncing it as involving a second-hand principle which diverts an original force or usurps an original power. The other way, by contrast, is to overturn the law by descending towards the consequences. [...] The first way of overturning the law is ironic, where irony appears as an art of principles, of ascent towards the principles and of overturning principles. The second is humor.*[252]

Authors like Friedrich Nietzsche (1844–1900) and Søren Kierkegaard made use of both instruments in order to destroy the metaphysical systems of their epoch, whose dreams of omnipotence implied the annihilation of the

> *logos of the solitary and the singular, the logos of the "private thinker". Both Kierkegaard and Nietzsche develop the opposition between the private thinker, the thinker-comet and bearer of repetition, and the public professor and doctor of law, whose second-hand discourse proceeds by mediation and finds its moralising source in the generality of concepts (cf. Kierkegaard against Hegel, Nietzsche against Kant and Hegel; and from this point of view, Peguy against the Sorbonne). Job is infinite contestation and Abraham infinite resignation, but these are one and the same thing. Job challenges the law in an ironic manner, refusing all second-hand explanations and dismissing the general in order to reach the most singular as principle or as universal. Abraham submits humorously to the law, but finds in that submission precisely the singularity of his only son whom the law commanded him to sacrifice [...] In Nietzsche's striking atheism, hatred of the law and* amor fati *(love of fate), aggression and acquiescence are the two faces of Zarathustra, gathered from the Bible and turned back against it.* [253]

Job questions directly God's goodness, "why are you doing this to me?"; he challenges the principle at stake: in this sense is he ironic. Abraham submits himself to God's will, but in a way that obliges God to change it; he cunningly respects the principle, carrying it to contradiction in its consequences: in this sense is he humorous.

This does not mean that Kierkegaard and Nietzsche shared the same goals: the former was promoting religious belief, which the latter rejected vehemently.[254] What matters for Deleuze, and for the present chapter, is their common appeal to irony and humour, both of which are seen as the two utensils capable of subverting the conceptual cages within which Kant and Hegel tried to reduce all possible human experience.

Humour descends from the caging structure to its contradictory or paradoxical consequences, finding loopholes that can make the whole structure collapse. Irony, on its part, "is the art of problems and questions. Irony consists in treating things and beings as so many responses to hidden questions, so many cases for problems to be resolved."[255]

The special art of irony, according to Deleuze, was born philosophically within Plato's dialogues, but can itself be used against any Platonism, idealism and ambitious metaphysics:

> *We are reminded of the grand finale of the Sophist... The Eleatic Stranger gives a definition of the sophist such that he can no longer be distinguished from Socrates himself: the ironic imitator who proceeds by brief arguments (questions and problems) [...inasmuch as] irony itself is a multiplicity – or rather, the art of multiplicities; the art of grasping the Ideas and the problems they incarnate in things, and of grasping the things as incarnations, as cases of solution for the problems of Ideas.*[256]

Irony shows in this way its anarchic nature. Despite its propaedeutic use in Plato's works, the corrosive spirit of this dialectical instrument is capable of overturning the ruling concepts. Irony is a revolutionary instrument of the intellect—the eternal challenge to absolute power. Irony cannot be just a moment in the construction of a metaphysical system, for it ends up attacking any stable result of the dialectical enterprise.[257]

Irony preserves nonetheless a cognitive aspiration that humour rejects. The ironic procedure is an inquisitive one, as if a higher or deeper understanding were attainable behind, beyond or underneath the questioned system of knowledge. Humour, as seen, detests higher or deeper levels; its dimension is not a dialectical game of questions and problems, but a disruptive game of paradoxes, in which "that which is the most profound is the immediate... Paradox appears as a dismissal of depth, a display of events at the surface, and a deployment of language along its limit. Humor is the art of the surface, which is opposed to the old irony, the art of depths and heights."[258]

Under this perspective, irony is opposed to humour, insofar as it aims at going even higher than the principle at stake. However, in order to challenge the existing principle, irony must accept the rules of its opponent and play consistently with them. According to Deleuze's account, irony is an inquisitive method and cannot escape the fixed boundaries of an individual intellect engaged in a discussion. Irony requires at least two voices challenging each other, a set of shared rules, and a binding dialectical logic. Humour does not. Humour plays on a different level, bringing about all the arbitrariness that any logic, any set of rules and any dialogue may entail. Humour descends into the chaotic, egalitarian context of the surface, the zero-level of non-sense where every series has its origin, linguistic sense included. Humour discloses the surface of singular events, which admits the coexistence of contradictory elements, so that irony *qua* dialectical interplay founded upon strict logic is unavoidably ruled out:

> *What all the figures of irony have in common is that they confine the singularity within the limits of the individual or the person. Thus, irony only in appearance assumes the role of a vagabond. But this is why all these figures are threatened by an intimate enemy who works on them from within: the undifferentiated ground, the groundless abyss... that represents tragic thought and the tragic tone with which irony maintains the most ambivalent relations. It is Dionysus, present beneath Socrates, but it is also the demon who holds up to God and to his creatures the mirror wherein universal individuality dissolves. It is the chaos which brings about the undoing of the person [...] The tragic and the ironic give way to a new value, that of humor. For if irony is the coextensiveness of being with the individual, or of the I with representation, humor is the coextensiveness of sense with nonsense. Humor is the art of surfaces and of the doubles, of nomad singularities and of the always displaced aleatory point; it is the art of the static genesis, the savoir-faire of the pure event, and the 'fourth person singular' – with every*

signification, denotation, and manifestation suspended, all height and depth abolished.[259]

The difference between irony and humour can probably explain why the history of thought enlists many more cases of irony than of humour. What kind of representational knowledge can be achieved from the latter? The former, albeit by way of conflict, deepens somewhat the present knowledge and allows it to progress further; its distinctive aim has somehow always been the quest for higher or deeper principles, rather than their sheer frustration, humiliation and pulverisation. From resignation and dust, what sort of higher awareness or profound knowledge could be ever achieved?

The contrast between irony and humour is not limited to cognitive, theoretical or philosophical areas. Once again, as already seen in the case of masochism, Deleuze's notions find an application in literary and psycho-pathological contexts. Deleuze argues that irony is the distinctive trait of the Marquis de Sade's (1740–1814) libertine heroes and heroines, as opposed to Sacher-Masoch's, for:

> *Irony is still in the process or movement which bypasses the law as merely secondary power and aims at transcending it toward a higher principle. But what if the higher principle no longer exist, and if the Good can no longer provide a basis for the law or justification of its power? [...] We now note a new attempt to transcend the law, this time no longer in the direction of the Good as superior principle and ground of the law, but in the direction of its opposite, the Idea of Evil, the supreme principle of wickedness, which subverts the law and turns Platonism upside down.*[260]

According to Deleuze, the sadist challenges ironically the Platonic ideal of a reality gravitating around the notion of the Good, by means of the only alternative principle that can be found, i.e. evil. "The ironic sadist is a logician of principles", as opposed to "the humorist, a logician of consequences", whose distinctive feature is a self-interested twist of the law by deceitful submission to it.[261]

The sadist cannot admit any form of submission, she does not pulverise the law by carrying it to paradoxical outcomes, but rather faces the law, arming herself with the consistent conceptual load of a better alternative, a more fundamental principle. And she is so engaged in this battle, that she can lose her own ego, i.e. her Freudian reality principle, her sense of reality. As Deleuze writes, this is the distinctive pathological expression of sadism:

> *The sadist's superego is so strong that he has become identified with it; he is his own superego and can only find an ego in the external world. What normally confers a moral character on the superego is the internal and complementary ego upon which it exerts its severity, and equally the maternal element which fosters the close interaction between ego and superego. But when the superego runs wild, expelling the ego along with the mother-image, then its fundamental immorality exhibits itself as sadism. The ultimate victims of the sadist are the mother and the ego.*[262]

After presenting an extensive account of Deleuze's notion of humour I now crystallise humour's distinguishing features by way of a couple of representative terms. By doing this, I intend to initiate an ironic analysis of humour—a game of questions and problems.

Superficiality and Displacement

The first representative term is *superficiality*, in the specific sense that humour is said to be "the art of surface". Its function is the disclosure of the dynamic, magmatic, uncontrollable surface of singular events to which all forms of being can be reconnected ontologically. Humour reveals to us, according to Deleuze, that a "groundless abyss" sub-tends to our cognitive and existential constructions; an abyss whose oneness, specificity and constitutive difference cannot be mastered by any of those conceptual, perceptual, or even sensorial representations that we can creatively concoct.

As previously mentioned, intellectual and perceptual representations imply the subsumption of experience under a categorical structure of understanding. Subsumption works as a process of collocation of experience under cognitive umbrella-terms, which eliminate by definition the ontologically singular, i.e. the unique phenomenon and/or event, *in lieu* of the logically particular, each unique phenomenon and/or event being then an occurrence of the general.

Paradoxes, puns and nonsense provide us with a refreshing hint at the nameless multiplicity of being upon which we all stand, and they show as well the limits of the mechanism of classification or 'pigeon-holing' proper to perceptual and conceptual understanding.[263] These linguistic short-circuits break down the reassuring homogenisation of diversity brought about by representation, which combines together the multifarious received information into consistent patterns (or "common sense") and redistributes it usefully within the spatio-temporal archive of the accepted understanding (or "good sense").[264]

Following Deleuze's argument, humour's basic function is thus an anarchic, iconoclastic de-structuring: humour laughs at the naked emperor. But at the same time, it projects us beyond the emperor himself, leading us into the ground from which every kingdom, every power, every hierarchy arises. Humour discloses before us the land of co-original non-sense and sense, the ungraspable abyss out of which everything comes as pure singularity. Why is humour called "the art of surface", then? Why not rather "the art of the unseen depth"?

Deleuze makes a somewhat ambiguous use of geological terms suggesting different levels, strata or depths, which are encountered along the "descent" of humour towards the surface of singular events (e.g. "sense in itself" and "sense emerging from bodily *eros*", "passive" and "active genesis", "language" and "orality", "surface" and "subtending substance"); however, he is always consistent in stressing and calling the role of humour as "the art of the surface".[265] In so doing, Deleuze's chief aim is to provide a definition of humour that highlights its anti-hierarchical and anti-representational character.

Having this goal, Deleuze ends up neglecting its revelatory aspect, the relevance of which I am emphasising instead. Deleuze adumbrates humour's audacious camouflaged profundity in favour of its witty open playfulness. But humour is like a lady who forgets her gloves at the ball, so that the noble host will have to visit her in order to return them. How much intrigue, premeditation and lust behind a seemingly trivial mistake!

Similarly operate the powerful insights that humour, as described by Deleuze himself, can bring about. The declared richness of meanings, connections and signals entailed by a humorous remark, a paradox, or apparent nonsense, may be well interpreted as the access to a new depth, rather than a mere displacement, or the simple loss of previous grounds. An abyss is opened under our feet by virtue of humour: what is deeper than an abyss? Is not the intuition of a surface of being, out of which all events come as singularities, the achievement of a new depth?

It may well be the case that, as humour's revelatory aspect is concerned, the conceptual depth (or peak) that applies is not identical to that of traditional metaphysics; but it is nevertheless a depth offering us a glimpse of the utmost nature of beings. Although such a nature is "superficial" and approached *via negativa*, it is a step underneath (or above) the level of commonsensical or even scientific representation. Besides, humour itself, as Deleuze understands it, originates from the depths of our faculties.[266]

Logical paradoxes, typically, are the fruit of attentive studies and careful formal analyses. Zen masters had to spend long periods of segregation and meditation before they acquired their wisdom and started uttering perplexing koans. Yiddish nonsense is a prerogative of rabbis and vagabonds, namely individuals who have lived a life of separation from both "common sense" and "good sense".

Deleuze's humour is said to be an art and, as such, it needs time and effort to be practiced in order to be learnt and applied successfully: *Übung macht den Meister*. This is true even if humour is wisdom of a peculiar sort, since it implies the negation of the generally accepted wisdom. Under this respect, humour is not unlike irony: it challenges the official power, and it aims towards a new power, namely the power of the surface of being, from which everything else arises. By disclosing the source of being, of both sense and non-sense, Deleuze's humour reaches this new horizon more efficiently than irony itself, for irony operates within the limits of the given logico-linguistic categories.

The second representative term is *displacement*. Humour displaces by switching always from a supposed meaning to a different meaning, which cannot be handled within the given context. Using a Heideggerian expression, humour guides us through a *Lichtung*, an opening whence new vistas can be entertained. Humour leads us to the presence of a self-concealing manifestation of being that we had never explored before and that we did not even expect to find along our path.[267] It is in this way that humour challenges the principles and the most basic assumptions of any systematic thinking, conceptual scheme or theory.

Humour's *modus operandi* is different from the one followed by irony, but less radically opposed to it than Deleuze argues. Humour can be understood as irony in disguise, being its distinctive specialty to infiltrate the system being criticised and cause lethal damages from the inside. Irony, on the other hand, prefers assaulting directly the system from the outside, without subterfuge. The aim is the same, though. The productivity of new thought is the same too: both humour and irony can be precious sources of new insights.

I do not deny that humour displaces our ordinary patterns of understanding, thus manifesting a peculiar resistance of thought, as if such a thought were lazily entrenched within the categories of our representational faculties. Certainly, humour's intervention breaks down the alliance between good sense and common sense, which are both intended to grasp the whole of being and allocate it in well-ordered progressive conceptual pigeonholes along the arrow of conventional time. In any case, neither condition seems to exhaust the creative power of humour. Paradoxes do not only displace us and show us the limits of language and conceptualisation in general, but also promote the understanding of both language and conceptualisation by virtue of the "epiphanies of the limit" for which they allow, at least on occasion.

In the first place, I must admit that not all displacements appear to be humorous: being lost in the Amazon forest is not humorous, no matter one's survival skills. But more congruously to Deleuze's ontology, not all paradoxes, nonsense, puns, etc. can be humorous. If intended in the commonsensical sense of the word, Deleuze's humour is often a humourless humour. In other terms, thus interpreted, Deleuze's notion would be too broad, describing as humorous authors, insights, and experiences, which nobody but Deleuze would call humorous. Despite their familiarity and aptitude *vis-à-vis* paradoxes, logicians and mathematicians such as William of Ockham, Kurt Gödel (1906–1978) and Bertrand Russell (1872–1970) do not belong to the same group of people as witty *literati* Giovanni Boccaccio (1313–1375), Nikolay V. Gogol (1809–1852) and Daniil Kharms (1905–1945), but they would nevertheless comply with Deleuze's requirements in order to be enlisted as humourists. Or, taking a case dear to Deleuze, Lewis Carroll's (1832–1898) writings are humorous indeed, whereas Reverend Dodgson's are not, despite them being one and the same person.

In the second place, the very Deleuzian notion of humour can be too broad, as it applies to paradoxes, nonsense and puns, whose "disclosing" force and "displacing" ability are almost zero. They can "descend" from principles to consequences, they can break down the principles, they can create displacement, they can play on the surface of sense and non-sense, but they can be at the same time non-humorous as long as they do not disclose any particularly relevant unseen depth. In other words, the "descent" of humour knows many degrees. There are in fact humourless paradoxes, pure logical knots, whose description as humorous would be rather bewildering: they do not disclose anything, they do not show any "epiphany of the limit", but only how to solve the problem or that the problem was badly put. *Reductio ad absurdum* is regularly used in mathematics to reinforce the representational logical system in which the reduction is implemented.

There is humourless nonsense too, mere communicative failure, whose description as humorous would be an exaggeration. Not all slips are Freudian slips: there are temporal, functional, procedural slips, and many other banal mistakes. Finally, there are humourless puns, simple attempts at humour, whose description as humorous would be an undeserved compliment. They are endeavours, which do not reach their target and do not provoke any other displacement than misplacement. They would produce nothing but embarrassment —imagine somebody telling a blasphemous joke at the CDU national congress.

In the third place, Deleuze seems oblivious of the tragic element implied by humour's genesis, namely the element of destruction, uncertainty and disorientation that the disclosure of the surface of being entails. His oblivion is shown by certain *interpretations* that Deleuze gives about a few references of his, where he skips the tragic in favour of an almost exclusive ironic or burlesque interpretation of humour. In other terms, Deleuze turns tragedy into comedy, the tragic into comic, without recognising their co-existence, co-determination and mutual need. Thus, not only is Deleuze's notion of humour too broad and counterintuitive, but also too poor. Such is the case of his interpretation of Franz Kafka's work, for instance:

> *Une seule chose fait de la peine à Kafka et le met en colère, en indignation : qu'on le traite d'écrivain intimiste, trouvant un refuge dans la littérature, auteur de la solitude, de la culpabilité, du malheur intime. C'est pourtant sa faute, parce qu'il a brandi tout ça... pour devancer le piège et par l'humour. Il y a le rire de Kafka, rire très joyeux, que l'on comprend si mal pour les mêmes raisons. C'est pour les mêmes raisons stupides que l'on a prétendu voir un refuge loin de la vie dans la littérature de Kafka, et aussi une angoisse, la marque d'une impuissance et d'une culpabilité, le signe d'une tragédie intérieure triste. Deux principes seulement pour épouser Kafka : c'est un auteur qui rit, profondément joyeux, d'une joie de vivre, malgré et avec ses déclarations de clown, qu'il tend comme un piège ou comme un*

cirque. D'un bout à l'autre, c'est un auteur politique, devin du monde futur, parce qu'il a comme deux pôles qu'il va savoir unifier dans un agacement tout à fait nouveau: loin d'être écrivain retire dans sa chambre, sa chambre lui sert a un double flux, celui d'un bureaucrate de grand avenir, branche sur les agencements réels en train de se faire; et celui d'un nomade en train de fuir a la façon la plus actuelle, qui se branche sur le socialisme, l'anarchisme, les mouvements sociaux.[268]

I do not deny that Kafka was a refined humourist, but rather wonder how it is possible to underestimate those elements in his writings that express terrible anguish, misanthropy and despair. Despite the burlesque side, despite the theatrical play of human inconsistencies and foolishness, despite the ironic challenge against the power-structures, despite the constructive critical spirit sometimes perceivable behind the lines, can we really minimise the tragic side, the feelings of impotence and eradication, the sense of frustration pervading his prose, the traumatic cases of his personal life, the isolation in which he spent most of his existence?

Deleuze's accent on the humorous flank of Kafka's literature goes too far. Deleuze is somehow forcing an asymmetry between these two complementary elements of Kafka's creativity. And more critically, I would claim that Kafka's humour could not even live without an equal amount of laughter and tragedy, of amusement and despair. Humour was said to arise from tragedy and irony, even if only in a single passage that does not find many echoes in the rest of Deleuze's production. Why does Deleuze forget about this point when discussing Kafka? Why does Deleuze minimise the interplay of the two genetic elements, i.e. irony and tragedy?[269]

My only explanation is that Deleuze does not want to stress the possibility of a co-original co-existence of two opposite elements. Tragedy and irony, if such were the case in the birth of humour, could constitute a dialectic duo of Hegelian memory: a duo whose central feature is *negation* (or opposition). And Deleuze does not like negation at all, insofar as it manifests a presupposed ontology of identity, an altar on which the original difference of multiple singularities is sacrificed to the gods of representation, conceptual consistency and comprehensiveness—the gods of "common sense" and "good sense".

A relevant part of Deleuze's production deals in fact with the delineation of an ontological distinction of difference and negation (or opposition), the latter being interpreted as a representational oversimplification of the more fundamental difference:

The negative is an illusion, no more than a shadow of problems [...] Critiques of the negative are never decisive as long as they invoke the rights of a first concept (the One, order being); they are no more so as long as they are content to translate opposition into limitation. The critique of the negative is effective only when it denounces the interchangeability of opposition and limitation, thereby denouncing the hypothetical conceptual element which necessarily sustains one or the other, or even one by means of the other. In short, the critique of the negative must be conducted on the basis of the ideal, differential and problematic element, on the basis of the Idea. It is the notion of multiplicity which denounces simultaneously order and disorder, and (non)-being or ?-being which denounces simultaneously both being and non-being. The complicity of the negative and the hypothetical must everywhere be dissolved in favour of a more profound link between difference and the problematic.[270]

Even admitting that difference and the problematic are the original ground of the negative, and therefore of opposition, why should one neglect the opposition of ironic, or even humorous, and tragic in Kafka's work? How can it be possible to underestimate the eerie pendulum swinging between the monstrous metamorphosis of Gregor Samsa and life seen from a bug's perspective, or the irreversible ruin of K's destiny and the lunacy of the bureaucrats around him? How not to appreciate Kafka's subtlety, without the oppositions underlying humorous moments: sense and non-sense, functional and dysfunctional, dead and living, honest and corrupt, facetious and tragic?

The interpretation of a piece of literature or of an artist's work is a representational matter. Interpretation always takes place at the conceptual or linguistic level and negation, or opposition, is a valuable conceptual tool at such a level—*at least* at such a level. Without the assertion of an egalitarian interplay of the two elements of irony and tragedy, it is difficult to fully understand Kafka's prose, as well as to realise why he should be humorous in Deleuze's own terms.

Kafka's case is not an isolated inconvenient, because with the exception of the long passage quoted from *The Logic of Sense*, Deleuze tends to treat humour as non-tragic in most of his writings, such as Deleuze's interpretation of Friedrich Nietzsche's works.[271] In *Nietzsche and Philosophy*, Deleuze focuses his attention on the affirmative side of Zarathustra's teachings, in a way that regularly minimises the contradictions embodied by Zarathustra himself (the ancient Persian mystic being Nietzsche's literary alter ego). Zarathustra affirms, for sure, but he also negates. Zarathustra is not the Overman, but the one who announces his coming. Zarathustra dances, Zarathustra laughs, Zarathustra despises the ass and the demon of nihilism—all of this is joyful affirmation; but Zarathustra lays sick in his cave, he rests melancholic in the graveyard, and he is incapable of getting rid of his inner demon, namely the tragic, heavy side of the same message. *Also Sprach Zarathustra* ends with an unfulfilled hope of realisation of the prophet's teachings, with an unresolved tension between the spirit of affirmation of utter contingency and the weakness of the human being in becoming able to affirm such affirmation.[272]

In his study of humour, Deleuze takes minimal notice of tragedy, pain, or weakness. His overall attitude towards the "darkness" of the "groundless abyss" recalls Nietzsche's warning in the *Fröhliche Wissenschaft* and specifically the powerful allegory therein contained of the Enlightenment philosophers, who quietly discuss in the public market their proudly Newtonian and unchristian materialism, without realising the terrible existential implications of their own thoughts—an arrogant ignorance or trained indifference, against which went the desperate cry of Nietzsche's madman in the book: "*Gott ist tot!*"²⁷³

Deleuze himself appears insensitive to the despair and loss that Diogenes and Chrysippus' "descent" brings about. Where do our previous convictions go, after recognising that they were mere contingent illusions? What confidence can we have in our faculties when they are shown to be so poorly gifted? What kind of astonishment may follow from the intuition of the "groundless abyss" of being?

A third case can be envisaged in Deleuze's *Cinema 1. The Movement-Image*. Interpreting Charlie Chaplin's (1889–1977) genius of the burlesque, Deleuze notes the interplay of comic and tragic elements that made Chaplin's movies so original and successful, but ends up always highlighting the former and minimising the latter:

> *If we want to define Chaplin's originality, to find what gave him an incomparable place in the burlesque, we must look elsewhere. For Chaplin knew how to select gestures which were close to each other and corresponding situations which were far apart, so as to make their relationship produce a particularly intense emotion at the same time as laughter, and to redouble the laughter through this emotion. [...] No case can be made for a tragic Chaplin. There is certainly no case for saying that we laugh, whereas we should cry.*²⁷⁴

Even when laughter becomes less relevant, as in the case of Chaplin's late production, Deleuze finds always a way to reduce the importance of the field of oppositions in which Chaplin's creativity moved, preferring to switch his attention to another theme:

> *Chaplin's last films* [The Great Dictator *and* Monsieur Verdoux] *both discover sound and put Charlie to death... Here the same principle seems to gain a new power... In these two films, does Chaplin want to tell us that there is a Hitler, a potential murderer in each of us? And that it is only situations which make us good*

or evil, victims or executioners, capable of loving and destroying? Whether or not such ideas are profound or platitudinous, this does not seem consistent with Chaplin's way of looking at things, except in a very secondary way. For what is still more important than the two opposing situations of good and evil are the underlying discourses, *which are expressed as such at the end of these films.*[275]

How to deny the importance of these discourses? Are these oppositions, along which both movies run, secondary? Deleuze's interpretation sounds once again exaggerated. Deleuze seems to ignore and dismiss as secondary the constitutive grounding profound role that such oppositions play in function of the final "discourses".

Deleuze underestimates the drama behind the witty remarks of the Cynic and Stoic sages of old, though his interpretation of Kafka is probably the most evident exemplification of his indifference towards the tragic side of the humorous experience, Nietzsche's and Chaplin's cases suggesting an even broader 'allergy' to opposition *in se et per se*. However it is taken, Deleuze's indifference makes it difficult to appreciate the many bittersweet ambiguities that so often appear in humourists' works, such as Eugène Labiche's (1815–1888) clever plays, Samuel Beckett's (1906–1989) theatre of the absurd, or the largely anonymous traditional Yiddish tales. Is Deleuze really portraying the essential features of humour? Is he realising that a demon accompanies humour's "descent" into the "groundless abyss" of singularities? Could language ever gain a destructive character, without the presence of a demonic figure inside it?

Anticipating what follows, we could say that it is indeed a very special kind of ambiguity, or ambivalence, which can be described as the crucial ingredient for successful humour, also and above all with respect to Deleuze's account of it *qua* art of the surface. The previously selected features of humour, namely its superficiality and displacement, are applicable to paradoxes, puns and nonsense, when these are expressed in a way that makes them become humorous. Superficiality and displacement, more in general, may convey the insightful disclosure of the groundless abyss of singularities, if and only if they are linked to a certain interpretative pattern that can cast a particular light on them, i.e. a humorous light. And in order to understand how humour may arise, we must call in for another intellectual: Luigi Pirandello.

Pirandello and Humour

Among the many characteristics mentioned by authors who have tried to give a definition of the notion of humour, there are:

> *[A] fundamental "contradiction" which is usually said to derive principally from the discord which feeling and meditation discover either between real life and the human ideal or between human aspirations and human frailty and miseries, and whose main effect is a certain perplexity between weeping and laughing; the skepticism which gives color to all humorous observations and descriptions; and finally, the minutely and even cunningly analytical process of that skepticism.*[276]

Despite the insights that such definitions may provide "one can reach an understanding, in general terms, of what humor is, but it will undeniably be an understanding which is too summary."[277] And more pessimistically, it is actually quite hopeless to try to infer how humour arises by giving definitions of this sort, insofar as:

> *[T]o start from these characteristics is not the best way to arrive to an understanding of the true essence of humor, for it always happens that the characteristic that is taken as fundamental is the one that is found to be common to several works or to several writers studied with special interest. The result is that there are as many definitions of humor as characteristics that have been found, and all of them naturally have an element of truth, and yet none is the true definition.*[278]

A better approach to the problem is suggested. Instead of attempting a self-defeating quest for clear-cut definitions:

> *Let us see, then, without further digression, what is the process that results in the particular representation which is customarily called humor; let us see if this representation has its own distinctive traits, and what is their origin, and if there exists a special way of looking at the world which constitutes precisely the substance and explanation of humor.*[279]

Pirandello chooses to move through the observation of the creative process giving rise to humorous contexts. Pirandello being a humourist himself, the description of this process follows quite natural and detailed to him, and a precise explanation of the interplay of consciousness, reflection and feeling, is thus delineated:

> *[T]he work of art is created by the free movement of inner life which organizes the ideas and images into a harmonious form, in which all the elements correspond with one another and with the generating idea that coordinates them. Reflection does not remain inactive, of course, during the conception and during the execution of the work of art... [But] consciousness does not illuminate the whole realm of spirit; particularly in a creative artist consciousness is not an inner light distinct from thought, which might allow the will to draw from it images and ideas as from a rich source. Consciousness, in short, is... an inner mirror in which thought contemplates itself. One could say rather that consciousness is thought which sees itself watching over what it does spontaneously. As a rule, in the moment of artistic conception, reflection is hidden and remains, as it were, invisible: in the artist, reflection is almost a form of feeling.*[280]

Gifted with a form of contemplative, subconscious, spontaneous reflection, the humourist seems to differ from other artists because:

> *[D]uring the conception of all works of humor, reflection is not hidden, it does not remain invisible: it is not, that is, almost a form of feeling or almost a mirror in which feeling contemplates*

itself; rather, it places itself squarely before the feeling, in a judging attitude, and, detaching itself from it, analyzes and disassembles its imagery; from this analysis and decomposition, however, there arises or emerges a new feeling which could be called and in fact I call the feeling of the opposite.[281]

By way of example:

I see an old lady whose hair is dyed and completely smeared with some kind of horrible ointment; she is all made-up in a clumsy and awkward fashion and is all dolled-up like a young girl. I begin to laugh. I perceive that she is the opposite of what a respectable old lady should be. Now I could stop here at this initial and superficial comic reaction: the comic consists precisely of this perception of the opposite. But if, at this point, reflection interferes in me to suggest that perhaps this old lady finds no pleasure in dressing up like an exotic parrot, and that perhaps she is distressed by it and does it only because she pitifully deceives herself into believing that, by making herself up like that and by concealing her wrinkles and gray hair, she may be able to hold the love of her much younger husband – if reflection comes to suggest all this, then I can no longer laugh at her as I did first, exactly because the inner working of reflection has made me go beyond, or rather enter deeper into, the initial stage of awareness: from the beginning perception of the opposite, reflection has made me shift to a feeling of the opposite. And herein lies the precise difference between the comic and humor.[282]

Pirandello provides further examples taken from a number of European literary sources. In all of them Pirandello individuates a play of oppositions as the core of their humorous moments, or as the description that they somehow provide when confronting related expressive realities such as the ironic, the satirical and the comic.

Pirandello and Deleuze

Combining now together Deleuze's notion of humour with Pirandello's one, it can be said that the latter gives us elements to better understand the dialectic of superficial and deep implied by Deleuze's account of humour. I am suggesting this in order to achieve a narrower, more sophisticated definition of humour, which may be more consistent with the commonsensical perception of what is humorous. Pirandello's account of humour can refine and improve Deleuze's own notion of humour and help us realise why Deleuze may have minimised the tragic side in his accounts of Kafka, Nietzsche and Chaplin.

Pirandello's description of the phenomenon of humour implies, in fact, a very Deleuzian 'superficial depth'. The humourist is said to succeed in being humorous by reflecting on the comic and bringing about the tragic behind it. This reflection, this deepening action of special reflection, this original scrutiny of the data of experience, is said to be not fully conscious. According to Pirandello, the humourist is gifted with a natural disposition to reveal the opposite, as if there took place a conscious reflection in what she does, even if all happens actually in a spontaneous manner. Not dissimilarly from Diogenes or Chrysippus, the humourist is pointing at what lies behind a given experience, breaking down the immediate perception of the phenomenon, which was built on the existing representational frame that we all absorb as social linguistic animals.[283]

Pirandello's notion sounds more adequate in order to describe the phenomenon of humour as something connected with laughter, irony, the comic, the burlesque. Deleuze's notion seems too broad with respect to the commonsensical conception of humour, which would hardly consider logical paradoxes or philosophical knots something humorous. They can become such, of course, but if presented in a humorous way. And Pirandello knew how to make people laugh—it was part of his job as a playwright and novelist— and had probably a better understanding of what humour is considered to be like by his human fellows, i.e. his audiences and readers. It is not by coincidence that he prefers following a

Bergsonian kind of inquiry with regard to the process of creation of something humorous, rather than to the definition of humour as such.[284]

Pirandello's conception is helpful with regard to Deleuze's own notion of humour, for it can add to Deleuze's insights those instruments that he would need in order to select and separate among cases of paradoxes, puns or nonsense that are actually humorous and the unsuccessful ones. Pirandello would make Deleuze capable of including under the term "humour" only those linguistic figures bringing us so down in the "descent" from the abstract principles they destroy, that we manage to experience an actual disclosure of the "groundless abyss" where sense and non-sense co-originate. In order to obtain this seemingly desirable result, Deleuze should then endorse Pirandello's understanding of humour as coming out of the "feeling of the opposite".[285]

Pirandello's account can help us understand why Deleuze adopted such an unusual concept of humour, as well as why he did ostracise the tragic component involved in the humorous. Pirandello's notion of humour provides in fact a reason in favour of a more tolerant approach to negation, in the form of opposition. According to Pirandello's work, anything humorous implies opposition at several levels, and not only at representational ones. His characterisation of opposition suggests that contradiction does not exist only at the level of the first synthesis of time and space, i.e. the level of conceptual constructions, but also in the deeper layers that allow these constructions to subsist, both in temporal and in spatial terms. Pirandello is evidently aware of them; he is almost a "Deleuzian" thinker *ante litteram*:

> *Life is a continual flux which we try to stop, to fix in stable and determined forms, both inside and outside ourselves, because we are already fixed forms, forms which move in the midst of other immobile forms and which however can follow the flow of life until the movement, gradually showing and becoming more and more rigid, eventually ceases... But within ourselves... there are restless souls, almost in a continuous state of fusion, who are*

disdainful of becoming congealed or solidified into a particular form of personality. But even for the more peaceful souls, who have settled into one form or other, fusion is always possible: the flux of life is in all of us.[286]

The flux of life is such that:

[C]ontrast reveals itself to be irreparable and its conflicting elements prove as inseparable as the shadow from the body. In this rapid vision of humor we have seen it expand gradually, go beyond the limits of our individual being, where is rooted, and extend itself all around us. [...] Bare life, nature itself without any order, at least without any apparent order, bristling with contradictions, seems to the humorist to be very far from the ideal contrivances of ordinary artistic creations, in which all the elements are visibly held together in close interaction and collaboration.[287]

Nature is much more chaotic than artistic or, more broadly, intellectual representations suggest. Opposition, negation, is found in the flux of life, and it founds the ambiguous character that Pirandello describes as crucial for humour. Opposition is certainly rooted within the representation of the phenomenon (e.g. Pirandello's account of it), but also in the spontaneous representation of the artist (e.g. *Don Quixote*'s self-referential chapters) as well as in the superficial level of the comic (i.e. the perception of the opposite); and, similarly, it can be found in the constitutive level of the humorous (i.e. the feeling of the opposite), or even more deeply in the chaotic flux of being itself (e.g. the co-original ground of sense and non-sense).

This fundamental chaos is revealed by opposition and negation occurring in art, philosophy and common sense. Each of these human activities:

[G]enerally abstracts and concentrates; that is, it catches and represents the essential characteristic ideality of both men and things. Now it seems to the humorist that all this oversimplifies

nature and tends to make life too reasonable or at least too coherent... does not take into account, as it should, the causes, the real causes, that often move this poor human soul to the most mindless and totally unpredictable actions.[288]

Had Deleuze agreed on a more punctual definition of humour, closer to Pirandello's one, he would have committed himself to a reconsideration of the notion of negation. This would have taken place at least with regard to the forms of opposition and contradiction, which are the two that Pirandello refers to primarily. Yet Deleuze seems to be obsessed by the idea of avoiding negation in principle, insofar as it entails the model of recognition or representation, i.e. of the notion of mirroring essences and principles of identity.

In reply to Deleuze's negative attitude towards negation (or opposition, contradiction), it must be firstly stated that negation is absolutely consistent in the realm of representation, to which humour belongs as a linguistic phenomenon. That humour may in addition open the abyss of non-reducible singularities, this is a further characteristic, with which one deals in a second time, and that constitutes a virtue of humour in Deleuze's own view, but not a dismissal of its representational origin *tout-court*. Humour must be expressed through words, after all.[289]

Secondly, it must be stated that Pirandello's notion of humour entails an opposition that is not only representational, but presentational too, or pre-representational. It does not only deal with how we reconstruct and reflect on a state of affairs, but on how it strikes on the humourist's disposition too, forcing her to think or to react in a spontaneous manner entailing the "feeling of the opposite". More radically, in the cases of the non-humourist and the mere comic, there is already enough to suggest that opposition may subsist at a pre-representational level.

The experience of laughter is, as we all know, often anterior to any explicit conceptualisation, i.e. to any active synthesis of conscious thought, for it is frequently immediate, uncontrolled and unexplained. There is indeed the recognition of an abnormality, but it seems to be instinctive, as the self-imposing power of an externally existing contradiction, rather than the instruction of one built by means of conscious comparison of *Vorstellungen*. Using Deleuze's terminology, laughter would work as a "passive synthesis", an aggression from the experiential level that we cannot reject, a fundamental "encounter". As Henri Bergson (1859–1941) had already observed, it is not rare that a person may laugh at a scene in a play before that same person can formulate an account of the causes for her action.[290]

Concluding Remarks

We should then reconsider the possibility of readmitting opposition and negation within the ontological ground of experience, in virtue of a peculiar sort of "transcendental exercise" ignored by Deleuze: laughing. If humour discloses the great surface of differential singularities and if it implies an opposition, then we should infer that the great surface of differential singularities includes opposed singularities, or oppositions as singularity. I do not argue in favour of either, but only wish to stress that if the two premises are correct—and the former is surely correct in Deleuze's own view—then we should accept opposition, contradiction, negation, inside Deleuze's theoretical panorama. In spite of his rejection of the ontology of identity, negation would thus find a way to survive, as a part—sometimes even an important part, as in the case of humour—of his ontology of difference. Negation could be considered one of the many faces of difference at its deeper levels, i.e. one of the many expressions of being.

Certain passages in Deleuze's ontological writings seem to corroborate this hypothesis. For instance, in *Difference and Repetition*, Deleuze claims that every intensity implies all the others, but that each of them develops according to the values peculiar to itself, so that every intensity eventually differs from those having other peculiar values.[291] Now, if this is the destiny of every intensity, i.e. the fundamental manifestation of difference in Deleuze's ontology, is it not plausible to say that every development of an intensity denies the identities which do not share the same peculiar values from manifesting themselves in the same circumstances? There could be a shift of level, a point of discontinuity, where the other intensities might enact their own actualisation, but as long as this is not the case, those peculiar explications will be simply virtual, and therefore denied from being actualised. Could not this temporary exclusion at one level of time, i.e. the present, be seen as a case of negation?

If such were the case, there should be a reintroduction of the notion of identity-to-itself, with respect to each intensity's peculiar values, which would operate like its individuating connotations. In other terms, when Deleuze distinguishes among various intensities on the basis of their peculiar values, he is providing a set of connotative coordinates to individuate them. Representation, then, would have found yet another way to infiltrate our thought, or make it possible in the very first place.

Chapter 8: Reflections on Gadamer's Hermeneutics and Vico's Thought

In his 1960 *magnum opus*, the book entitled *Truth and Method*, Hans-Georg Gadamer claims to be embracing the intellectual heritage of Giambattista Vico, especially with regard to the notion of common sense or, in the Latin original, *sensus communis*.[292] On this subject, the text by Vico to which Gadamer pays the highest tributes is *De nostri temporis studi ratione* (1709), i.e. neither *De antiquissima italorum sapientia ex linguae latinae originibus eruenda* (1710) nor his *Principi di scienza nuova* (commonly known as *Scienza nuova*, 3rd definitive ed., 1744, 1st ed. 1725), which are Vico's most famous works. Indeed, Gadamer dislikes these two later works of Vico's, because they entail a faith in the human ability to achieve a flawless, clear, method-centred understanding of historical reality, reflecting an overall positive trust in human rationality that, in Gadamer's opinion, does not connote Vico's earlier work.[293]

Giambattista Vico

When scrutinising Vico's writings, Gadamer retrieves in them a notable philosophical stance that is:

1. Antagonistic to the cultural imperialism of the natural sciences, i.e. opposed to the idea that all valuable knowledge about humankind can be attained *via* a single rational method of inquiry, as ideally sought after in the natural sciences: "[T]he human sciences are a long way from regarding themselves as simply inferior to the natural sciences", writes Gadamer, for they are "the true heirs of humanism".[294]
2. Contingency-oriented or categorically historical, i.e. regarding the goal of a definitive, unchanging account of humankind based upon the natural sciences as impossible: "[I]t is senseless to speak of a perfect knowledge of history".[295]

3. Scholarship-oriented and ecumenical, i.e. regarding the goal of a definitive, unchanging account of humankind based upon the natural sciences as undesirable, so as to avoid "the conquest of mythos by logos".[296]
4. Dialogical and open-ended, i.e. appealing not exclusively to the ideal of pure reason or *sophia* (i.e. knowing that, propositional knowledge), but also to the ever-growing practical reason or *phronesis* (i.e. knowing how, practical knowledge): under this perspective, Gadamer acknowledges "the hermeneutic relevance of Aristotle", who developed an alternative model of rationality capable of "placing limits on the intellectualism of Socrates and Plato".[297]

In the oration *De nostri temporis*, which was delivered as professor of rhetoric at the University of Naples, Vico is said to be articulating one of the earliest scholarly reactions to the cultural imperialism of the then-growing scientific paradigm, which was going to blossom in full-fledged positivism in the 19th and 20th centuries. According to Gadamer, *De nostri temporis* was meant to cool down the enthusiastic, unconditional support that Descartes' rationalism and Galileo's physics had been receiving at the time. As later history showed, Vico's attempt was not paid much heed to by his colleagues, until the overall faith in science's manifest destiny was shaken by the technologically advanced global onslaughts of the modern era, long after his death.

Gadamer argues convincingly that *De nostri temporis* was intended to remind 18th-century intellectuals that not all fields of research are alike, and that, possibly, all disciplines perform a valid role in exploring the manifold reality of our world, including older humanistic disciplines. According to Vico, Gadamer insists, worldly and, even more so, otherworldly entities cannot be investigated all in the same way, as the Cartesians and the sycophants of the mechanical science of his day wrongly aspired to.[298]

If anything, Vico thought that any younger, growing discipline could gain only strength by reflecting upon the knowledge possessed by the older disciplines, which carry within themselves centuries of intellectual inquiry and research—Vico's own philosophy and rhetoric being among them: "Let us now scrutinize these advantages of our study methods, and try to ascertain whether these methods lack some of the good qualities possessed by those of the antiquity: or whether, instead, they are impaired by faults from which ancient methods were exempt."[299]

In *De antiquissima*, which is another oration delivered by Vico as professor of rhetoric in Naples, the same thinker famously states that "*verum* and *factum* are interchangeable"; "*verum*" meaning for Vico "entirely intelligible" and not just "true".[300] The human being is thought capable of knowing in an entirely intelligible manner only what she herself makes, e.g. legal institutions, national myths, works of literature, and, more broadly, history or, as Wilhelm Dilthey (1833–1911) would later rephrase it, all things belonging to the realm of the Spirit (*Geist*). People have created and create these kinds of phenomena, according to Vico, and we alone *qua* people can determine why.

This is not the case with the objects studied by the natural sciences, since God alone knows for what purpose they were created. The realm of human activity, on the opposite, can be known down to its deepest origins. This half of the phenomenal universe, which indeed was neglected by Cartesians such as Nicolas Malebranche (1638–1715) and Antoine Arnauld (1612–1694), can be examined right down to the level of the *principia*, i.e. the reasons, causes and motives that generated them; the other half cannot.[301]

Through his sharp distinction of entities and related fields of investigation, Vico wanted to warn the intellectual community of his time about the dangers of rampant scientism, and particularly about the intellectual ideal that a comprehensive, coherent, and exhaustive picture of the world could be obtained by following the methodological lines of natural science alone. Vico, who had been educated in the humanistic spirit of the classics, deemed this intellectual ideal to be simply wrong and, from a cultural point of view, nightmarish. The reduction of all knowledge to the natural sciences would have meant the dissolution of the immense heritage of the *artes liberales* and of rhetoric *in primis*; a heritage that many intellectuals of modern Europe were patently mocking as obsolete, stuffy and useless, showing as much arrogance as they showed enthusiasm for Galileo's new science.[302]

The old wisdom contained in the organisation of human knowledge into *trivium* and *quadrivium* was clearly lost on these worshippers of new approaches to knowledge, as it still is on their contemporary heirs, who regularly fail to see how that ancient distinction suggests that any advanced scientific study—the *quadrivium*'s arithmetic, music, geometry and astronomy—presupposes prior competence in thinking and talking—the *trivium*'s grammar, dialectic and rhetoric. Steeped in classical wisdom, Vico was quite simply immune from this kind of error.[303]

Vico's ambitious *Scienza nuova* combined *filosofia* [philosophy], i.e. the formulation of adequate theoretical categories of explanation and related hypotheses, with *filologia* [philology], i.e. the acquisition of empirical data confirming or falsifying such hypotheses, or calling for a reformulation of the explanatory categories. Nowadays we would probably refer to this *scienza nuova* with the name of "abduction" and regard it as an obvious way of doing serious scientific research. Vico saw the need for this method three centuries ago, though, when the empiricist's induction and the rationalist's deduction were the only options on the field.

Moreover, connected with his new and more open methodological approach, came also Vico's re-evaluation of imagination and sensation as valuable cognitive faculties, as well as his re-evaluation of imagination's and sensation's by-products as cognitively relevant. Mythology, poetry and the fine arts, if understood in their own terms, were seen by Vico as capable of conveying as much information about the world as did physics, geometry or astronomy, which rely instead on reason alone.

Critical Literature

The separation between the natural and the human sciences, the re-evaluation of the humanistic tradition, and the stress on the cognitive relevance of imagination and sensation make of Vico a suitable candidate for Gadamer's development of a historical, humanistic and dialectical model of reason to be applied to the interpretation of reality. Yet, the enthusiasm with which Gadamer incorporates Vico into his hermeneutical project leads him also to overlook a few substantive differences between him and Vico. This is, at least, the conclusion reached by two eminent Vico scholars, namely Christoph Jermann[304] and J.D. Schaeffer,[305] who represent the leading voices in the skeletal contingent of commentators investigating Gadamer's reading of Vico, and whose interests and critical concerns I obviously share.[306]

Jermann's main accusation concerns Gadamer's use of Vico's philosophy to stress the point that scholars should just abandon the hope of a foundational justification of the social sciences. However, if we were truer to Vico's own understanding, the mere given of human historical determination of knowledge does not logically imply that reflective activity cannot transcend it altogether. Thus, Jermann claims that Gadamer is following a Kantian line of thought, which assumes *a priori* that we deal with phenomena alone and that we can never be sure that these phenomena do correspond, even just partially or sufficiently, to noumena or things-in-themselves. In this manner, as Jermann continues, Gadamer manifests a dogmatic attitude, a sort of peculiar sceptical dogmatism, whereas his own hermeneutics should always keep the door open to different possibilities, i.e. a constructive scepticism.

On his part, Schaeffer argues that Gadamer's hermeneutics is unappealing because its willingness to embrace contingency and uncertainty makes it politically and socially impotent, whereas Vico's own new science is not. According to Schaeffer's account, Gadamer's philosophical hermeneutics cannot escape being trapped within a set of socio-historically shared prejudices that cannot be brought to the surface, thoroughly investigated, and, if necessary or desired, radically modified. Gadamer does not give us a way to fundamentally re-discuss what the ancients, or even the moderns, have left behind for us to live by and contend with. Our past is still here, it influences us, and we cannot do much about it, for we cannot transcend it. Its authority is absolute: once the 'fathers' have been given, as in a sort of primeval revelation, nothing else can be expected but re-working inside their primeval framework. Tradition, so it would seem, cannot be challenged, but only embraced.

Both Jermann and Schaeffer highlight how Gadamer adopts Vico's notion of an active, critical and judging *sensus communis*, and misrepresents it in terms of an inherited sensitivity, a passive set of emotional attitudes that the members of a community have as their default, and on the basis of which such members develop personal attitudes towards novel objects of experience, particularly in the case of moral and aesthetic experiences. Their conclusion is that Vico's *sensus communis* is turned by Gadamer into a Kantian equivalent of taste, or into a sort of Heideggerian *Vorurteil* [prejudice] conditioning the way in which we can plausibly experience reality. No genuine intellectual judgement is left on the scene.

In his *magnum opus*, Gadamer does affirms that the proper location of *sensus communis* is "the heart" not the mind.[307] *Im Herzen* [in the heart] does *sensus communis* constitute a background of instincts and hopes, which are eminently expressed through the authorities of the community, be they religious, political, literary or philosophical.[308]

Vico, though, says that *sensus communis* is "judgment... shared by an entire class, an entire people, an entire nation, or the entire human race."[309] This is different from Gadamer's rendering of it, namely "the concrete generality that represents the community of a group, a people, a nation, or the whole human race."[310] Vico sees the *sensus communis* as an actively judging faculty possessed by both the community and the individual, not as some culturally fabricated Kantian template of conditioned responses to *stimuli* that the subject inherits inside the ethnos to which she belongs. As Vico writes: "*Sensus communis* is the criterion taught to the nations by divine providence to define what is certain in the natural law of the *gentes*. And the nations reach this certainty by recognizing the underlying agreements which despite variations of detail obtain among them all in respect of this law."[311]

On this point, Schaeffer underlines how the Greek model of philosophy that Gadamer marries, or hopes to marry, is opposed to the practice-oriented and undogmatic Roman rhetorical model espoused by Vico. The former model is the archetypal example of a philosophy that can determine what is real and what is apparent, what is absolute and what is relative, what is unchangeable and what is mutable. Such a declaredly powerful philosophy does not sound much like the historicistic, humanistic and dialogical project espoused by Gadamer himself, who does not question the supremacy of the Greek tradition over the Western civilization, nor notices that *theoria* and not *phronesis* was, for the Greeks of the Golden Age, the highest moment of contemplative illumination.

Giambattista Vico, according to Schaeffer, was willing to challenge such authoritative assumptions, on the basis of the Roman rhetorical tradition, which trained people to argue from both sides of any argument and *ipso facto* educated them to a modicum of scepticism under all circumstances. In his *Scienza nuova*, Vico placed the Greeks at the end of a process of cultural and philosophical development that had begun in Egypt and continued in Mesopotamia, hence suggesting both a rationalistic and a decadent character to the Greek tradition, which necessitated the rediscovery, aid and completion that imagination and perception could provide.

Whether Schaeffer is entirely correct or not, it is certainly true that Vico, in the same paragraph just quoted, claimed *sensus communis* to constitute the deep layer of individual and collective drives and evaluations allowing "the community to form judgments about needs and utilities". In a holistic perspective, *sensus communis* was taken by Vico *qua* inherited and dynamic "moral sense of a community", as well as the "public ground of truth" for that community. The roles it plays are therefore complex and multifarious, covering both moral and epistemological domains, whereas Gadamer seems to reduce them to emotional inputs inside the ethical and aesthetic spheres.

Schaeffer's critique does not stop here, for he writes that Gadamer's whole project is "hardly defensible" because it combines contradictory elements within itself. Schaeffer argues that Gadamer, on the one hand, endorses a passive acceptance of authority and, on the other hand, wants to characterise his own philosophical work as a

Heideggerian, post-metaphysical affirmation of historical contingency in Western thought. Indeed, as already noticed in Jermann's article, Gadamer assumes that no absolute standard of rationality can be attained by the human being. Our judgments cannot but rely on a shifting, fluid structure of contingent beliefs and prejudices about the phenomena we observe and discuss. At the same time, Gadamer states that our beliefs and prejudices cannot be entirely identified and corrected either; some of them, probably the oldest and most deeply rooted in our culture, may then actually operate as a noumenical foundation of sort for our beliefs.

As a supplement to Jermann's and Schaeffer's studies, I would like to point out *why* the active, judging character of Vico's *sensus communis* gets lost in Gadamer's treatment of it. I do this by highlighting a second origin of Gadamer's notion of *sensus communis* that has so far escaped the notice of the critical commentators: German Pietism.

Pietism

Gadamer's *Truth and Method* gives ample room to the description of Lord Shaftsbury's (1671–1713) celebrated treatment of "common sense" as an unscientific source of wisdom, but even more room is given therein to little-known Friedrich Christoph Oetinger's (1702–1782) account of the same topic. These two thinkers are mentioned along with Vico as the co-originators of the concept of *sensus communis* in the *Kulturgeschichte* of modern Europe.

However, Oetinger is quoted in a far richer and more detailed way than Shaftsbury. The former's contribution to the understanding of this notion seems to play a special role in Gadamer's book, equal if not superior to Vico's own. Oetinger's name is unlikely to sound familiar to contemporary philosophers' ears, for his legacy has been generally limited to theology and theosophy.

Oetinger's name, if ever, is usually heard along those of Jakob Boehme (1575–1624) and Emanuel Swedenborg (1688–1772), who are probably the two best known voices of German Pietism, i.e. the modern-era Lutheran sect aiming at the restoration of an experiential, faith-centred and morally rigorous Protestant Christianity.

Originally, from the late 16th century through the end of the 17th, German Pietism had intended to represent a reaction to the defensive, heavily dogmatic spirit of Lutheran Confessionalism, which held to Martin Luther's (1483—1546) doctrinal tenets as rigidly as the Catholics did to the Pope's, and which regarded all other Protestant positions with suspicion, whether they be Calvinist, Anabaptist or Philippist. This rigid closure was seen by the Pietist movement as a betrayal of the universalistic intents of the Reformation itself, and as a contribution to the climate of intolerance that devastated Germany until 1648.[312] Attacking what they saw as the self-righteousness of the self-appointed sole and true interpreters of Luther's dictates, Pietist authors like Johann Arndt (1555–1621) and Philip Jacob Spener (1635–1705) thought that the stress should be posited on Luther's *sacerdotium universale*, and on the personal experience of faith that each believer can and must gain in order to be saved.

After the end of the Thirty Years War, religious matters were undergoing a more and more thorough process of secularisation. The marriage between the young Lutheran Church and State authority, aimed at eliminating most of the Roman influence, saw the Reformation mired in endless theological diatribes, split in proliferating factions, bent under increasing political subjection and, above all, stained with the blood of almost two hundred years of savage butchery. Such a legacy could not but lead to less and less sincere interest for religion, whether traditional or reformed, which often turned religious practice into social formalism, especially in the educated class. In this climate of increasing secularisation, rationalism found ways to grow stronger and stronger, also among theologians.

Common Sense

Oetinger shared with the rationalist tendencies of his day a somewhat similar rejection of theological Byzantinism. Yet, he opposed the general intellectualistic turn of his age. Reason was not the answer, according to him; if anything, reason was the cause of the problem. Pietism had individuated a different path to follow, i.e. faith.

Faith and its ultimate truths, according to Pietism, had to be rediscovered as the source of salvific knowledge, which was revealed in the Bible, and which could be appreciated by pure souls alone, i.e. free from intellectualistic prejudice. In his works, Oetinger tried himself to revive the flame of enthusiastic mysticism, in opposition to what he saw as a cold-headed threat against religion.

Emblematically, Oetinger's declared enemy was, perhaps unsurprisingly, the philosopher and mathematician Leibniz, who wanted to reduce all knowledge and understanding to a simple matter of *calculus metaphysicus*. Taken as the most representative voice of rationalism, Leibniz was accused of writing against faith and the intimate experience of God. By exalting reason as the only true gift from God, and the instrument for our salvation, Leibniz rejected natural dispositions and instincts as confused representations, whereas Oetinger saw them as the necessary prerequisites for any deep, authentic religious experience.

Gadamer characterises Oetinger's position on the notion of *sensus communis* as that of a follower and developer of Shaftesbury's anti-enlightenment line. For Gadamer, Oetinger wants: "[T]o delimit the claims of science, i.e. of demonstration... for the preacher, who seeks to reach the hearts of his congregation"; with Oetinger, "we find [*sensus communis*] in an expressly hermeneutical application".[313]

Gadamer's reading of Oetinger's "hermeneutical application" of *sensus communis* is not meant to be in opposition to Vico's. Gadamer believes their conceptions to be analogous. As Gadamer claims, Vico "was not alone in his appeal to the sensus communis".[314] This is Gadamer's mistake, though: Vico's understanding of *sensus communis* did never oppose rationality and natural dispositions. Vico intended these two sides to work together.

On the contrary, in his *Inquisitio*, Oetinger writes about *sensus communis* as the source of all truths that the erudite have vainly tried to make explicit and to elucidate *in toto*. As Oetinger continues, for this is not possible, since the *sensus communis* underlies any activity of this kind and makes it feasible in the first place.[315] As a consequence of such a foundational role, *sensus communis* is bound to "remain hidden" to rational scrutiny.[316]

Oetinger suggests that this *sensus communis* actually pervades the whole of nature, thereby generating all forms of life. *Sensus communis*, at a deeper level, could be described as life itself, or a vivifying spirit:[317] "the breath of life insufflated into the organic body".[318] Human rationality, which is just one of the many expressions of life, cannot reflect upon its origin and embrace it completely, for its origin is going to be always behind its eyes and its being itself.[319]

> *Sensus communis is the living and penetrating perception of the objects that are evident to the whole of humankind, obtained through immediate contact with, and intuition of, these [objects]; such [objects] being the simplest, most useful, and most necessary [...] It is self-evident, without resolution of its origin into principles; we experience it through acquaintance and joy; and it can be expressed in distinct notes, relations, and proportions through external comparison with objects, but not through determinations of measure, number, and weight.*[320]

Reason cannot grasp, seize, and delineate *sensus communis*. Still, reason's realm is connected deeply with *sensus communis*, for only the latter can ground the former and turn it into a fruitful instrument of knowledge. "If we want to move from the unknown to the known", as Oetinger writes, "reason must never override *sensum*".[321]

Whether this *sensum* is interpreted as the *sensus communis* itself or one of our perceptive senses, it is not clear from the passage. However, the difference would be minimal, since all the senses are said to be grounded in the *sensus communis* and are an extension of its perceptual force. Physics, philosophy, music can be there thanks to the previous presence of such an experiential and ontological basis which, incidentally, resembles more and more God, His Providence, or the Holy Ghost.

It must not surprise us, then, if Oetinger regards Biblical hermeneutics as the best way to realise the truth of his statements. "Solomon's Wisdom" is the path to follow to acquire adequate knowledge and "only the right heart can comprehend it... In Solomon, heart and *sensus communis* are one. Saying it in French – *l'intérieur*".[322] In opposition to this Solomonic *forum internum* is the *extérieur*, i.e. the realm of reason, which Oetinger defines as "the complex of notions obtained through ordered alteration of the intuitive and symbolic experiences [of *sensus communis*]".[323]

The objects of reason are not the same as those of *sensus communis*, even if they are grounded in this *sensus*. The scientific achievements of chemistry, psychology, or metaphysics, namely "the objects of reason", are not so certain and definitive as the perception of *sensus communis*: human reason, after being "elevated through principles of analysis", allows only for the determination of "truths that come and go in vain succession and circularity, always the same from the most ancient times, now rejected, then restated... The objects of *sensus communis*", instead, "are truths of all times and places, useful to all men, easy to apprehend", such as "moral and pedagogical notions regarding friendship, conduct, justice and equity, the idea of God's justice, man's wisdom, opposition to evil, promotion of the good", namely objects that are ends at the very same time and for the realisation of which God Himself placed inside the human heart a "secret impulse" towards the "conservation of such things".[324]

Indications of the presence of such a "secret impulse" may be found in the fables of the ancients, "as well as in the mottoes and proverbs of all nations", whose teachings of wisdom, practical rules of conduct, laws and institutions embody traces of this "secret impulse", which is bound to contrast the "inclinations to evil" that are also present in the human bosom.[325]

Evil would seem to contradict the presence of the "secret impulse" just mentioned, but Oetinger believes they can be actually harmonised with each other. As Oetinger explains, the inclinations to evil can be subsumed under the very same logic that sees God granting us *sensus communis* in the first place, which carries:

"within itself the instinct for, and internal attraction to, the presence of God in bodies, as well as intimate signs for the perception of God in souls, in order to distinguish in the universe the things that have maximal proximity to men's happiness and life, and to discern among them the simplest, the most useful, and the most necessary."[326]

If God's gift is coupled with the consideration that reason alone cannot lead us to moral perfection, then we may perceive the Superior Will operating behind all this. It is in the midst of this conflict, in fact, that the mystery of salvation lies. It is in the depths of this gap, namely the gap between true *sensus communis* towards goodness and the evident human inclinations towards the opposite of goodness, that man can gain access to Heaven, or lose it. Since reason cannot detect and explain adequately the positive *datum* lying inside us, and since our imperfect nature may easily fall prey to sin, the human being must be able to rely on the mysterious, aboriginal, pre-rational impulse that she feels inside herself. She must learn not to rely on her mind alone. She must learn not to fall victim to the chaotic flux of perceptions that she vainly tries to unify under concepts. She must be able to perceive the principle of unity and harmony already present within herself. She must gain Solomon's wisdom and rely on her heart: she must have faith. This is the subtle, dramatic challenge, as Oetinger concludes, through which "God anticipates the judgment of men".[327]

Concluding Remarks

For the sake of my investigation, the most important element that can be found in these passages quoted from Oetinger's *Inquisitio* is the Pascalian shift from mind to heart. That which Gadamer needs is there: *sensus communis qua* passive set of emotional dispositions excluding judgment and, more broadly, reason. Gadamer's reading of Oetinger is correct. Oetinger does advocate a shift from the *esprit de géométrie* to the *esprit de finesse*, the latter informing Oetinger's notion of *sensus communis*, as it is distinguished and separated from our *esprit de géométrie*.

This sharp distinction and separation is the core of the difference from Vico's actual stance on the matter, though. Vico would never substitute the former for the latter, even if Gadamer combines the two authors together, indifferent to the fact that Vico's holistic attitude may contradict Oetinger's appeal to the mystery of God's judgment, which involves an ultimate *aut-aut* between mind and heart. For Oetinger, that which informs and supports our judgment is irremediably hidden behind judgment itself. No ultimate revelation of the fundamental structures of our understanding is possible. We can define reason and its features, but *sensus communis* remains ungraspable: "We were able to define reason; we were not able to define *sensus communis* adequately. It is in fact a complex of instincts. And instincts cannot be discerned completely, nor can they be determinate".[328]

Gadamer celebrates Oetinger as a brilliant philosophical mind precisely for this reason and is thus depicted as playing "also a highly original philosophical role" that was meant "to have a large influence in the epoch of German Idealism", Oetinger's *sensus communis* anticipating features of the Hegelian notion of Spirit.[329]

In order to understand why Gadamer misinterpreted Vico's thought in the way denounced by Jermann and Schaeffer, it is reasonable to assume that Gadamer, if not even German culture as a whole, is indebted more to Oetinger and Pietism than it is to Vico.[330] After all, Vico's thought had some impact on Italian culture in the 18th century and, to a lesser extent, Spanish culture, but it did not spread widely across the rest of Europe until the 20th Century, when he was eventually saluted as 'the Italian Hegel'.[331]

It may be worth highlighting how the overall sensibilities of Oetinger and Gadamer seem to be alike. Gadamer too has limited faith in our rational abilities. As Jermann's study also highlights, Gadamer intends to dismiss any attempt to found rationally the social sciences once and for all, in a way akin to the natural sciences. Even Oetinger's fideism resonates in Gadamer, and not solely in connection with received cultural tradition: "Our technological progress has become our destiny, in good and evil. Which political system to arrange to control technology? Democracy? I don't know...

It is a worrying situation in which we are living. We can still hope that some power will eventually rescue us. Maybe this power is God."[332]

I do not take this short passage as the ultimate and sole expression of the ground beneath Gadamer's philosophical enterprise. However, I do consider it representative of a religious nuance colouring the background of his enterprise, as reflected in Gadamer's interests in theology and Biblical studies.[333] Such a religious element may help explain the conservative character of Gadamer's philosophical hermeneutics, which cherishes and celebrates the past while chaining ourselves to it and our chances for change to a significant extent, as observed and frequently complained about by many commentators.[334]

Chapter 9: Reflections on Pareto's Rhetoric

Given the absence of literature on Pareto's treatment of rhetoric, at least as far as the Anglophone world is concerned, it is my aim to offer one.[335] By recovering Pareto's treatment of rhetoric in the *mare magnum* of words and thoughts contained in his humongous *Trattato di sociologia generale* (1916; translated into English as *The Mind and Society*), I therefore contribute something novel and, I hope, interesting, to contemporary Pareto studies. Moreover, my endeavour should appeal to scholars in rhetoric and communication studies at large, for it contains a Paretian elucidation of rhetoric and of the psycho-social forces allowing for persuasive communication.[336]

First, I provide a brief account of rhetoric's two paradigmatic Western interpretations and assessments, i.e. Plato's and Aristotle's. Then, I outline Pareto's interpretation and assessment of rhetoric. Specifically, after presenting his dismissal of rhetoric as commonly practiced in speech and writing, I dwell on Pareto's more complex discussion of rhetorical reasoning *qua* derivation and non-logical action.

Although Pareto's understanding of rhetoric is *prima facie* analogous to Plato's and remains as suspicious concerning rhetoric's aims, I argue that it contains some Aristotelian elements, of which Pareto himself might have been unaware. I intend to 'extract' Pareto's treatment of rhetoric from his most famous work. From a rhetorical point of view, my unveiling an unexpected Aristotelian flavour should let this chapter be more enjoyable, hence more likely to persuade. Lastly, I comment on the persistence of rhetorical elements within Pareto's own work and the persisting relevance of rhetoric for an adequate understanding of communication.

Two Contrasting Views of Rhetoric

Rhetoric suffers from bad reputation; the origin of the word itself may explain why. Although *rhēsis* ["saying" or "speech"] can be retrieved in the writings of Homer (9th century BC?) and Herodotus (5th century BC), and *rhētōr* [orator] in Euripides' (ca. 480–406 BC), *rhētorikē* ["rhetoric" proper] as such appears for the first time in Plato's *Gorgias*. In this dialogue, "rhetoric" designates the sophistic *technē* ["art" or "technique"] for seducing gullible audiences and winning arguments at all costs, i.e. without any consideration for what is actually true and good. According to Plato, rhetoric stands in stark opposition to philosophy, just like the much-admired Gorgias stood in stark opposition to the widely resented Socrates, whose quest for truth and goodness in the democratic city-state of Athens had ended in tragedy.

For Plato, rhetoric sides with murky common opinion and with fickle popular acclaim, whilst philosophy sides bravely with the unchanging light of pure knowledge and steadfast virtue, at which only the select few can gaze veritably.[337] Compared to philosophy, rhetoric's powers are shallow, misguided and overestimated. They resemble those of cuisine and fashion in comparison with those of medicine and gymnastics. The former disciplines may produce the semblance of wellbeing, sometimes more convincingly than the latter. Nevertheless, it is solely medicine and gymnastics that can truly confer wellbeing.[338]

As widespread and influential as Plato's negative assessment of rhetoric may have been up to our times, none less than Aristotle came to the rescue of this art, soon after Plato's judgment had been passed. Aristotle was far less dismissive of common opinion than Plato and he could not seriously entertain the notion that a discipline as successful and as widely cultivated as rhetoric was devoid of important elements of truthfulness and goodness. Thus, Aristotle's vast corpus of scholarly and scientific studies includes a lengthy treatise devoted to rhetoric, probably the first one in history, in which he presents not only a detailed account of the art of rhetoric itself, but also a fundamental pedagogical justification for it.

According to Aristotle, rhetoric is necessary first and foremost to teach the uneducated and persuade the uneducable: "[B]efore some audiences not even the possession of the exactest knowledge will make it easy for what we say to produce conviction".[339] Few are able to acquire the complex wisdom of the philosopher—Plato and Aristotle agree on the elitist character of higher knowledge—but even those who are able to do so must be first introduced to it gradually and by means of simpler, ordinary intellectual references. To this end, rhetoric is regularly employed, for it alone can address and guide the emotion so that it may cooperate, rather than interfere, with reason. Therefore, rhetoric cannot be dismissed as inherently bad.

A First View of Rhetoric by Pareto

Pareto's declared aims are descriptive, not normative: he is "looking strictly for what *is*" and not for "what *must* or *ought to* be".[340] Nominally at least, Pareto differs from both Plato and Aristotle, whose aim was to improve the human condition, not just to describe it. In actual fact, Pareto even claims that Aristotle's big mistake was to abandon sheer empirical research, which he had pioneered laudably, in preference to "the mania for achieving some practical result".[341]

This difference in aims notwithstanding, Pareto would seem to favour straightforwardly Plato's view of rhetoric rather than Aristotle's. Although he is hardly ever sympathetic to the founder of philosophy, which Pareto regards in essence as confused and unscientific gobbledygook, he nevertheless agrees with Plato in rejecting rhetoric as an alleged source of knowledge.[342] Pareto straightforwardly and repeatedly equates rhetoric to demagogic sophistry, hollow formalism, bombastic wordiness and preposterous verbiage:

- "But rhetoricians, sophists, and casuists have their uses, because they bake a bread that is suited to the teeth of the mass of people in a population."[343]

- "The gods of Homer, with whom Plato picks his quarrel, were alive in the minds of millions upon millions of human beings. The god of Plato was never alive, and he has remained a rhetorical exercise on the part of a few dreamers."[344]
- "Of the aggressive anti-German platforms of candidates running for the French National Assembly, Bismarck said: 'Too much rhetoric! . . . They remind me of Jules Favre. On two or three occasions he tried that grand language on me. But it did not last long. I always brought him down to earth with a jesting remark'."[345]
- "The description that Sallust gives of it in his *Bellum Catilinae*, is so ridiculously rhetorical as hardly to pass as a cheap melodrama."[346]

Revealingly, Augustine's (354–430 AD) apostolate and its rhetorical "antitheses... double meanings... and other cavillings", which generations of literary experts have admired, are dubbed "wretched and inept".[347] Pareto's stance could not be any more adamant.

If truth be told, the very focus upon persuasion that characterises rhetoric causes Pareto to doubt its value, inasmuch as amongst the "excellent methods of persuasion" that he lists in his work are included sarcastically to "roast" opponents "at the stake" and "vilify" them, as done by Calvin (1509–1564) with "poor Servetus" (1509–1553)—the "logico-experimental value" of such methods being "exactly zero".[348]

Pareto's negative evaluation of rhetoric reverberates in his 1897 article on "The New Theories of Economics". In it, Pareto states that rhetoric pertains to the domain of art, not to the domain of science. And for Pareto, art's defining aim is persuasion, not seeking the truth, which instead science alone pursues *via* its logico-experimental method:

As a matter of fact, art has always preceded science. When in the course of the evolution of human knowledge art and science have drifted apart, critics have never been wanting who were ready to assert that science was productive of no useful results. Criticisms of this kind are largely founded on the fact that a science has not nearly so immediate a utility as the cognate art. It is also to be said that art cannot confine itself to its teaching function; it must also demonstrate its persuasive power. Consequently art is obliged to make use of certain rhetorical devices with which science has nothing to do... Science considers means of expression solely from the point of view of their power to disclose the truth, whereas art must primarily consider their efficiency as means of persuasion. From this it follows that economic science will not hesitate to use mathematics, philology, physiology, etc.; whereas art can draw upon these sciences to but a very limited extent for fear of not being understood by the majority of those it undertakes to persuade.[349]

By "logico-experimental" Pareto means, in essence, internal consistency plus experience- and observation-based hypotheses that are tested empirically. Pareto is a radical empiricist, to the point of stating: "From our point of view not even logic supplies necessary inferences, except when such inferences are mere tautologies. Logic derives its efficacy from experience and from nothing else."[350]

It is then somewhat ironic that such an emphasis on experience, which is logically always controvertible, turns scientific reasoning into reasoning upon the probable i.e. that which Aristotle described as rhetorical reasoning. In any case, for Pareto, reason stands clearly on one side, whereas on the other side stands unreason: "Passions, accords of sentiment, vagueness of terms, are of great efficacy in everything that is not logico-experimental."[351] *Mutatis mutandis* and despite the overall positivistic spirit of Pareto's thought, his distinction between art and science mirrors the stark opposition between rhetoric and philosophy that characterises Plato's *Gorgias*.

Only on infrequent, marginal occasions does *The Mind and Society* depict, or refer to, rhetoric more neutrally, i.e. as a body of technical notions and a source of linguistic insight:

> *Grammar answers the general questions. Morphology yields the elements of language—substantives, adjectives, verbs, and so on. Syntax shows how they are combined... Grammatical analysis yields the elements (substantives, verbs, and the like); logical analysis shows how they are combined and the significance they acquire through the combination... [R]hetoric deals with the passage more especially under its subjective aspect.*[352]

Similarly, as he cites Father Marie-Joseph Lagrange OP (1855–1930), Pareto employs the rhetorician's jargon: "Because people speak, abusively—the figure is called *catachresis* in rhetoric—of a 'religion of honour', that definition has to be accounted for in the definition of religion in general!"[353]

Further rhetorical figures or tropes are mentioned by Pareto, such as "proverbs",[354] "personifications"[355] and "[m]etaphors, allegories, analogies" *qua* "indefinite terms" that may be useful "as a way of getting from the known to the unknown", but not "as demonstration" based upon logical inference and repeated empirical observation.[356] Still, even in this connection, Pareto cannot refrain from passing negative comments about such tropes, which he describes as instruments "to swindle many ignorant people" since "one would have to be an idiot indeed not to find a way to infer anything one chose from such pronouncements."[357]

According to Pareto, rhetoric is not a crucial human activity, at least *vis-à-vis* the pressing demands of everyday life: "Rhetorical and philosophical divagations are largely a luxury, and practical life demands something else. People want to know how they should conduct themselves in order to achieve 'happiness' in the ordinary sense of the word as material well-being."[358]

A Brief Overview of Pareto's Key-terms

Additional, more articulate considerations pertaining to rhetoric are contained in the initial paragraphs of chapter IX of *The Mind and Society*. This chapter introduces Pareto's theory of derivations and supplies a transition from the second volume, which is entitled

"Analysis of Sentiment" and is devoted to the presentation of his theory of residues.

"Residue" and "derivation" are terms that Pareto coined afresh and as conspicuously artificial as possible. His intentions were praiseworthy, for he wished to prevent established habits of thought from reducing the theories presented in his treatise to some other, previous, possibly erroneous conception. Nonetheless, in so doing, Pareto opened the door to different readings of his new terminology and to a heap of thorny hermeneutical issues.[359]

Henceforth, before tackling Pareto's more articulate considerations on rhetoric in "Sentiment in Thinking", it may be advisable to explain briefly what is meant by "residues" and "derivations" in the present book chapter and how they relate to the fundamental Paretian issue of the non-logicality of a hefty proportion of human agency.

Residues

Residues are what we can conceive of human behaviour, as this is revealed in linguistic usages, when all contingent circumstances are taken away. Termed as Pareto does, they "correspond to certain instincts in human beings, and for that reason they are usually wanting in definiteness, in exact delimitation".[360] Therefore, "residues" convey unchanging, universal "instincts and sentiments"[361] that are likely to have fuelled human behaviour in all ages and civilisations, individually as well as collectively. "Great social currents" may "often produce general changes" in religions, philosophies, political theories, morals, yet "leaving residues unaffected".[362] Together with "appetites, tastes, inclinations, and ... interests" these unchanging instincts and sentiments form the basic set of psychic forces determining any "social equilibrium".[363]

Residues can underlie logical behaviour, i.e. behaviour of which a satisfactory assessment can be given by the objective logico-experimental method (e.g. subjective interests leading to objectively logical economic behaviour). However, Pareto focuses upon their role with respect to non-logical behaviour, i.e. behaviour which escapes or contradicts the objective logico-experimental method.

Distinctively, *The Mind and Society* reviews six main classes of residues: "instinct for combinations", "group-persistence", "need of expressing sentiments by external acts", "residues connected with society", "integrity of the individual and his appurtenances" and "the sex residue".[364] In essence, before any verbal rationalisation of our actions occurs, the actions themselves were set in motion by urges to make, preserve, do, fit in, self-preserve, and/or be gratified in our lust, whether we were conscious of such urges or not.

For the sake of brevity and reader-friendliness, Pareto treats "residues" and "sentiments" as equivalent "convenient makeshifts", albeit as a competent, self-aware man of science, he emphasises the abstract, functional, symbolic character of the terms that he uses.[365] There is nothing deeper, eternal or dogmatic about them: they "are the products of logical activity on the part of scholars".[366]

Derivations

Derivations are the contingent, non-logical expression of residues in language: "Where there is no explaining, there is no derivation."[367] Together, residues and derivations explain why we are motivated to act, why and which reasons we provide most commonly for our actions, and how these reasons have typically very little to do with the actual motives of our actions. Most human beings, most of the time, act straightforwardly upon their residues or sentiments (and tastes, interests, etc.),[368] i.e. the underlying field of psychic forces to which we refer abstractly as "residues" or "sentiments".[369] The same human beings, though, like to think that they have good reasons for doing what they do. "The usual purpose of a derivation", Pareto writes, "is to satisfy with pseudo-logic the need of logic, of thinking, that the human being feels".[370] Therefore, human beings shall seek *post factum* linguistically expressible rationalisations of their behaviour.

Derivations vary in type, complexity (e.g. derivations may combine together in complex non-logical theories or "derivatives") and they vary with each individual's intellectual abilities, social setting and historical conditions.[371] Specifically, Pareto reviews four main classes of derivations: "assertion" (e.g. 'X is B'), "authority" (e.g. 'God says that X is B'), "accords with sentiments or principles" (e.g. 'honour demands that X is B') and "verbal proofs" (e.g. a syllogism concluding that 'X is B').[372] These are accompanied and made physically possible by non-linguistic corporeal activities or "manifestations".[373]

Non-logical conduct

As a trained economist, Pareto grew disillusioned with the inability of economics to predict human behaviour, which regularly falls short of the self-interested rationality conventionally assumed by the heirs of Adam Smith (1723–1790).[374] Pareto's *Mind and Society* aimed precisely at casting light upon the vast universe of "non-logical" behaviour.[375] According to Pareto, there exist several forms of human agency that either contradict or elude the logico-experimental method and that can be properly understood if and only if close attention is paid to the species-defining emotional magma seething under the familiar veneer of linguistic rationalisations.

Pareto reviews the following main types of non-logical behaviour: purely habitual or instinctive behaviour (e.g. faithful adherence to Hesiod's obscure precept "not to befoul rivers at their mouth");[376] conduct that is meaningful subjectively but not objectively (e.g. "sacrifices to Poseidon" to secure "a favourable voyage");[377] activities that are objectively consistent and purposeful, yet performed subjectively without any awareness of the actual reasons (e.g. faithful adherence to Hesiod's contagion-reducing precept "not to befoul drinking water");[378] activities that are objectively consistent and purposeful, yet performed subjectively on account of different reasons, whether the results are subjectively acceptable (e.g. the ancient gods-fearing augur forestalling "some decision ... harmful to the Roman People" because of negative omens)[379] or unacceptable (e.g. the decline in prices and, eventually, profits, caused by profit-maximising "wage-cutting" operated by capitalists "working under conditions of free competition").[380]

Pareto believes the first and third type of actions to be fairly widespread amongst "savages and primitive peoples", whilst more advanced peoples are bound to transform these actions into tokens of the second and fourth type, as "travellers are bent on learning at all costs the reasons for the conduct they observe."[381]

A Second View of Rhetoric by Pareto

It may sound bewildering that the alleged reasons for human action may have so thin a connection with the actual motives of the same. Indeed, Pareto wonders himself: "how can the many men of genius who have dealt practically and theoretically with human societies have failed to notice the fact?"[382]

Less bewildering is the answer that he gives to his own question: "the role played by sentiment has in fact been often perceived; but indistinctly, so that it has never been given a complete theory and its importance has never been accurately evaluated."[383] It is not that human beings have been completely blind to the power of emotion over their own minds and to the infelicity of the many apparent reasons that are routinely utilised in order to justify our actions. Rather, according to Pareto, none before him has ever undertaken as thorough, comprehensive and scientific a study of these phenomena as the one embodied by *The Mind and Society*.

Concerning an ancient attempt, Pareto recalls Aristotle's discussion of the rhetorical syllogism or "enthymeme" i.e. "a judgment that is combined with a statement of its reason" or, in the language of "modern logicians ... a syllogism in which one of the premises is not stated".[384] In other words, rhetorical syllogisms are abbreviated arguments.[385]

Both Aristotle and Pareto acknowledge that any items of communication that were so carefully crafted as to contain each and every logical step from the premises to the conclusion would be very hard to bear. If one wishes to be persuasive, as Pareto concedes, one must avoid being "cumbersome, tedious, unreadable".[386]

This being the point about which Pareto cares most, the rhetorical abbreviation of syllogisms allows the speaker to hide whichever premises may be logically fallacious or unconvincing. Since the syllogistic form is meant to make the elements of an argument most explicit, persuasiveness is bound to be lost whenever there are within it logically erroneous or dubious terms and/or premises. On the contrary, in an enthymeme, "things may be so arranged that the proposition not stated is the one where the logical weakness is most apparent".[387]

Emblematically, Pareto cites an Aristotelian enthymeme that reads as follows: "Nourish not, being mortal, immortal wrath."[388] Nothing could seem more obvious and persuasive. Nonetheless, were we to reconstruct it as a proper logical syllogism, then it would read: "Man is mortal. A mortal cannot nourish immortal wrath. Therefore a man cannot nourish immortal wrath."[389] Thus presented, though, the syllogism would fail to convey the actual meaning of the original statement. In it, according to Pareto, "immortal" is used equivocally to mean "for too long a time" as opposed to the actual opposite of mortal. Despite that, "immortal" is preferred to the correct expression "for too long a time" because of the contrast that it generates *vis-à-vis* "mortal".[390] If we wished to disambiguate the terms utilised, then the logically accurate rendition of the syllogism at issue would be: "Man is mortal. A mortal must not nourish wrath for too long a time. Therefore man must not nourish wrath for too long a time."[391]

However, this rendition would reveal the weak spot of the whole reasoning, i.e. the unsubstantiated premise that a mortal must not nourish wrath for too long a time. Instead, this premise is suppressed in the enthymeme. The enthymeme, rather than a succinct syllogism, becomes a sheer assertion, i.e. a derivation. According to Pareto, assertions possess the colourings of logical thinking, but in fact rely upon residues for their persuasiveness. Insofar as "the assertion ... subsist of itself by virtue of a certain inherent persuasiveness independent of experience ... it is a derivation."[392]

As for the residues at play in the enthymeme "vivisected" above, Pareto observes, in the first place, the intentionally misleading "linking of names and things",[393] which regularly "suggest certain experimental, or even imaginary, property of things".[394] In the second place, an even more profoundly ingrained residue is at work, namely an instinct of "sociality".[395] To be exact, this instinct is rooted in the "need of uniformity"[396] that most human beings commonly experience, as they desire to be "connected with society".[397] That is the ultimate source of persuasiveness of the Aristotelian enthymeme's injunction against those who do not forgive. This is an immensely powerful residue, given that "[t]he larger and more effective portion of the residues prevalent in society cannot be altogether unfavourable to its preservation; for if that were the case, the society would break down and cease to exist."[398]

The logically minded person might be tempted to believe that enthymemes are acceptable because they are part of a larger syllogism. Nonetheless, as the previous example aims at revealing, it is not the case. According to Pareto, although enthymemes may be reconstructed as syllogisms, their persuasiveness is not due to their truncated yet persisting participation in a broader logical deduction. Rather, their "persuasive force" is due to "the sentiments that they arouse".[399]

The Aristotelian enthymeme scrutinised by Pareto follows the general strategy that he outlines in an earlier section of his work, in which he states:

> [I]n a reasoning developing by accord of sentiments, the syllogism may be as sound as sound can be; because, in reality and taking due account all along of the indefiniteness of terms in ordinary language, if the sentiments aroused by [the thing lying within the experimental domain] A accord with the sentiments aroused by [another thing lying outside that domain] X, and the sentiments aroused by X with the sentiments aroused by [the thing lying within the experimental domain] B, it will follow that on the whole the sentiments aroused by A will accord with the sentiments aroused by B.[400]

Hidden within the semblance of a logical piece of reasoning, there reside deep-rooted sentiments determining human action. As they persuade pseudo-logically the audience to behave in accordance with sentiments elicited by the skilled rhetorician, enthymemes turn out to be splendid tokens of non-logical behaviour. Furthermore, whichever fallacy may have been exploited by the rhetorician, this does not have to be "a deceit, a trick, a logical action" calculated to deceive, but itself an action "without conscious design" that leads to conjoin "sentiments together over the path" desired by the rhetorician.[401]

What spurs the rhetorician to concoct cunning items of pseudo-logical reasoning is typically as deep-seated and invisible a sentimental drive as the one, or the several, deployed therein. "Oftentimes the person who would persuade others begins by persuading himself... Unbelieving apostles are rare and ineffective, but ubiquitous and ubiquitously effective is the apostle who believes."[402]

Even if Pareto's opinion of rhetoric remains negative—as with the swift 'Platonesque' dismissal highlighted as his "first view"—this ancient discipline becomes something more than sheer obfuscation in Pareto's "second view", given that rhetorical syllogisms seem capable of revealing outstanding examples of non-logical behaviour at two different levels of analysis. Aristotelian enthymemes may be something that Pareto does not like very much, but they can be useful to articulate and explain Pareto's own theory of residues and derivations.

The Unseen Aristotelian Character of Pareto's Second View of Rhetoric

Undetected fallacies, shameless sophisms, heaps of rhetorical tropes and figures inhabit the most esteemed treatises and scholarly endeavours. According to Pareto, they seem to determine the appeal and popularity of such endeavours, as "the persuasive force" of "literature, from simple fairy-stories all the way along to the most complicated theological, ethical, metaphysical, 'positivistic', and like disquisitions" resides "in the residues and interests that they call into play".[403]

The sociologist that Pareto wants to be and to beget should "not stop with the reflection that a certain argument is inconclusive, idiotic, absurd, but ask ... whether it may not be expressing sentiments beneficial to society, and expressing them in a manner calculated to persuade."[404] Whilst addressing the Aristotelian enthymeme discussed in the previous section, Pareto expresses his genuine conviction that the sociologist's *defining* task is to explain why such a flabbergasting amount of intellectual self-deception may be possible:

> *When the logician has discovered the error in a reasoning, when he can put his finger on the fallacy in it, his work is done. But that is where the work of the sociologist begins, for he must find out why the false argument is accepted, why the sophistry persuades. Tricks of sophistry that are mere finesses in logic are of little or no interest to him, for they elicit no very wide response among men. But the fallacious, or for that matter the sound, theories that enjoy wide acceptance are of the greatest concern to him. It is the province of logic to tell why a reasoning is false. It is the business of sociology to explain its wide acceptance.*[405]

Even if a full treatment of Aristotle's position would exceed the boundaries of the present chapter, a few summary reflections may suffice to highlight the points of contact between "the hermit of Céligny"—as Pareto was nicknamed during the later years of his life—and the Stagirite. I shall start with the passage just quoted, for it possesses an exquisitely Aristotelian colour, well beyond Pareto's own recognition.[406]

Understanding the sophist's success

Pareto argues that understanding the truth depends as well on being able to understand why that which is false can be mistaken so often and so widely for that which is true. Whether Pareto was aware of it or not, this was one of the aims of Aristotle, according to whom: "The true and the approximately true are apprehended by the same faculty".[407] Emblematically, Aristotle distinguished carefully between enthymemes that are actual abbreviated syllogisms and enthymemes that are so only on the face of it.[408] Similarly, he distinguished between rhetoric and sophistry on moral grounds.[409] He was so concerned with keeping these two dimensions distinct, that he devoted two distinct works to them, namely his *Rhetoric* (or *Ars Rhetorica*) and the *Sophistici Elenchi* comprised in his *Organon*.[410]

The rhetorician envisioned by Aristotle "must be able to employ persuasion, just as strict reasoning can be employed, on opposite sides of a question, not in order that we may in practice employ it in both ways ... but in order that we may see clearly what the facts are, and that, if another man argues unfairly, we on our part may be able to refute him".[411] It is only by grasping the ways in which the sophist succeeds that the rhetorician can defeat her. Certainly, Aristotle knew that rhetoric could easily degenerate into sophistry, but "if it be objected that one who uses such power of speech unjustly might do great harm", it is also true that "[a] man can confer the greatest of benefits by a right use of [it]".[412]

In order to use the power of speech justly, and to counter the sophist who may be using it unjustly, one must know how such a power operates: "[I]t is absurd to hold that a man ought to be ashamed of being unable to defend himself with his limbs, but not of being unable to defend himself with speech and reason, when the use of rational speech is more distinctive of a human being."[413] Aristotle's rhetorician is not a sophist and, as such, she should be able to unmask the latter's tricks and explain why they are successful, exactly like Pareto's sociologist.[414]

Using art when science fails

Aristotle's acceptance of rhetoric for pedagogical aims reverberates too in Pareto's acknowledgment of the elitist character of higher forms of knowledge: "As regards persuasion, [logico-experimental] proofs are convincing only to minds trained to logico-experimental thinking", i.e. a tiny fraction of the world's population.[415] "If a person would persuade another on matters pertaining to experimental science, he chiefly and, better yet, exclusively, states facts and logical implications of facts."[416] In contrast, if the same person wishes to persuade "another on matters pertaining to ... social science, [then] his chief appeal is to sentiments, with a supplement of facts and logical inference of facts."[417]

Even in his own beloved field of scientific research about social phenomena, Pareto obliquely concedes that any intelligent person, "if he were to disregard sentiments, he would persuade very few and in all probability fail to get a hearing at all".[418] As he writes: "In practical life" one must be able and willing to cope with "the approximate" and choose the imperfect language "that awakens favourable sentiments" rather than "unfavourable sentiments".[419] Therefore, the rhetorically challenged social scientist would be in the same unfortunate position as those "good souls" who "have imagined that they could destroy Christianity by proving the historical unreality of Jesus." Shut within the gates of the scholarly community, "they persuade people who are already persuaded".[420]

As elitist as Aristotle himself, for whom the heights of philosophical reason eluded most human beings and indeed the whole female half of humankind, Pareto argues that "nearly all human beings are in the habit of thinking synthetically, and find it hard to grasp, in fact are quite unable to grasp, a scientific analysis".[421] Logically, it follows that other ways have to be found in order to convey scientific and other sensible information to the less capable. Historically, such has been the province of arts such as rhetoric. Pareto, indirectly, agrees: "the function of art" is to deal with phenomena "synthetically and must not separate the elements", for this, "moreover, is an effective method of persuasion".[422] In short, there would appear to be ample room for rhetoric in the modern world, and legitimately so.

Understanding human sentiments

Anticipating Pareto's concern for residues, Aristotle's own understanding of rhetoric is accompanied by a lengthy analysis of the emotions that should complement any good rhetorical syllogism in order for it to be persuasive.[423] Far from being elusive on this point, Aristotle presents what Roland Barthes (1915–1980) calls "a classificatory psychology" that illustrates what human emotions are believed to be like and to what sort of characteristic stimuli they respond.[424]

Love, anger, fear and many other passions are scrutinised with care. Aristotle instructs the speaker on how such stimuli are activated, for it is also by affecting passions that her message can get across to her audience—and the sophist's too. To this, he adds a discussion of the emotions that the audience should project onto the speaker, or the character traits that the speaker should lead the audience to attribute to her.[425] These are the recommended "airs" of wisdom (or objectivity), virtue (or frankness) and amiability. A successful orator, or a person who attempts to address successfully a composite audience, must come across as someone who acknowledges different points of view, is committed to her own, and is somewhat approachable and pleasant.

To sum up, Aristotle offers not solely a sophisticated discussion of how to reason in order to be persuasive. He offers a sophisticated discussion of the emotional or, in a Paretian sense, of the eminently non-logical factors at play in persuasive communication. Bearing this in mind, then Aristotle's enthymemes may be something more than apparent abbreviated syllogisms, which actually rely upon residues alone for their persuasiveness. Aristotle's enthymemes, being directed to a composite audience, would seem to be so built as to appeal to the logically minded person, who reconstructs them as proper syllogisms, as well as to those persons who would not be able to grasp the logical proofs, in part or even *in toto*. Why use solely one shiny yet often blunt javelin—reason—when jagged stones—passions—and a multi-layered armour—character—can lead to victory?[426]

Using rhetoric for the good of society

Despite his professions of sheer empiricism and neutrality, value-laden elements persist in Pareto, including his approach to rhetoric. What is more, some of these elements are reminiscent of Aristotle's concern with the common good that the rhetorician's skilful civic discourse ought to promote.[427] Precisely, Pareto is not content with determining only whether a given set of propositions "is a sound reasoning or a sophistry".[428] Nor is he pleased with merely assessing "the relation of the derivation to experimental reality".[429] A "third problem" is left on the table: "the question of their social utility".[430]

Pareto is quite open to the notion that by reiterating "something that was already present in the mind of the searcher, and not infrequently in the opinions of the community to which he belongs", the successful rhetorician "may frequently lead to results that are socially beneficial".[431] After all, "[t]he masses at large pay little attention to the sources of their rules. They are satisfied so long as society has rules that are accepted and obeyed" and, in general, with whichever course of action that "saves the country and preserves its freedom".[432]

I am not claiming that Pareto argues his points primarily so as to produce social utilities, but that he does so while also having social utilities in mind. His main focus may be upon the objective study of the non-logical features of human behaviour but, as already quoted, Pareto claims Servetus to be "poor" when he was burnt alive and Augustine's preaching to be "wretched and inept", whilst he writes uneasily about the many "varieties of asceticism" *qua* "perversions of the instinct of sociality", since "without that instinct human society could not exist".[433] Detached, observation-aimed value-neutrality may be commended by Pareto, but it is not always his *forte*.

Additionally, it should be noted that Aristotle, early as well as late Scholasticism, plus following influential Italian political economists and jurists such as Antonio Genovesi (1713–1769) and Luigi Taparelli (1793–1862) had long argued that sound ethics (e.g. integrity, dutifulness, generosity), civic virtues (e.g. mutual trust, honourability, law-abidingness) and relational goods (e.g. love, friendship, fellowship) are of fundamental importance for any well-ordered polity and, *a fortiori*, any prosperous economic order.[434] Any society where people are not adequately socialised, mutually well-meaning and habitually cooperative cannot but be uncivil; and even if wealth gets created therein by many and accumulated by some, happiness remains private rather than public. Limited by the methodological adoption of the strictly individualistic and fiercely competitive philosophical anthropology characterising classical economics, Pareto cannot be as keenly aware and as openly commending of such aspects of human behaviour, several of which he dubs "non-logical". Yet Pareto's *Mind and Society* acknowledges that, somehow, these aspects do lead to social equilibrium, e.g. in § 1931. Moreover, when orthodox economic rationality leads instead to socially paradoxical and ethically despicable outcomes (e.g. killing unproductive, resource-consuming elderly or severely handicapped persons), Pareto is more than willing to bring back into play methodologically unwarranted and theoretically ungrounded "sacred moral duties" as a sort of *deus ex machina*, despite his own declared inability to provide a "rational ethics" based upon the anthropological assumptions of his economic and sociological theories.[435]

A Third View of Rhetoric, within Pareto

Pareto agrees with Auguste Comte (1798–1857)—a rare event indeed—upon the idea that the Stagirite too, like all ancient thinkers, sought the "convenience ... to be believed without being pestered for proofs".[436] However, Pareto's own monumental *Trattato* would not pass the scrutiny of a social scientist looking for properly conducted quantitative studies. Though humongous and filled with explanatory diagrams, *The Mind and Society* reads itself like a commented collection of noble opinions from the past, not unlike Aristotle's *Ars Rhetorica*.[437] This is a criticism vented repeatedly at Pareto by statistics- and protocol-loving sociologists.[438]

Whether such a criticism is fair or unfair, I shall not judge. Rather, it is my contention that rhetoric persists within *The Mind and Society* in many other ways. For the sake of order and illustration, I am to present these ways following Aristotle's designation of the three main parts of rhetorical activity. These parts are the well-known first three canons of classical rhetoric, each dealing respectively with: what one is to say in order to prove a given point (*inventio*), in what order (*dispositio*) and in what sort of style, i.e. that style which is appropriate to specific aims and circumstances (*elocutio*).[439]

Inventio

The "invention" of Aristotelian and, in general, of classical rhetoric does not refer to inventing something, e.g. constructing a new engine or developing a new computer programme. Rather, it refers to retrieving something in an inventory. This "something" is the set of proofs that one should produce in order to argue for or against a given point, namely the thesis—if it is a broad issue—or hypothesis—if it is a specific issue—of the person whose aim is to persuade, that is to say, the rhetorician. The "inventory" is the vast field of commonsensical and technical information available to the rhetorician. The rhetorician can make use of it as sheer factual data (i.e. so-called "external" or "non-technical" proofs equally available to her potential adversaries) or, more creatively, as examples, parables, fables or premises for rhetorical syllogisms supporting the thesis/hypothesis under consideration (i.e. "internal" or "technical" proofs that the rhetorician has to come up with).[440]

Typically, the clearer, more probable and intuitive are the chosen proofs, the more likely is the rhetorician to succeed. Operating within the frame of presuppositions and prejudices of one's audience is generally a recipe for success, from pub talks to peer-reviewing academe. In addition, the rhetorician must take into account what is to be said in order to be perceived as a person of good character, plus anything that may be of relevance as regards directing the emotional dispositions of the specific audience addressed.

Under this perspective, even the seemingly soulless, cold, artificial, formal and symbolic language of mathematics, which is perhaps the paramount example of objectivity in the realm of human knowledge, possesses rhetorical features. It is the likeliest case of emphasis upon character, inasmuch as such a language "hides" the individual mathematician completely, depriving her apparently of stylistic devices to a much higher extent than other technical fields allowing for the use of at least some ordinary language. Thus, Pareto's own diagram-expressed "coldness" is a rhetorical strategy.[441]

In primis, Pareto's claims of neutral aloofness are intended to manifest the logical character of the proofs that are provided by him *qua* logico-experimental discourse directed at a broadly and loosely positivistic audience of peers, whether contemporary sociologists would call his discourse "science" or not. Secondly, when Pareto states that he "is interested strictly in uniformities", draws unnecessary albeit helpful diagrams, and fills pages with remote events from classical antiquity so as "to choose from the multitude of facts such as, in my judgment, will exert least influence upon sentiments", he is attempting to attain an air of wisdom.[442] This is the case whether Pareto is actually delivering value-neutral scientific observations or not.

Analogously, when Pareto retreats from the much-highlighted value-neutrality of his work and expresses worries about society's enduring wellbeing,[443] he is accepting the risk of appearing inconsistent for the sake of sounding committed to a basic notion of social welfare that would be rejected by no reader of his, not even the quite rare Leopardi-like pessimist.[444] As for Pareto's amiability, *The Mind and Society* may not be very reader-friendly, due to its remarkable size and conceptual complexity. Pareto himself was also a surly man, at least according to the records. Still, his lengthy treatise is ripe with qualifications, exculpations and appraisals aimed at showing humour, moderation and self-irony, even in connection with thinkers and thoughts of which Pareto disapproved.[445]

What is more, along with the reason- and character-centred proofs, Pareto's work is not devoid of appeals to sentiment. As he discusses in paragraph 817, scientific discourse comprises assertions that the untrained mind does not grasp as links in a long chain of logical inferences springing from empirical data. Most people, in other words, are to focus chiefly upon the most striking assertions presented by the scientist, whose "persuasiveness" in modern society is due to the three causes: "A vague feeling that a person who expresses in such a form *must* be right"; "[a] feeling that such a select form is authoritative"; and "[t]he more or less vague notion that the authority is justified".[446]

Consistently, Pareto's own science of society is going to gain acceptance amongst sections of his audience *via* such a sentimental avenue, given that scientific authority is at the same time "a tool of proof and a tool of persuasion".[447] Pareto states as well that "an assertion is accepted and gains prestige through the sentiments of various kinds which it excites", and that it is bound to be "more effective in verse than in prose, in print rather than in manuscript, in a book rather than in a newspaper, in a newspaper rather than in the spoken word".[448] How much more powerful is the same assertion going to sound in an awe-inspiring, complicated, diagram-filled treatise of general sociology?

The noted economist Albert Otto Hirschman (1915–2012) believes that even stronger emotional components permeate Pareto's allegedly value-neutral study of social phenomena. As contended in his *Rhetoric of Reaction*, Pareto's work epitomises turn-of-the century reactionary thought appealing to rhetorical strategies centred upon feelings of perversity, futility and jeopardy. The targets of these feelings are, typically, the introduction of universal suffrage, redistributive State policies, and socialism. Hirschman's case is well-argued, rich in textual references and pregnant with insights *vis-à-vis* the non-logical and eminently persuasive components of Pareto's oeuvre.[449]

Pareto's repeated attacks against the sort of State intervention favoured by early-twentieth-century growing—albeit far-from-predominant—socialists as gluttonous "spoliation" by yet another "plutocracy" are said to rest upon a sense of futility, rather than upon any extensive and prolonged empirical study of fairly novel democratic regimes.[450] Pareto's theory of the "circulation of the elites" and his famous 80–20 principle or "Pareto's Law" express the inevitable persistence of inequality within human society.[451]

However, as the young parliamentary democracies of the 1920s are concerned, they do not substantiate it empirically. Rather, Pareto's "circulation" theory and his "Law" are either "self-fulfilling" hypotheses—for they exhorted the inter-war-period reader to react against democratic and socialist aims (e.g. fascist reaction by Mussolini (1883–1945) in Italy)—or "self-refuting" ones—for they could and, in fact, did lead other watchful readers to anticipate and fix various shortcomings and inconsistencies of the novel political system (e.g. the egalitarian accomplishments of Scandinavian social-democracy).[452] Either way, they are no longer components of a candid, detached analysis of socio-historical patterns, but an incitement to influence such patterns.

Although Hirschman does not dwell on it, a touch of perversity colours Pareto's rendering of the unexpected outcomes of socialist policies. Talking once more about unobservable future developments of a young and polymorphous political streak, Pareto claims that socialism would destroy the one truly productive class, upon which the nation's wealth depends, i.e. the capitalist class. Socialism would thus obtain the opposite result of what it intends to achieve: it would grant poverty for all instead of widespread wealth.[453]

Finally, I would add that many, if not most, amongst Pareto's readers belonged to the wealthy section of their native societies. Henceforth, Pareto's prospect of an electorally sanctioned socialist "spoliation" implied that they and their actual personal wealth would be placed in jeopardy. It is plausible to assume that Pareto made these readers feel threatened in their wallet and in urgent need of protection. His much-debated connection with the "red-flood-damming" Italian fascism of the inter-war period resides therein, more than in any old-age honour and *post mortem* glorification that Mussolini's regime may have showered onto Pareto.

Dispositio

The concluding paragraphs of Aristotle's *Ars Rhetorica* are devoted to the parts comprised in the well-ordered speech.[454] They are basically "two", i.e. "the presentation of a problem" and "its demonstration".[455] The former includes preamble and narration; the latter argumentation, interrogations and epilogue.

Aristotle's conception of *taxis* or *dispositio* has been discussed, verified, sub-divided and enriched by generations of successive rhetoricians. In essence, it has endured: any persuasive piece of communication, whether spoken or written, must be well-organised, and this principle applies also to contemporary social and natural sciences.[456]

As for the persistence of *dispositio* in Pareto, it is pretty obvious. There is no element that is delivered casually, as exemplified by: the work's division into volumes, chapters and paragraphs; the logical steps from methodological considerations and considerations of the object of inquiry (volume I) to the presentation of Pareto's theory of residues (volume II) and derivations (volume III); its application to the study of "the general form of society" and "social equilibrium" (volume IV); the epilogue-like index-summary of theorems (volume IV). Inside this larger organised framework—Pareto's "system" or general sociology—further internally organised pieces of persuasive communication are delivered: the study of each and every class of residues identified; their substantiation with examples; the discussion of further implications arising thereof; the careful cross-referencing seeking internal consistency and underscoring that of the overall framework.

Elocutio

The third canon of rhetoric deals with style. As Aristotle observes, it is not enough to have something to say and, for that matter, to know in which order to present it, for *how* this something is delivered is itself of crucial importance too.[457] A well-substantiated and orderly speech or essay may fail to persuade because the language it employs is either dull or inappropriate. Therefore, attention must be paid to its form. Quintilian (ca. 35–ca. 100 AD) expresses this notion as the distinction between *res*—the things to be said—and *verba*—the words chosen to say the things.[458]

A first implication of this simple but fundamental consideration is that one's speech or written work must be appropriate to the circumstances. Classically, three standard "genres" of discourse were acknowledged and discussed by rhetoricians: the judicial or forensic, dealing eminently with past events and the truth or falsity of accusations; the deliberative or political, dealing eminently with future events and the utility or liability of law proposals; the epideictic or laudatory, dealing eminently with present events and the praise or blame to be ascribed to a person, activity or institution. Historically, further genres came about, including the edifying sermon of the clergyman, the educating lecture of the teacher and, as argued by Alan G. Gross (b. 1936), the knowledge-building study of the scientist.

Gross suggests that science constitutes yet another finely developed rhetorical endeavour, which may resemble or combine the three classical genres summarised above.[459] Analogously to the forensic genre, the scientist's study can attempt to demonstrate a certain point by "reconstruct[ing] past science".[460] Also, it can attempt "to direct future research", like the political genre.[461] It can attempt as well to commend and recommend those "appropriate methods" that constitute genuine science, as opposed to detestable pseudo-science, thus exemplifying the laudatory genre.[462]

If Gross is correct, then the scientist's study is so much more than "uninterpreted brute facts" and Pareto demonstrates it, for he engages in all three attempts blatantly and repeatedly.[463] In his vast treatise, the hermit of Céligny not only cast a piercing glance at the knowledge of social affairs accumulated up to his own day, which includes the treatment of rhetoric recovered in the present book chapter. Moreover, he wishes to guide the intelligent researcher away from the mire of "humanitarian ... metaphysical ... Christian, Catholic, and similar sociologies" and towards "a sociology that is purely experimental".[464] His admiration for "chemistry, physics, and other such sciences" is never disguised, for "it is through them alone that we manage to gain some knowledge of the forces which are at work in society".[465]

Gross' remarks lead us to a second implication too. Choice and composition of words must be such as to gain and keep the attention of the audience, in order to maximise one's persuasiveness. This is the realm of rhetorical figures or tropes, which Pareto's *Mind and Society* addresses. Since his study of derivations constitutes an impressive classification of linguistic expressions, it should not come as a surprise that it may overlap with the classifications of linguistic expressions produced by rhetoricians in the past twenty-five centuries. As shown in the section of this chapter devoted to the first Paretian view of rhetoric, he acknowledges several tropes that are commonly delivered in human language so as to be persuasive. Furthermore, Pareto makes himself use of several others.[466]

Some tropes, like *dialogismus* (i.e. speaking as someone else, e.g. quoting Condorcet (1743–1794) and other Enlightenment thinkers)[467] and *procatalepsis* (i.e. refuting anticipated objections, e.g. "A reader might observe ...")[468] have been the standard fare of scientific literature to the present day, albeit many a scientist may not be aware of them as tokens of rhetoric. Others are fairly incendiary and far less common in scientific literature, such as *ecphonesis* or *exclamatio* (i.e. an emotional ejaculation, e.g. "Well said!")[469] and *ironia* (i.e. speaking so as to imply the contrary of what one says for the purpose of derision or jest, e.g. "I do not deny ... may be").[470]

Overall, there is no lack of tropes in the nearly 2,000 pages of Pareto's *magnum opus*, as one can spot *inter alia* instances of *aporia* or *addubitatio* (i.e. asking oneself what is the best or appropriate way to approach something, e.g. "Who can mark the boundaries ..."),[471] *articulus* (i.e. joining several phrases or words successively without any conjunctions, e.g. "Theories, their principles, their implications"),[472] *correctio* (i.e. amending of a term or phrase just employed or a further specifying of meaning, especially by indicating what something is *not*, e.g. "Our aim is to distinguish, not to compare, and much less ..."),[473] *dicaelogia* (i.e. admitting a charge, but excusing it by necessity, e.g. "the theories of pure or mathematical economics have to be supplemented ... So far no other method has been found")[474] and metaphors or *translatio* (i.e. referring to one thing as another, e.g. "general principles" as "lords").[475]

Concluding Remarks

In all probability, Pareto gives Aristotle less credit than he deserves. Though himself—and timidly—indebted to previous thinkers, Pareto underplays the Stagirite's contribution to the understanding of sentiment, especially in connection with rhetoric. Revealingly, in addition to the enthymeme discussed in the central part of this book chapter, Aristotle's *Ars Rhetorica* is cited in *The Mind and Society* as giving "good counsel" as concerns "[t]erms designating things and arousing incidental sentiments, or incidental sentiments determining choice of terms" (e.g. Orestes as "matricide" or "avenger of his father").[476] It is also swiftly mentioned in connection with an insightful account "of the traits of man according to age" as well as "the effects on character of noble birth, wealth, and power", namely of "the domain of non-logical conduct".[477]

However, no substantial recognition or rendition of this work is present in Pareto's *Treatise*; rather, the reader finds the eventual condemnation of the Aristotelian enthymeme selected as a token of derivation. Not satisfied with this, Pareto includes a value-laden, sarcastic dismissal of Aristotle's metaphysical "escape" from the "desperate cases" of the latter's own making.[478] After all, even if more empirically minded than Plato, Aristotle was still an unscientific metaphysician. Nonetheless, as I hope to have been able to show, there are more points of contact between Pareto and Aristotle than the former acknowledges.

It cannot be excluded that Pareto's own classical training might have led him to perceive rhetoric as hopelessly antiquated and not to consider that this discipline, by having dealt with linguistic communication "especially under its subjective aspect" for twenty-four centuries, had possibly achieved more than just engendering generations of sophists.[479] Pareto's own vibrant dislike for unscientific endeavours and moralistic or political projects that did not coincide with his own made it unlikely for Aristotle and rhetoric in general to be treated very gently.[480]

Nevertheless, the above-sketched list of tropes alone suggests that rhetoric can hardly be avoided, even with regard to scientific discourse.[481] Having mapped centuries of linguistic usages, rhetoric is very likely to encroach the road of anyone who utters a phrase aimed, if not to persuade, at least to catch the ear and/or mind of the audience. All forms of linguistic communication, inasmuch as this is subjectively apprehended, display an unavoidable rhetorical dimension, for they seek to establish a modicum of identification between the speaker and the audience, hence of trust and attention, without which persuasion would be impossible, including persuasion based upon rational argumentation.[482] Somehow, as shown, Pareto recognises this last point.[483]

At a deeper level, language is essentially metaphorical. Although this notion has become popular only in the postmodern era, especially thanks to the investigations of Belgian literary theorist Paul de Man (1919–1983), it had already been formulated by Nietzsche, whose thought Pareto acknowledges to some extent.[484] Pareto himself recognises repeatedly the essentially arbitrary and pragmatic function of language, including the carefully stipulated, artificial, ambiguities-devoid language of "logico-experimental science".[485]

Even so, Pareto was not in for a full-fledged study of rhetoric. Too many and too different were the aims of his masterpiece, not least to overcome the predictive limitations of economics by instituting a new science of social phenomena modelled along the lines of well-established natural sciences. Perhaps, had Pareto recognised more explicitly the wealth of knowledge contained in so old-fashioned a discipline as rhetoric, then the persuasive power of his own new scientific endeavour would have been lessened considerably, especially in the positivistic academic climate of his day.[486] His discourse, in other words, would have been inappropriate to the circumstances.[487]

Chapter 10: Reflections on Moral Philosophy in Pascal's *Thoughts*

Should I be asked to give an immediate answer to the question "what is morality?", I would say: "an instance of civil commons", that is, an instance of "social constructs which enable universal access to human life goods without which people's capacities are always reduced or destroyed."[488] In line with my axiological studies, I would place myself in the ideal position of an external observer and determine what role morality has been playing *vis-à-vis* the most regular aim displayed by human beings, both individually and collectively: to lead a tolerable life. Referring to the civil commons would give a description of morality that focuses upon its life-enhancing function. It would be a description of morality from the *outside*.

Another description is possible, however, that focuses upon the feelings of outrage, remorse, shame, distress, empathy, pleasure, pain, as well as the calls of duty and the spontaneous sense of what is right and what is wrong that populate at least *my* experience of morality—*inside*. All these emotions, their related beliefs, the reasoning processes that they set in motion, the subsequent acts of will and the corresponding physical actions that one imagines and hopes to materialise, and the effective words by which a person can elicit such emotions in another human soul constitute the domain of morality as *felt being* or *lived personal experience*.

It is primarily within this latter domain that Blaise Pascal[489] develops his reflections on morality, which, despite his enduring fame as a scientist and a thinker, have received very little attention by modern Anglophone ethicists, who have written instead endless volumes on the epistemology of his wager or *le pari*—itself a piece of apologetics and an early example of game theory.[490] They have typically labelled Pascal a "philosopher of religion" and pretty much left him there, as marginal as religion itself seems to be these days.[491]

Yet, Pascal did have a moral philosophy of his own and one that can help us answer the question "what is morality?" from the perspective of lived personal experience; if anything, Pascal's religious focus is as much a result of his moral philosophy as his moral philosophy is the result of his religious focus: "Man's true nature, his true good, true virtue, and true religion, are things that cannot be known separately".[492]

It may not be an easy moral philosophy to detect, for it is scattered across his unsystematic maxims, short reflections and aphorisms, themselves scattered across a number of differing manuscripts. Reconstructing and outlining it here is the chief aim of this chapter.

The Heart

According to Pascal, morality is behaviour consistent with the correct apprehension of moral value, i.e. goodness, through "the heart, which perceive[s] wisdom".[493] The *heart* [coeur] is the faculty that feels or senses good and bad or, in other words, it is the moral *sense*, perhaps an organ of perception, analogous to hearing[494] or seeing—hence Pascal's writing in the same passage about "the eyes of the heart".[495]

And if the eyes can see many things, so does the heart deliver much more than just the immediate apprehension of moral truths or values, whether "explicitable" (e.g. "homicide is wrong") or not, since *all* forms of knowledge rely upon first principles that cannot be rationally demonstrated, but only *intuited*:[496]

> *We know the truth not only through our reason but also through our heart. It is through the latter that we know first principles, and reason, which has no part in it, tries in vain to challenge them. The skeptics, who have only this for their object, labor uselessly. We know we are not dreaming, however powerless we are to prove it by reason. This inability demonstrates only the weakness of our reason, and not, as they claim, the uncertainty of all knowledge. For knowledge of first principles, such as*

space, time, motion, number is as firm as any we derive from reasoning. Reason must use this knowledge from the heart and instinct, and base all its arguments on it. The heart feels that there are three dimensions in space... Principles are felt, propositions are proved; all with certainty, though in different ways.[497]

Analogous remarks appear in his 1658 *Art of Persuasion*, where Pascal discusses the importance of rhetoric and distinguishes between knowledge that enters the heart through the spirit, and knowledge that enters the spirit through the heart.[498]

Perhaps the heart should be better described as a skill than a faculty, indeed one relying upon long-internalised skills, such as seeing or hearing; this is certainly a difficult issue to resolve, given the ambiguity of many passages in Pascal's work. Whichever description may be the likelier, the actual crux of Pascal's emphasis is the following: sane human beings grasp and believe in the existence of, say, space, time, extended bodies, moral wrongfulness, and upon them build their sciences, whether these eventually reflect adequately the original intuition or not.

"Ethics" itself, albeit "special", is, for Pascal, a "universal science".[499] What is important in it, is to rely upon correct intuited principles, which we may have experienced in childhood if we had good enough a natural disposition,[500] and before education, local customs[501] or excessive faith in discursive or demonstrative reason could lead us astray:[502] "Wisdom leads us back to childhood".[503] Some human beings, according to Pascal, are fortunate enough as to be able to attain religious faith through the same mode of apprehension:

As if reason alone were capable of teaching us! Would to God, on the contrary, that we never had need of it, and that we knew everything by instinct and intuition. But nature has refused us this good, giving us instead very little knowledge of this kind... That is why those to whom God has given religion by intuition of the heart are very fortunate and, in fact, properly convinced.[504]

The least fortunate, instead, who are devoid of a piously "incline[d] heart"[505] or have been hardened[506] or corrupted to the extreme point of cynical disinterest for the most important things, such as the fate of our immortal soul,[507] may have to think through Pascal's wager or "machine" and determine whether it is advantageous to lead a pious life rather than a selfish one.[508]

The Spirit for Fine Things

It is important to highlight that the heart's sentiments combine emotional, intellectual and volitional elements. We may separate them *in abstracto*, but they are joined in actual experience. These sentiments are "internal and *immediate* feeling[s]",[509] but they are also forms of comprehension, insofar as they engender certain beliefs and interpretations,[510] and they prompt us into action, including successive discursive or demonstrative rational processes.[511] They are part and parcel of that *ésprit de finesse* that allows the person to grasp truths about reality, which the *ésprit de géométrie* cannot attain by way of articulate reasoning.[512] As Pascal famously asserted: "*The heart has its reasons*, which reason does not know."[513]

Typically, philosophers have emphasised the negative part of this statement. However, the positive is at least as important. Pascal was an intuitionist and believed sentiments to be the springboard of morality; but he was no sentimentalist or, to use a 20th-century label, no emotivist. "Religion", as he writes, "is not contrary to reason".[514] Echoing old scholastic wisdom on this matter, i.e. the principle of *recta ratio*, Pascal states that "[t]he principle of morality" is "to think well".[515]

Pascal does not posit an impassable contradiction between blind subjective bodily passion on the one end, and cognising objective disembodied reason on the other. Rather, he tries to reveal how different types or levels of belief, certainty and knowledge, wisdom included, can be acquired through our different faculties, one of which, the heart, characterised sometimes as "instinct", can grasp fundamental truths that discursive or demonstrative reason cannot grasp.[516] Science itself would not be possible if we were not trustful enough in our intuitions, which give us certainty in our indemonstrable first principles and spur us to investigate that which we do not yet know.[517] Pascal condemns "Two excesses. Excluding reason, admitting only reason."[518]

The notion of a golden mean between too much and too little of something is a recurrent theme in Pascal's thoughts and it applies, *inter alia*, to the effect of age on judgment,[519] thinking,[520] the distance from an object of observation,[521] the speed of one's reading[522] and the constitution of virtue.[523] Whether it can be attained, however, is doubtful, given the dual nature itself of man,[524] who is a "thinking reed" cast between two opposed infinities (i.e. meaninglessness and all-embracing thought), experiencing opposed tendencies (e.g. fear and courage, pain and pleasure) and possessing two opposed natures (i.e. animal and angelic) revealing his being an admixture of contradictory elements (i.e. body and soul); Jesus Christ alone seems capable of embodying opposites successfully and in His success does He signal the path to salvation.[525]

True to his intellectual hero, Augustine of Hippo's motto *"credo ut intelligam"*,[526] Pascal sees the limits of human reasoning and believes our sentiments to be able to spur,[527] integrate[528] and, when necessary, substitute our discursive or demonstrative reason.[529] A famous mathematician and physicist, Pascal reminds himself nonetheless to "write against those who delve too deeply in the sciences. Descartes" *in primis*.[530] There are much more important subjects than the scientific ones, such as "the study of man",[531] to which ordinary science can contribute nothing, for it cannot address the ultimate questions of our existence.[532] The strictly rational conceptual tools of science are inadequate: "The heart has its order; the mind has its own, which consists of principle and demonstration. The heart has another. We do not prove that we should be loved by displaying in order the causes of love. That would be absurd."[533]

Gifted with good intuition, a humble child may attain moral truths that adults, even the keenest scientist or theologian, fail regularly to grasp, for they attempt to do without the heart—not to mention those who fall prey to their basest impulses instead.[534] As Pascal puts it: "The greatness of wisdom... is invisible to carnal or intelligent men. These are three different orders. Of kind."[535] The most intelligent philosopher's reason may demonstrate, while the libertine's embodied will may desire; but only the sage's pure heart loves, allowing for forms of understanding that escape reason. To expect that one faculty or one mode of reasoning suffices for all possible domains of experience and investigation is a foolish form of epistemic "tyranny".[536] For Pascal, there are "different kinds of right thinking: some in a certain order of things, and not in other orders, where they talk nonsense".[537]

There is no lack of vagueness and ambiguity in Pascal's writings. For one, "heart" itself is not used only as the term denoting our faculty of intuition, but also more loosely as referring to will or desire,[538] mere feeling,[539] and a person's soul or character (especially in connection with the Old Testament's use of it).[540] It does not help either that Pascal stresses so often the opposition between heart and reason, as though they were irreconcilable enemies at "war" with each other—and here we get truly to the negative part of the cited famous statement about heart's reasons.[541]

Pascal is not advocating irrationalism, rather a form of understanding that does not rely primarily upon abstract conceptual expression (e.g. Descartes' ethically "useless" rationalism),[542] logical reasoning (e.g. the "corrupt" Jesuits' casuistry attacked most forcefully in his 1656–7 *Provincial Letters*)[543] and algorithmic computation (e.g. his own calculations of utility for the libertine's sake).[544]

Uncertainties

As difficult to pinpoint as it may be—for Pascal never offers more than a sketchy phenomenology of the heart in action[545]—his account of moral experience entails an embodied rationality that is intuitive rather than discursive or syllogistic, concomitant and intertwined with emotions and wilfulness, and capable of grasping objective truths about the world that only the trained sceptical ignorance of philosophers can doubt of. As Pascal writes, "We know this in a thousand things"[546]

Whether in matters of mathematics, love, or religion, intuition anticipates, grounds and eludes whatever subsequent reasoning we may attempt to build upon it. As morals are concerned, Pascal believes logical reflection to be inadequate within the domain of the intuitive spirit for fine things, or "*ésprit de finesse*", as opposed to the logical spirit of geometry, the "*ésprit de géométrie*". Whilst the former is subtly acute, delicately nuanced, highly personal, and mixed in its being both cognitive and affective, the latter is forcefully trenchant, rigorously explicit, methodically interpersonal and allegedly purely rational.

These two forms of comprehension are not mutually exclusive in absolute terms. For example, a mathematician may sense analogies or truths and conjure thereof new hypotheses, which he can test according to standard geometric methodology. Moreover, explicit knowledge may be internalised to the point of becoming intuitive, as with the acquisition of a skill.[547]

Pascal knew that these two forms of comprehension could subsist separately as well, however. A mystic, for one, could cultivate the former to the point of becoming unfamiliar with the latter: "Those who are accustomed to judge by feeling do not understand matters involving reasoning. For they want first to penetrate at a glance, and are not used to looking for principles."[548] On their part, persons relying upon logical reasoning can become so removed from their own heart and the realm of intuition that they end up quite ignorant of them both and incapable of ascribing any order or intelligibility to them: "And others, on the contrary, who are accustomed to reason from principles and being unable to see at a glance".[549]

Immediate, intuitive apprehensions of good and bad are not the end of Pascal's moral philosophy. Rather, they are its beginning.

In primis, there is the issue that we might be mistaken in our apprehensions, which may then require correction, as when we hear "cabbage" instead of "baggage" inside a noisy place or claim to have seen a certain individual when in fact we had seen another. Still, this is not an issue that Pascal is interested in as such. His focus is moral and apologetic, not epistemological. As Richard Rorty would possibly put it, it is *relevance*, not *rigour*, that which guides Pascal's endeavour.[550] Pascal wants to help his fellows to become wiser and lead a better life, now and after our death, not to get entangled into technical debates.

Secondly, Pascal cautions us against over-rationalisation as a path leading away from our intuitions' potential clarity: "Reason acts slowly, and with so many perspectives, on so many principles, which must be always present, that it constantly falls asleep or wanders, when it fails to have its principles present. Feeling does not act in this way; it acts instantaneously, and is always ready to act. We must then put our faith in feeling, or it will always be vacillating".[551] Consistently, he warns his readers against people who no longer have any "common sense", such as "academics, students, and that is the nastiest type of man I know."[552]

Imagination

Pascal is much more intrigued by the fact that despite our possible immediate grasp of moral value, human behaviour is all but consistent with it. Even moral philosophers, who might be inclined to making morality an important feature in their lives, fall prey of professional pride, personal pettiness and subjective resentment. A devout Catholic, Pascal was well aware of the endless list of sins that human beings are capable of. How can we sense what is good and bad and, between the two, opt for the latter?

Pascal's penultimate answer to this crucial ethical question lies in his account of *imagination*, which reshapes and reinterprets the immediate givens of the heart. And this is *bad*. Far from extolling the virtues of this faculty, which Romantic and post-modern philosophers have done aplenty in later centuries, Pascal worries about the imagination's "dominant" role within the human psyche and its ability to distort in self-serving fashions the data of sentiment, which is particularly prone to being twisted in over-intellectualising minds: "I am not speaking of fools; I am speaking of the wisest, and they are those whom imagination is best entitled to persuade. Reason may well protest; it cannot determine the price of things."[553]

Reason does not fix values within and around us; imagination does. Appealing to our "proud" and selfish thirst for power, knowledge and pleasure, "imagination... has established a second nature in man" and "disposes of everything. It creates beauty, justice, and happiness, which are the whole of the world."[554] Instead of allowing the humble acknowledgment of our helplessness and imperfection, which is grounded in our feelings[555] and is rationally as undeniable as our mortality,[556] imagination leads each person to attribute an overwhelming amount of value upon herself and "makes [her]self the center of everything", when it is quite obvious that she is not.[557]

Far from the exaltation of *amour-propre* or "self-love" that will characterise much French and Scottish Enlightenment moral philosophy, Pascal writes:

> *The nature of self-love and of this human self is to love only self and consider only self. But what will it do? It cannot prevent the object it loves from being full of faults and wretchedness. It wants to be great and sees itself small; it wants to be happy, and sees itself wretched; it wants to be perfect and sees itself full of imperfections; it wants to be the object of men's love and esteem and sees that its defects deserve only their dislike and contempt... No doubt it is an evil to be full of faults; but it is a still greater evil to be full of them and to be unwilling to recognize them, since this adds the further evil of a deliberate illusion.*[558]

The power of imagination can be so deep-reaching that we may no longer be able to distinguish between sentiment and the fantasies that imagination—occasionally called "fancy"—delivers in order to please our self-love:

> *All our reasoning reduces to giving in to feeling. But fancy is similar and opposite to feeling, so that we cannot distinguish between these two opposites. One person says that my feeling is*

fancy, another that his fancy is feeling. We should have a rule. Reason is proposed, but it is pliable in every direction. And so there is no rule [...] It is a nothing that our imagination enlarges into a mountain: another turn of the imagination makes us discover this without difficulty [...] We need a fixed point in order to judge... The harbour decides for those who are on a ship. But where will we find a harbour in morals?[559]

In the midst of such uncertainty and confusion, which are epitomised by the madness of human love affairs, given that intuition itself can become as unreliable a source of belief as reason is, tradition can come of use and help us.[560] When something is not "demonstrable" and "doubting" leads nowhere, "submission" becomes reasonable.[561]

Submission

In Pascal's case, that means submission to religious tradition, and specifically to the Catholic one;[562] in this sense, then, "all morality is concupiscence and grace".[563] "Religion is such a great thing", as Pascal writes, also because it grants "[c]omprehension of the words 'good' and 'evil'."[564] Submission to religious tradition means, in essence, to follow "[t]wo laws" that "suffice to rule the whole Christian Republic better than all political laws" i.e. to love God and to love one's neighbour, as per Matthew 22:35;[565] "charity" or love "in morals" being able "to produce fruits against concupiscence"[566] and turn the energy of potentially sinful "passions" into "virtues".[567] In particular, Christ's two laws go to the very heart of human behaviour towards oneself and others, hence they can make the eradication of vice fairly effective, since "[t]here are vices that take hold of us through other ones, and that, when the trunk is removed, are carried away like branches".[568]

Nonetheless, even within religion does imagination make moral life difficult: "Men often take their imagination for their heart, and they believe they are converted as soon as they think of being converted.";[569] they can therefore remain "duplicitous in heart... neither fish nor fowl";[570] their "blinded" minds leading to quarrels, schisms and sectarianism that "destroy... morals";[571] their misplaced self-confidence making them "sinners, who believe themselves righteous",[572] "corrupt the laws" of "the Church",[573] and "do evil... completely and cheerfully... out of conscience".[574]

Consistent with his picture of the human being as an erring wanderer prone to error yet also capable of greatness, Pascal offers no easy path to wisdom, which may be perceived at times, even patently exemplified in saints and sages, but still eludes us in spite of our best efforts to grasp it and make it truly ours.

Self-deception

According to Pascal, imagination is the first step in a process of moral self-deception, which reasoning can take farther by adding the uncertainty of sceptical considerations to the distortions of the imagination and making religious self-correction ineffective. We may even be most thoughtful and honestly good-willed, but without divine grace there is little likelihood of success. The good may still escape us—even the brightest and most celebrated minds among us can fail. As Pascal remarks, there are "[t]wo hundred eighty kinds of supreme good in Montaigne".[575] To which he adds, humbly: "It is not in Montaigne, but in myself, that I find everything I see in him."[576]

Starting a theme that will play an important role in the moral philosophy of 20th-century French existentialists, Pascal deems self-deception the main springboard of immorality, not our inability to perceive what is right or wrong, or our incapacity to comprehend what is good and what is bad. Quite the opposite, according to Pascal, we would appear to have the faculties needed to perceive and understand all this; but we possess another, imagination, which, combined with our passions and with self-love in particular, distorts our perceptions and understanding to the utmost degree.[577]

The imagination's detrimental deceptions are, for Pascal, one of the consequences of the Biblical fall, i.e. the ultimate cause of immorality. According to him humankind, having tasted perfection before the fall, is now condemned to sense and seek truths that, however, escape us.[578] More than religion itself, then, we need God's help: His grace alone can save us, "enlighten" us, give us the wisdom that innocent children and some pious souls are capable of, and therefore help us make proper use of the faculties that we are endowed with, and upon which we rely in order to lead a good life, a religious life, and an eternal life in the sight of God.[579]

Concluding Remarks

Reading a classic is always a worthy endeavour, especially if it offers opportunities for genuine philosophical meditation. Additionally, there are some more specific reasons why I think that rediscovering Pascal may be advisable for today's Anglophone ethicists.

First of all, his moral conceptions and his celebrated literary style highlight the importance in human morality of sentiments. This is no minor issue, for the impact of sentiments upon people's actual behaviour tends to be much stronger than that of abstractions or complex reasoning. Abstraction and complex reasoning are relied upon in somewhat particular circumstances, such as bioethical committee's deliberations about technology-driven dilemmas and adjudications by courts of justice. Under normal circumstances, mothers, teachers, priests, novelists and TV stars affect people's sentiments to a much greater degree than any ethicist or judge, shaping *a fortiori* people's moral and immoral behaviours.

As Richard Rorty noted, Harriet Beecher Stowe's (1811–1896) *Uncle Tom's Cabin* did much more to let Americans see the true horror of slavery than all liberal philosophers since John Locke's (1632–1704) day.[580] Nevertheless, philosophers have been pursuing relentlessly the path of abstraction and complex reasoning, leaving that of sentiment to others. Now, if we wish to engage in meta-ethics alone, such a division of labour may be fine. But if we want to change the world a little, whether as educators or public intellectuals, then some familiarity with the realm of sentiments may be a boon, since we may aim at "impassioning" rhetorically rather than just "instructing" scientifically, as Pascal would word it.[581]

Secondly, moral intuitionism has been on the rise over recent decades because of its recurrent empirical substantiation in psychology.[582] Still, as far as I know, the only philosopher who has taken seriously Pascal's notion of a different, heartfelt understanding —embedded, embodied, united with sentiments—and built an ethics upon it is Max Scheler (1874–1928). Amongst contemporary Anglophone intuitionists, Pascal is as absent as is Scheler himself, who has long lost the enormous popularity that he enjoyed in the early 20th century. Nonetheless, Pascal's moral philosophy is based upon the notion of intuition and constitutes an attempt that treads upon the tight rope set between rationalism and sentimentalism—and a moral philosophy that can be mined for its wealth of psychological insights and for its enduring rhetorical refinement.

Thirdly, Pascal's approach is relevant because it makes the ground of moral value *independent* of the individual, who can only apprehend it for what it is, lest her imagination is so corrupt as to distort apprehension. In that case, Jesus Christ, that is, revealed religion, is the fixed point of equilibrium that Pascal opts for.[583] Since the global affirmation of industrial society, we live in the first age in human history in which our species has become a threat to its own survival, as another religious-minded ethicist, Hans Jonas (1903–1993), underscored repeatedly in the 20th century.[584] Pascal's moral philosophy is relevant in this respect because, like Jonas', it reminds us of the possibility that the ground of moral value may not be individualistic, relativistic, or even anthropocentric. The risk of species-wide annihilation may reveal something much more objective, such as planet-wide life-conditions and eco-system-wide life-needs, which we can only acknowledge and comply with, lest we prefer perishing to living, hence destroying the fundamental precondition for all preferences. As such a reminder, Pascal's moral philosophy can then serve as a token of civil commons.

Chapter 11: Reflections on Richard Rorty's Hortative "We"

With the publication of Richard Rorty's *Philosophy and the Mirror of Nature* in 1979, the ancient discipline of rhetoric started regaining ground inside Anglophone philosophy. Following a series of conferences held in the mid-1980s at Iowa and Temple Universities, the "Project on the Rhetoric of Inquiry" (POROI) was launched. Some of the works published therein were penned by Richard Rorty, whose influence was steadily growing. Indeed, Herbert W. Simons credits Rorty with coining the slogan the "rhetorical turn" at one of these meetings.[585] According to the same account, Rorty treated this "turn" as the third step in an intellectual process that:

1. had shifted philosophy's focus away from both raw data and pure ideas and towards language, i.e. the "linguistic turn";
2. thus making philosophers aware of the inevitable element of interpretation or hermeneutics involved in it, i.e. the "interpretative turn";
3. and eventually of the aim that most articulate discursive activities pursue, i.e. persuasion, hence the "rhetorical turn" (rhetoric being understood since Aristotle as the discipline studying all the available means of persuasion under given circumstances).

Simons' account is merely a token of the scholarly literature dealing with Rorty and his association with rhetoric. Among the more carefully conducted studies are those by Paul Trembath and by Áine Kelly, who have investigated Rorty's emphatic metaphors of "writing" and "narrative" as ways to persuade readers to think differently about philosophy.[586] Janet Horne has mused on Rorty's shift from foundationalist argumentation within a narrow set of discipline-defining "philosophical" issues to an anti-foundationalist "conversation" about new and broader ones, *qua* establishment of novel rhetorical "topics".⁵⁸⁷ Péter Csato has classified Rorty's "rhetorical strategies" of "conversation... irony... appropriation... and exclusion" and their relevance in promoting the neo-pragmatist agenda.⁵⁸⁸

This chapter adds one element to the existing literature; namely, it specifies the quintessentially rhetorical character of Rorty's recurrent use of the personal pronoun "we" and its relevance with regard to a more nuanced understanding of his political thought. Rorty is said to have turned to "political theory" in the 1980s and undergone a "political turn" in the 1990s. Rorty himself links his use of the personal pronoun "we" to his advocacy of ethnocentrism and cultural politics.⁵⁸⁹ At the same time, Rorty's political thought has been widely criticised, with some of the criticism being precisely directed at his use of "we". It is not least by way of responding to such criticism that Rorty has clarified his position on the question "who are we?"

I review here some of this criticism in order to highlight the cooperative dimension of his philosophy (the "we" that is constituted by "him and his critics" in their ongoing conversation). This is crucial for filtering out the evaluation of his later writing as successful. I discuss Rorty and his political philosophy at its best, before considering the problems that remain unsolved and suggesting how Rorty's pragmatist politics can be further developed.

Rorty's (In)famous "We"

Rorty is likely to have started using "we so-and-so" in his *Philosophy as a Mirror of Nature*. From the early 1980s onwards, this became a characteristic feature of his writing style as he began attaching various group labels to the chosen plural pronoun. The (non-comprehensive) groups' list is nothing short of impressive: we moderns; we latecomers; we in the twentieth century; we Westerners; we of the West; we Western philosophers; we contemporary inheritors of the Cartesian distinction between mind and matter; we heirs of the Enlightenment; we Europeans, we Americans; we Anglo-Americans, we Anglo-Saxons; we rich, fat, tired North-Americans; we liberals in the United States; we Western liberals; we liberals; we twentieth century liberals; we bourgeois liberals; we postmodern bourgeois liberals; we tragic liberals; we liberal reformists; we liberal intellectuals; we decent, liberal, humanitarian types; we Alexandrians; we downbeat, Alexandrian, social democratic liberals; us twentieth century Western social democrats; we powerful, discursive types; we partisans of solidarity; we atheists; we ironists; we fuzzies; we new fuzzies, we pragmatists; we new pragmatists; we anti-essentialists; we anti-foundationalists; we nominalists; we Wittgensteinian nominalists; us Wittgensteinians; we pragmatic Wittgensteinian therapists; we therapeutic philosophers; we Deweyans; we enlightened post-Kuhnians; us shepherds of Being; we analytic philosophers; we philosophers; us insiders; we in the humanities; we philosophy professors; we humans.

This use of "we" did not escape the attention of readers. Rebecca Comay accused it of being so vague and parochial as to underplay the enduring divisions of class, gender and race within modern Western societies and thus of ultimately serving the status quo by reinforcing the self-reassuring platitudes of the dominant "we".[590] Michael Billig called it the "syntax of hegemony", simply a clever way of rhetorically embellishing straightforward nationalism.[591] Similarly, according to Lynn Baker, Rorty's approach prevented people from challenging the existing forms of oppression, for all they had at their disposal was an over-stretched and underdefined "we".[592] Richard Bernstein too noted the indeterminacy of Rorty's favourite pronoun: "Sometimes it seems as if what Rorty means by 'we' are 'all those who agree with me'."[593] Mark Kingwell condemned it as a poor linguistic choice, coming across as ambiguous and self-enclosing especially when combined with "ethnocentricity" and anti-metaphysical stances.[594] As Susan Haack argued, Rorty's "we" may even fail to include great pragmatists such as Charles Sanders Peirce (1839–1914), given the many points of disagreement between them.[595] Echoing this criticism, Jonathan Rée described Rorty's "we" as a "histrionic" device to side with any 'rebel' group attacking academe's "self-appointed guardians of philosophical propriety".⁵⁹⁶ In the same year, Jenny Teichman offered her own vitriolic dismissal of Rorty's "we":

> *The we-talk so typical of this author... appears now and then, as when he insists (thump, thump, thump) that "we no longer believe in God." Who is this "we"? one asks. Well plainly it is he, Rorty—and come to that it is also me most of the time. At this point, however, a list of real, contemporary, living-and-breathing, God-believing philosophers, physicists, biologists, academic lawyers—and even a few professors of theology—appear before the mind's eye. Rorty must be living a pretty hermetic kind of life if he has never heard of these other we's. And what about the teeming Hindu millions of India and Nepal and Sri Lanka?... Perhaps, for Rorty, these people are not we. Perhaps they are only* them.⁵⁹⁷

Rare have been the positive appraisals of Rorty's "we". Daniel Conway sees it as a wake-up call for all modern liberals who are committed to the same civic goals as Rorty, while for Mario Moussa it is a "short-hand reference to a forum where ideally all members of a democracy participate in making the decisions that affect them".⁵⁹⁸ More commonly, Rorty's acolytes do not focus on the pronoun itself, but on Rorty's works and civic commitments as a whole, or on specific aspects thereof.⁵⁹⁹

Non-negative appraisals have been quite neutral, as Anthony Gottlieb's claim that "Mr. Rorty cannot admit to his own originality—to do so would, presumably, be a sin against the 'solidarity' that replaces objectivity as the main intellectual virtue in his world. So he is forever trying to place himself".⁶⁰⁰ Jean Bethke Elshtain writes: "My hunch is that this is because Rorty wants to embrace, not to debate, to draw us all under the big tent of 'we liberal ironists,' 'we pragmatists,' 'we antiessentialists,' we who 'don't do things this way,' we... we... we. ... Those of us who resist such 'we-ness' are left to sort out just how, why, and where we disagree."⁶⁰¹ And David Rondel similarly states:

> *I think Rorty's "We pragmatists", or "We postmodern bourgeois liberals" are no more problematic locutions than Nietzsche's "We moderns", "We fearless ones", or "We good Europeans." It is not that Nietzsche or Rorty are trying to gesture at some clearly distinguishable group of persons, they are issuing a rally-call. In any case, this is how I heard Rorty himself explain it at a 2004 conference at Emory University in Atlanta.*[602]

Rorty offers at least two further explanations. One is a direct response to Bernstein's criticism of the vagueness of "we pragmatists": "I am implicitly saying: try, for the nonce, ignoring the differences between Putnam and Peirce, Nietzsche and James, Davidson and Dewey, Sellars and Wittgenstein. Focus on the following similarities, and then other similarities may leap out at you."[603] Thus does Rorty describe his "we" as a self-aware attempt to encourage his audience to focus on what is held in common by various thinkers or schools of thought that are not normally regarded as forming a clear-cut, specific group, but rather possess beliefs or virtues that overlap to some extent, the relevance of which Rorty intends to highlight in connection with some particular argument.

The second explanation reveals the Sellarsian origins of Rorty's pronoun of choice: "I was trying to describe social progress in a way borrowed from Wilfred [sic] Sellars: the expansion of 'we' consciousness, that is, the ability to take more and more people of the sort fashionably called 'marginal' and think of them as one of us, included in us."[604] Back in 1989, Rorty had already revealed the Sellarsian origins of his own approach, though *via* the British conservative Michael Oakeshott (1901–1990): "morality is a matter of what he calls 'we-intentions,' that the core meaning of 'immoral action' is 'the sort of thing *we* don't do'."[605] A more recent article, though, shows just how marginally Sellarsian Rorty's appropriation of "we-intentions" has been.[606]

Be that as it may, if social amelioration is to be attained so that more individuals cooperate in the pursuit of moral or political ends, it is imperative that they perceive themselves and others as members of a larger human community—as "we". Rorty's references to

Sellars (1912–1989) reveal that his use of the "we", as a common rhetorical trope, is inclusive and specifically *hortatory*.[607]

A Rhetorical Analysis of "We"

Those who criticise Rorty's use of "we" seem to overlook the basic value of rhetorical strategies in human communication. They point to its vagueness, its being too broad and too narrow at the same time, seeing that the "we" does not clearly demarcate "us" from "them", while insisting on potential markers of such a demarcation (e.g., Dewey, fuzziness, solidarity, Wittgenstein). However, if its use is hortatory, then both a certain degree of vagueness and high context-dependence are advantages, not limitations.[608] Before explaining why this may be the case, I must briefly outline the principal features of classical rhetoric, part of which has already been briefly introduced in the chapter on Pareto.[609]

The first of the five tenets of classical rhetoric consists in finding things to say, that is, finding the rhetorical proofs of the thesis (a general point) or hypothesis (a more specific one) to be demonstrated.[610] Roman rhetoricians called this activity *inventio*, which refers to retrieving something from an inventory. The inventory is the vast field of commonsensical and technical information available to the rhetorician, who can use it as sheer factual data (i.e., external proofs that are equally available to others) or, more inventively, as examples, parables, fables or premises for rhetorical syllogisms (enthymemes) to support the thesis/hypothesis under consideration (i.e., internal proofs that the rhetorician has to create: the province of reasoning or *logos*). The clearer, more probable and intuitive the proofs are, the more likely the rhetorician is to succeed.

In addition, the rhetorician must take into account what is to be said in order to be perceived as a person of good character or *ethos*, as possessing the traits of wise objectivity *vis à-vis* the many ways in which a certain issue can be approached, of having a genuine commitment to one of these ways (the rhetorician is trying to prove a point, after all), and of overall amiability (an offensive person will have a harder time being listened to).

The rhetorician must consider everything that can affect the emotional disposition of the specific audience addressed: all forms of human communication involve as well an element of *pathos*. As already seen in the present book, even the positivist Vilfredo Pareto concluded that most people, including scientists, focus chiefly on the most emotionally charged assertions of authors or speakers, whose "persuasiveness" is due to three causes: "A vague feeling that a person who expresses in such a form *must* be right"; "[a] feeling that such a select form is authoritative"; and "the more or less vague notion that the authority is justified." Scientific authority is itself "a tool of proof and a tool of persuasion" and "an assertion is accepted and gains prestige through the sentiments of various kinds which it excites."[611]

The second tenet, *dispositio*, as found in the final paragraphs of Aristotle's *Ars Rhetorica*, relate to the arrangement of the parts that make up a well-ordered speech. Any persuasive piece of communication, whether spoken or written, must be well-organised, such as the standardised forms of scientific exposition.[612]

The third tenet, *elocutio* or style, is what rhetoric has most commonly been associated with and mistakenly reduced to down the centuries. It is not enough to have something to say and to know in which order to say it, because *how* the text is delivered is itself crucial. A well-substantiated and orderly speech or essay may fail to persuade because the language it employs is either dull or inappropriate. Attention, therefore, must also be paid to its form. Even great thoughts require the right choice of words to be persuasive.[613] This simple yet fundamental tenet implies that one's speech or written work must be appropriate to the circumstances.

Classical rhetoric listed three basic types of speeches/texts: (1) judicial, dealing mainly with past events and the truth or falsity of accusations; (2) political, dealing mainly with future events and the utility or liability of law proposals; and (3) epideictic, dealing mainly with current events and with ascribing praise or blame to a person, a course of action or an institution. Thus, the correct choice and arrangement of words must be such as to gain and keep the attention of the audience. This is the realm of rhetorical figures or tropes, which rhetoricians have studied and classified for over 2,500 years. They are, in fact, the language that we speak, for no communication is possible without them.

The fourth and fifth tenets are, respectively, *actio*, the actual delivery of a speech (still important at conferences and in the classroom), and *memoria*, the techniques of retaining what one has to say in mind.

Rhetoric is, in brief, inescapable, and although philosophers all too often equate *rhetoric* with empty verbiage, all forms and types of discourse—insofar as they attempt to persuade—are fundamentally rhetorical.[614]

If these five rhetorical tenets are applied to Rorty's use of "we", then its multiple meanings can be better grasped. As for *ethos*, Rorty's "we" facilitates his identification with a larger and quite diverse group of thinkers who share similar goals or methodologies, which enhances his *commitment*—since he has a declared aim—and *amiability*—for he reaches out to those who happen to esteem some of these thinkers. In a nutshell, Rorty's broad, yet graspable "we" indicates that he is neither devoid of an aim nor alone in his pursuit. Had he clearly signalled whom he sides with, he would have made enemies at the very start and compromised his chances to include, to be listened to, and perhaps to persuade as composite an audience as possible. And if he did not specify some criteria that are appropriate to the particular circumstances of his written text or speech, he would come across as truly vague, possibly irrelevant, even incompetent.

Concerning *pathos*, the "we" should appeal to the audiences' desire to be part of a larger whole engaged in a worthy endeavour; though Rorty's option may misfire and appear parochial, one should not underestimate the strong appeal of participation. Indeed, Pareto saw the most profoundly ingrained human "residue" or "sentiment" to be that of "sociality", given that "the larger and more effective portion of the residues prevalent in society cannot be altogether unfavourable to its preservation; for if that were the case, the society would break down and cease to exist."[615]

As for *logos*, Rorty's "we" is in part the result of his anti-foundationalist stance, his belief that all forms of argumentation are ultimately ethnocentric and based on the strongest convictions of the members of a community, whether these be the mathematically constructed fundamentals of physics or the gods of old, as W. V. O. Quine would have put it.[616] Rhetoric teaches that to be persuasive, a speaker must first engage the audience by presenting premises that possess the quality of verisimilitude, and can hence be accepted without controversy, so that the ensuing points may be made on a sufficiently solid basis. By using "we", Rorty attempts to engage his audience and produce as much initial agreement as possible. The various context-dependent qualifications of Rorty's "we" create a space for shared beliefs or, at least, shared knowledge, which facilitates the conceptual exchange between him and his audience.

As for style or *elocutio*, it was remarked already that Rorty's "we" is a case of *adhortatio*, an exhortation intended to move the audience's desires. However, it is also a *synecdoche*, for it makes use of the whole "we" to mean the part "I", as Teichman sneeringly stated, as well as implicitly including all potential members the author doesn't know who are his allies in his intellectual and political endeavours.[617] Equally, it is a case of *metonymy*, for "we *pragmatists*", "*irrationalists*" and so forth emphasise certain attributes of those who want to overcome one or more of philosophy's unsolved problems or engage in socially relevant activities that go beyond conceptual analysis. Furthermore, Rorty's stylistic choice includes *anaphora* (the repetition of the same word or group of words at the beginning of successive clauses, sentences, or lines) and *conduplicatio* (repetition of a word or words elsewhere), both of which phonetic forms attract attention and facilitate long-term retention of ideas.

Rorty's stylistic choices are not a sign of sloppiness or aimlessness, but rather sensibly selected rhetorical devices. Their relevance is even more pronounced once we recognise that Rorty's work has a deliberative or political dimension. Its main aim is not to assess whether certain things were true in the past or praise others, but to address the academic community at large, in its rich variety of cultural backgrounds, and to lead research onto new paths that focus on the social and moral usefulness of free thought ("relevance", "solidarity") rather than on the truthfulness of highly technical conclusions *via* strict protocols of investigation ("rigour", "objectivity"). One cannot engage such a large and diverse audience by using arcane formulations, but rather by using a lively prose style that strikes a balance between technical complexity, which shows inter alia the professional credibility of the writer, and overall clarity, the necessary condition for any successful communication.

Persuasion, it appears, may not be the ultimate criterion by which Rorty's endeavour should be measured—not even rhetorically. When we turn from classical rhetoric to looking at his use of the "we" in terms of modern rhetoric, drawn mainly from the works of Chaïm Perelman (1912–1984) and Kenneth Burke (1897–1993), his use appears sensible, if not apt. According to Perelman and Lucie Olbrechts-Tyteca (1899–1987), the question of the audience is paramount: "Since argumentation aims at securing the adherence of those to whom it is addressed, it is, in its entirety, relative to the audience to be influenced".[618] Rhetoric, in other words, records, systematises and teaches strategies aimed at engaging and maintaining the audience's attention, for no persuasion can take place without them. Persuasion thus falls within the province of the aims of rhetoric but does not exhaust it. For persuasion to be possible, the orator is first to "establish a sense of communion centered around particular values recognized by the audience".[619]

Rorty's "we" can be seen as pursuing Perelman's "adherence" by securing "communion" *via* a trope (or plurality of tropes) the aim of which is to capture the interest of academics at large and keep them listening to, or, to be more precise, reading Rorty's works.[620] For one, the repeated use of "we" in sentences and paragraphs can be taken as an example of *anaphora* or repetition, which brings distant things (e.g., dead philosophers) closer to the audience ("we") by restating again and again their presence, sensorial as well as conceptual.

The same "we" may also be an attempt to convince them of Rorty's theses, in line with Perelman's anti-foundationalism:

> *The man who requires that argumentation provide demonstrative proof of compelling force and will not be content with less in order to adhere to a thesis misunderstands as much as the fanatic the essential characteristic of argumentative procedure. For the very reason that argumentation aims at justifying choices, it cannot provide justifications that would tend to show that there is no choice, but that only one solution is open to those examining the problem.*[621]

Kenneth Burke, like Perelman, recognised that rhetoric aims at catching and sustaining the attention of the audience, prior to any persuasion, or even *independently* of it, since the speaker may simply wish to entertain the audience, to offer 'food for thought' rather than a specific conclusion, to converse without any predefined goal, or to keep disagreement on the level of conversation rather than resorting to insult or violence. Persuasion is not the only aim that rhetoric may serve:

> *We need never deny the presence of strife, enmity, factions, as a characteristic motive of rhetorical expression. We need not close our eyes to their almost tyrannous ubiquity in human relations; we can be on the alert always to see how such temptations to strife are implicit in the institutions that condition human relationships; yet we can at the same time always look beyond this order, to the principle of identification in general, a terministic choice justified by the facts that the identifications in the order of love are also characteristic of rhetorical expression.*[622]

For Burke, what matters is to create the right psychological conditions, so as to be able to carry forth a conversation and then, perhaps, achieve persuasion. Given the symbolic and agency-prone nature of humans, Burke thinks of linguistic communication as primarily a source of *motives*, and only secondarily as a form of persuasion. Thus "persuasion" itself is redefined by him in much broader terms than in classical rhetoric. For him persuasion is the attempt to lead a person to behave in a certain way, and to provide a motive for action, which too is taken to encompass all symbolic activities of the human mind: "Wherever there is persuasion, there is rhetoric. And wherever there is 'meaning' there is persuasion."[623] Rhetoric becomes for Burke "the use of words by human agents to form attitudes or induce actions in other human agents... *the use of language as a symbolic means of inducing cooperation in beings that by nature respond to symbols.*"[624]

Rooted in the scholastic notion of "substances" (e.g. physical objects, occupations, friends, activities, beliefs, values), which we share with those with whom we associate, Burke argues that we become "consubstantial" with others. In his analysis, "identification" replaces persuasion as the core of rhetoric: "you persuade a man only insofar as you can talk his language by speech, gesture, tonality, order, image, attitude, idea, *identifying* your ways with his."[625] What a speaker aims at is therefore "arousing and fulfillment of desires" or "the creation of an appetite in the mind of the auditor, and the adequate satisfying of that appetite."[626]

Analogously to what was pointed out on Rorty's "we" and Perelman's understanding of rhetoric, here too the "we" signals the initial embrace of the audience—or Burke's "identification"—by securing "consubstantiality" via a trope that aims at capturing the interest of the audience and keeping their attention for as long as possible. In other words, the aim of Rorty's "we" is to motivate his audience to read, discuss, and engage with his works, whether in eventual agreement or disagreement with him. Even bad publicity is publicity, after all.

Rorty's Political Philosophy of "We"

If it is the case that the rhetorical aim of Rorty's "we" is persuasion, communion, and identification, it is important to ask who is supposed to persuade whom, who to commune and identify with whom. The emphasis on a "we" cannot but mean that there is a "they".[627] Chantal Mouffe (b. 1943) has claimed that the "they" "represents the condition of possibility of the 'we', its 'constitutive outside'."[628] The opposite can probably be claimed too.[629] Who are "they"? Those to be persuaded, or those rallied against (these may, but need not, be identical), or those about whom the text remains silent, those who are neither to be persuaded nor even addressed?

Whatever the answer, the mere assertion of a "we" and a "they" may indicate a social ontology or criterion for distinguishing one group from another. Distinctions of this kind are often intimately related to and instrumental in politics. We find them in Carl Schmitt's (1888–1985) friend-foe distinction and in contemporary theories of the politics of difference. Rorty has affirmed that, in contrast with the philosophical question "what are we?" the question "who are we?" is "political", which brings us to a political analysis of Rorty's "we-talk".[630]

Compared with his much-discussed dismantling of representationalism, Rorty's political philosophy has met with little agreement. His politics has been considered "nowhere near the sophistication and expertise in his other work".[631] Thus his position has been said to remain "a distinctively minority one" and his destiny to be "rid[ing] off into battle mostly alone and unsupported".[632]

Rorty has been much criticised for rigidly holding onto a vocabulary of binary distinctions, which, to be sure, are the sort of distinctions he famously debunked in epistemology. His private-public distinction has been found unsound: for blindly reproducing the liberal division of these spheres in spite of their "historical and conceptual interrelations;"[633] for unduly relegating disagreement to the private sphere and stipulating a Rawlsian overlapping consensus in the public sphere;[634] for misguidedly not allowing irony into the public realm;[635] for suggesting the psychological impossibility of being an ironist privately and a staunch liberal publicly;[636] and for presupposing "one public space" only.[637]

In addition, Rorty has been criticised for holding an oversimplistic view of politics, understanding it as "a matter of pragmatic, short-term reforms and compromises",[638] and "at least in democratic countries, as something to be conducted in as plain, blunt, public, easy-to-handle language as possible."[639] His view of politics is all too naïve and ignorant of power relations,[640] of "the realities of power",[641] of the "antagonistic dimension" of "the political",[642] of "the narrative history of international capital",[643] or worse still, he is unwilling "to investigate and re-describe power and power relations".[644] Rorty is reproached for being disinclined to "discuss institutions" too,[645] and for being vague on practical implementation.[646] Ultimately, Rorty's pragmatism seems to lack practical relevance: it remains aloof and unworldly.[647]

Some criticism has been more directly aimed at Rorty's "we" in his discussions of solidarity, loyalty, community, ethnocentrism, and cultural politics. While attacking Claude Lévi-Strauss (1908–2009) for treating "human communities" as if they were (or were to be) "semantic monads, nearly windowless",[648] Clifford Geertz (1926–2006) charges Rorty as well with doing something very similar.[649] Others have repeated the same criticism,[650] or turned it into a critique of a homogeneous "we".[651] Rorty's embrace of "ethnocentrism"—"that we should be more willing than we are to celebrate bourgeois capitalist society as the best polity actualised so far"[652]—has stirred controversy and repudiation. Some have understood this as unwittingly advocating a version of (Samuel P.) Huntington-style (1927–2008) reactionary conservatism,[653] or, slightly more mildly, as "an *apologia* for the status quo",[654] that is, for a stars-and-stripes liberal democracy, which, moreover, he miscasts as a democracy in which genuine free discussion is the norm.[655]

Bernstein claims that "Rorty simply speaks globally about 'liberal democracy' without ever unpacking what it involves or doing justice to the enormous historical controversy about what liberal democracy is or ought to be", merely assuming that we all share "intuitions about what liberal democracy means or should mean."[656] That Rorty envisions the "we" of liberal democracy to become ever more inclusive has triggered the rejoinder that he allows only those to be included who are already subscribe to the "modish standards of polite liberal talk".[657] Nothing "alien" or "other" can challenge the supposed consensus of Rorty's "we", insofar as it has already become "non-alien", part of we's own: *eine Infragestellung des Eigenen durch das Eigene* (challenging what is proper to oneself by what is proper to oneself).[658]

Rorty's Ethnocentrism

Rorty started using the "we so-and-so" roughly at the same time he developed the notion of ethnocentrism. Contrary to what he later claimed,[659] he first used "ethnocentric" not in his 1984 essay "Solidarity or Objectivity?",[660] but at least as early as 1979 in his presidential address to the American Philosophical Association, where he mentioned the threatening "we" of the Orwellian state, blamed Jürgen Habermas's pragmatist line of transcendental defence against such threats, and urged pragmatists to "remain ethnocentric" ("ethnocentric" here denotes the opposite of "transcendental").[661]

Habermas, to be sure, is considered a pragmatist, but he is not part of Rorty's "we pragmatists". The reason for this was that Habermas had misguidedly resorted to an approach that he shared with those against whom he (i.e. Habermas) had set up his "line of defence" and that Rorty in his *Philosophy and the Mirror of Nature* had set out to debunk. Rorty identified this traditional approach to philosophy as Kantian, and although he initially criticised it exclusively in the context of epistemology and metaphysics, as a mistaken search for how the world really is and what notions such as truth, virtue, objectivity, and rationality really mean, he soon started applying his notion of antirepresentationalism to politics. In "Priority of Democracy to Philosophy", he writes:

> *What counts as rational or as fanatical is relative to the group to which we think it necessary to justify ourselves—to the body of shared belief that determines the reference of the word "we". The Kantian identification with a central transcultural and ahistorical self is thus replaced by a quasi-Hegelian*

identification with our own community, thought of as a historical product.[662]

In spite of his various adaptations of the notion of ethnocentrism, Rorty has kept steadfast as regards the work that this notion should do for him. He emphasises the antitranscendental (anti-Kantian, anti-Christian, anti-Platonic) meaning of "ethnocentrism" again and again.

For example, in his reply to Geertz, he refers to it as a "small, local, psychological problem" of bourgeois liberals "who have not yet gone postmodern".[663] He argues that when attempting to raise support for the disadvantaged, it is more persuasive, "morally as well as politically", to refer to hopeless young blacks in American cities as "one of us" in the sense of "fellow Americans" rather than of "fellow human beings".[664] Similarly, when he criticises Kantian moral philosophers such as Christine Korsgaard (b. 1952)—who would try, he says, to bring Nazis over to anti-Nazism—he states: "It is only *this* sort of claim that my ethnocentrism targets".[665] As David Hollinger explains:

As soon as the Kantians are disposed of, Rorty's vision of human solidarity takes on what most American intellectuals of the last half-century would recognize immediately as a decidedly anti-ethnocentric cast: this solidarity, says Rorty, should be understood as "the ability to think of people wildly different from ourselves as included in the range of 'us'." The circle of "we" thus embraces diversity; it is not a uniformitarian construct, predicating equality on sameness.[666]

Rorty's "anti-ethnocentric cast" is quite obvious unless one ignores the unconventional, novel use he makes of the term "ethnocentric", which means that any attempt to assess Rorty's ethnocentrism on the basis of the traditional meaning of "ethnos" would be to beg the question.[667]

Rorty's use of the term "ethnocentrism" has often been said to be rather loose and inconsistent,[668] as well as misleading; he himself has acknowledged that it is "misleadingly ambiguous",[669] so perhaps he never meant it to be anything other than a challenge to those who still fancy universalism,[670] or intentional provocation.[671] The ambiguity lies, as he explains, in that "one person's mild ethnocentrism is another's secondary narcissism or cultural imperialism".[672]

Rorty is aware of the negative connotations of the term and has always distinguished between two ethnocentrisms—his own and a "vicious" kind.[673] He would readily abandon the term if, as he says, he could come up with a better one.[674] So, what did Rorty mean to say that he could only say, for lack of a better term, by using "ethnocentrism"?

In one place he speaks of ethnocentrism as "an inescapable condition—roughly synonymous with 'human finitude'."[675] The term hence foregrounds what Wittgenstein called in *On Certainty* the "inherited background", against which we distinguish between true and false. Rorty sometimes follows the Wittgensteinian line quite explicitly, speaking of forms of life and alluding to the limits set by language. There is no doubt that for Rorty each person simultaneously belongs to several ethnoi.

As early as 1983, Rorty notes the "fact that most of us identify with a number of different communities", whether family, nation, churches and movements.[676] In his attempt to substitute the term "loyalty" for "justice", when it comes to questions of moral identity and ethnocentrism, Rorty writes that "*any* unforced agreement between individuals and groups about what to do will create a form of community", which potentially will "be the initial stage in expanding the circles of those whom each party to the agreement had previously taken to be 'people like ourselves'."[677]

Although he often clings to the opinion that smaller communities elicit more trust and loyalty than larger communities, particularly if the latter refers to humanity as such,[678] Rorty proposes the opposite: "what makes you loyal to a smaller group may give you reason to cooperate in constructing a larger group, a group to which you may, in time, become equally loyal or perhaps even more loyal."[679] Elsewhere, he expresses his hope for a "world republic".[680]

When he was criticised for not having a criterion for distinguishing one "we" from another, Rorty suggested a criterion drawing on Korsgaard's notion of a "different practical identity": that "we could not spin a coherent narrative about ourselves if we did what they do, and conversely", suggesting that "an inability to change while still keeping a sense of identity" is that which separates different communities. He went on to say: "'Sense of identity' is, I admit, a pretty fuzzy notion, but I do not think I can make the notion of 'Wir-gemeinschaft' any less fuzzy than that."[681]

In the same text, in response to Udo Tietz's claim that the attempt to define an ethnos by way of a linguistic community would result in having "already two physicists, say Albert Einstein and Niels Bohr, constitute their own ethnos",[682] Rorty wrote:

> *One of Tietz's most effective points is that, in my sense of "ethnocentric", you can be an ethnos all by yourself—a one-person ethnos. You can do this by having what in Contingency, Irony and Solidarity I called a "final vocabulary"—the vocabulary you fall back on when you defend an action which you [would] rather die than not have performed, but which strikes your interlocutors as crazy. In this sense, Socrates was an ethnos different from the one formed by most of his judges, and Nietzsche an ethnos different from that shared by Wilamowitz-Moellendorf and most of the other classic professors of the day. Such one-person ethnoi can be important engines of moral progress (or regress).*[683]

This statement should put to rest the claim that Rorty meant to stipulate a homogeneous "we" (elsewhere he explicitly writes of an "ever larger and more variegated ethnos").[684] Rorty's acceptance of one-person ethnoi recalls his exchange in 1984 with Foucault on the question of "we". Rorty complained that "there is no 'we' to be found in Foucault's writings",[685] to which Foucault replied by asking whether there must always be "a pre-existing and receptive 'we'" or whether the "we" could not also be the result of actions performed by an 'I'.[686]

Nonetheless, whenever Rorty discusses political issues, it is the nation that stands out as the most important community—the United States, in his case—which he considers a good example of a liberal society in "the West". The importance he attributes to the nation is manifest in his criticism of identity politics. More specifically, he argues that it is not enough to be politically active in a small community without any idea of how the political entity that has the monopoly of power—the nation state—should deal with affairs that have nothing to do with small communities.[687]

As regards the United States, he dithers between condemning it and praising it as "a great country".[688] The distinction between liberalism as it is experienced, and the only partially realised ideals of the liberal utopia is crucial to Rorty's entire project of being "frankly ethnocentric".[689] This distinction underlies the tension between the "we" of identity and the "we" of "we-intentions". When he speaks of our "inescapable condition", he is pointing out the limits imposed by always acting and thinking from where we stand, or, as he puts it, the "admission that we are just the historical moment that we are".[690]

Yet Rorty's liberal utopia is entirely directed at where we should go, at establishing "a democratic, progressive, pluralist community of the sort which Dewey dreamt".[691] The tension is dissolved once identity and the limits of contingency are no longer understood in an overly realist manner, once ideals in the form of edifying narratives, "us at our best",[692] are factored into an assessment of where "we" stand.

In a sense, when Rorty appeals to the common identity of "fellow Americans", he is gesturing towards what America could become; the "we" of identity is "mythic America" and amounts to a Rortyan we-intention: "The question 'who are we'?" as he writes, is "future-oriented".[693] This intended openness to the future may explain why Rorty always depicts his liberal utopia rather vaguely, say, as opposing cruelty, and refers rather sketchily to institutions such as elections or the rule of law.

The identification Rorty is speaking of in his use of the "we" is with the ideals that liberal institutions embody, and he is much less concerned with the differences and variants of their embodiments. Consider his reaction to criticism from the left, who, he writes,

> *think of themselves as standing outside of the sociopolitical culture of liberalism with which Dewey identified, a culture with which I continue to identify. So when I say ethnocentric things like "our culture" or "we liberals", their reaction is "who, we?" I, however, find it hard to see them as outsiders to this culture.*[694]

Rorty's identification with "the sociopolitical culture of liberalism" is the identification with the Enlightenment's political ideals (for why else would he use "we Europeans"?) without their metaphysics. Rorty's use of "we liberals" seeks to cover all kinds of political philosophies, which is why somebody like Laclau, a post-Marxist and radical democrat, is not contradicting himself when he explicitly "endorse[s]" Rorty's "liberal democratic framework".[695]

Inasmuch as real existing liberal democracies can be said to have lived up to their utopian promises (and who would say that they have not at all done so or have not when compared with other real existing frameworks?), Rorty insists that we should not be looking for alternative practices: "we do not need... 'a critique of liberal society'. We just need more liberal societies, and more liberal laws in force within each such society".[696]

Still, within liberal society, dissenters do play an important role:

> *We can only hope to transcend our acculturation if our culture contains (or, thanks to disruptions from outside or internal revolt, comes to contain) splits which supply toeholds for new initiatives. Without such splits—without tensions—which make people listen to unfamiliar ideas in the hope of finding means of overcoming those tensions—there is no such hope.*[697]

Later in the same article, Rorty reveals an often-neglected aspect of his political philosophy. In his pessimistic vision of "America, or the rich North Atlantic democracies generally, in the year in which I write (1990)", he conjectures that if things continue the way they are "for another generation, the countries in which it happens will be barbarised. Then it may become silly to hope for reform, and sensible to hope for revolution."[698]

No doubt, at the time and up until his passing away in 2007, Rorty did not think that the time for anything other than reform had come. But it is remarkable that in this footnote he historicises his own position, giving it the status of a suggestion, an argument of sorts, underlining that it too is contingent as much as anything else, or in his own words: "the only 'we' we need is a local and temporary one".[699]

Concluding Remarks

It is difficult to determine how persuasive Rorty was in his long career. Given the amount of literature produced on him, he was singularly successful in creating an audience for himself (i.e., gaining communion and identification). Compared with his colleagues, his views have been pondered upon by many more readers and experts outside the circles of professional philosophers. New readings of Rorty continue to appear. Leib, for example, emphasises the Rorty-Lyotard debate in 1984 at Johns Hopkins University that made Rorty "more sensitive to contestation, which always stands in the way of having a comfortable 'we' at the outset".[700] Hollinger, who detects "dead ends and contradictions" in Rorty's works, nonetheless claims that

> *they can help to inspire a postparticularistic or... "postethnic" disposition toward issues of affiliation in a variety of contexts. This disposition is not "an answer" to the problem of the ethnocentric circle; rather it is a willingness to engage that problem while remaining suspicious of the will to enclose.* [701]

Hollinger's project of *postethnicity* (the term was inspired by Laclau (1935–2014) and Mouffe's post-Marxism as both *post-*Marxist and post-*Marxist*) is still attractive. For one thing, Hollinger adequately addresses the issue of power:

> [N]o sooner do we ask, "How wide the circle of the we?" than we ought to ask, "What identifies the we?" and "How deep the structure of power within it?" and "How is the authority to set its boundaries distributed?"[702]

It is such readings that have made the best use of Rorty's oeuvre, for they use Rorty to go beyond him and thus come up with a better vocabulary, rather than offering the next quick dismissal of his ethnocentrism.

Rorty's notion of a one-person ethnoi deserves further attention, particularly because of its implications for his political philosophy. It appears, then, that Rorty's claim that what we need is "more liberalism", just like the leftist call for more radical change, cannot but be subject to the very same contingencies, the very same "inescapable condition", that provide the reasons to justify it.

Rorty's rhetoric of "we" is always relative to purpose, as is any term of commendation—such as utility or superiority—the pragmatist uses.[703] This suggests that to be really persuasive, any criticism of Rorty's "we" should focus on specific textual interventions that enable the critic to identify more precisely the audience addressed, or understood to be invoked, by Rorty's ubiquitous "we".

Chapter 12: *Gestalt* Psychology and the Tropes of Rhetoric

Rhetoric is possibly the oldest form of reflexive, organised inquiry in the nature, articulation and ends of human communication. Although the term itself is likely to have appeared for the first time in Plato's *Gorgias*, the study and the teaching of what Cicero (106–43 BC)[704] described as "the art of persuasion" had already been practiced extensively since at least the days of the legendary 5th-century orators Corax and Tisias.[705]

In contemporary academe, rhetoric still finds ample room for both study and teaching, not only in the field of rhetoric as such or within English and communication departments, but also amongst scholars in literature and poetry at large,[706] philosophers interested in argumentation and persuasion,[707] explorers of Greek and Roman antiquity,[708] educators cultivating their students' skills in public speaking and composition,[709] keen researchers in media and socio-political studies,[710] psychologists figuring out how people can change one another's beliefs and actions by talking or writing well,[711] or more practically oriented coaches in business,[712] marketing,[713] advertising,[714] graphic design,[715] IT development,[716] architecture,[717] political lobbying[718] and photography.[719] Indeed, as the vocational side of academic work is concerned, the study of rhetoric has found fertile soil in the domain of visual communication, which has become undoubtedly prominent in the age of televisual, phone-screen-based and computer-screen-based social interaction.[720]

Another line of study has been flourishing in the same domain over recent decades, i.e. the rediscovery and wide application of *Gestalt* psychology, especially with regard to the so-called "laws" or "principles" of organisation of human perception. No contemporary textbook, expert website or university course in visual communication can do without paying ample homage to the "forms" of perceptual organisation that Max Wertheimer (1880–1943), Wolfgang Köhler (1887–1967) and Kurt Koffka (1886–1941) identified and investigated in the first half of the 20th century ("structures" or "configurations" being equally valid translations of the German *Gestalten*).[721] Despite gradual marginalisation in universities and research centres during the Cold War years, *Gestalt* psychology never died out completely, unlike earlier schools of thought in psychology such as structuralism or functionalism, and much has been done since the fall of the Berlin Wall to further its founders' original discoveries,[722] including pursuing the genetic study of the forms of perception[723] and developing additional and/or substitutive laws or principles.[724]

Topic, Scientific Literature and Aims

Despite their conspicuous and simultaneous flourishing within the same set of academic and practical interests, one significant aspect of rhetoric, i.e. its tropes, and the *Gestalt* laws of perceptual organisation have hardly met each other. On the one end of the scholarly spectrum, contemporary rhetoricians have not been focussing particularly on tropes, but rather on broader theoretical issues such as the nature of human language, rationality and interpretation.[725] On the other end of the same spectrum, operating at a higher level of abstraction, "tropology" and "gestalts" *qua* cognitive schemata have been combined together in an interesting way by neuropsychologists.[726] However, with the noteworthy exception of Tucker, no researcher appears to have been interested in exploring how the rhetorical tropes observed and classified since classical antiquity may relate to the *Gestalt* laws so frequently presented in the textbooks of a vast array of disciplinary and vocational fields.[727]

Echoing older studies that were even more limited in scope—i.e. Talmy[728] and Koch[729] on metonymy—Tucker concentrates upon one of these laws, i.e. that of figure/ground, according to which perception is possible by means of the subject's projection of the object *qua* identifiable form or organised structure (i.e. a *Gestalt*) against a suitable background. As Tucker argues, rhetorical tropes are aptly called "figures" too, since they allow for human cognition to take place by letting congruous cognitive stimuli coalesce into intelligible structures shaping the objects of cognition, which are projected against the backdrop constituted by the remaining flux of potential information. The law of figure/ground applies to all rhetorical tropes, which he interprets in their diversity as cognitive schemata drawing the boundaries of graspable objects within the subject's field of cognisable experience (as a consequence, to avoid redundancies, I do not include the figure/ground law in the classificatory table presented below in this chapter).

In ordinary circumstances, we eventually recognise a human being in the fog when a coherent shape of a human body emerges from the haze. Analogously, we identify distinct phenomena as themselves, hence neither as nothing nor as something or anything else, by means of graspable forms or figures cast against the otherwise fuzzy field of cognitive stimuli with which we are presented in our environment. As neurologist David Rail writes: "Tropes shape thought so enabling our minds to echo our world."[730]

Tucker is noteworthy in suggesting that what is valid for perception in particular is valid for cognition in general, especially as comprehending linguistic meaning is concerned. In this, he is consistent with Rail's recent research in neuropsychology, but also and above all with Wertheimer's original claim that the laws or principles of organisation sought by *Gestalt* psychology do not deal with perception alone.[731]

Whilst his initial studies may have concentrated upon perception, Wertheimer's final goal was the understanding of the relationship between the whole and its parts at large, for *Gestalten* are supposed to be the cognitive structures whereby we interpret very many if not all phenomena, in very many if not all domains of existence, such as biology, society and the arts, which are among Wertheimer's own examples.

That tropes, along with other rhetorical devices, be cognitive schemata or important means of cognition rather than mere stylistic flourishes, is a notion that has been taken most seriously not only in psychology, but equally in as diverse fields of research as linguistics,[732] computer science[733] and business studies.[734]

In this chapter, I do not pursue any in-depth analysis of the nature of cognition according to psychology in general or *Gestalt* psychology in particular, nor do I offer a resolution of the methodological quagmires of the same, or even a sheer assessment of the plausibility of the latest developments in the field. Although the present research could possibly substantiate a tropology such as Rail's, my aims are more modest and make use of the time-tested *Gestalt* laws of organisation that populate standard textbooks in a variety of disciplines, so that the definitions of the laws presented below may result uncontroversial. Specifically, I aim at:

(1) Employing the long-established *Gestalt* laws as a tool to map the complex and heterogeneous realm of rhetorical tropes, which have been organised in a number of other ways since the days of Aristotle's pioneering treatise on rhetoric (do note that "tropes" and "figures" are used here as synonyms);[735] and

(2) substantiating Wertheimer's original claim that the laws or principles of organisation sought by *Gestalt* psychology do not deal with perception alone and that *Gestalt* psychology does actually work *qua* descriptive science of humankind's cognitive phenomena at large, by providing an exemplary, extensive and comprehensive application within a field of investigation, i.e. rhetorical tropes, relevant to all forms of human communication, scientific ones included.[736]

As concerns the latter aim, it should be noted that, whilst the list of tropes included in this chapter may appear perplexingly long and, possibly, even overwhelming to the reader, its vastness and completeness are crucial to establishing *via* substantial corroboration the scientific plausibility of the claim above and, *a fortiori*, to achieving the aim at issue. It is not just the rhetorical trope of emphasis that is at work here, but rather the painstaking demands for repeated observation, classificatory wealth and robust relevance that characterise psychology *qua* modern empirical science.

It should be noted too that the present chapter confines itself to the heterogeneous field of rhetorical tropes, which are one sub-set of issues in just one of the five canons of classical rhetoric, all of which are relevant to the known forms of human communication, scientific ones included.

Definitions

In order to pursue my aims, I make use of the following definitions of the *Gestalt* laws or principles of organisation.

I. The Law of Closure: Congruous cognitive elements (e.g. meanings in utterances, notes in a musical motive) tend to be grouped into complete structures; e.g., the following set of distinct segments is perceived as a rectangular shape:

II. The Law of Proximity: Congruous cognitive elements that are close together spatially tend to be structured as a group; e.g., the following set of circles is perceived as three horizontal sets rather than, say, twenty-three vertical sets:

ooooooooooooooooooooooo

ooooooooooooooooooooooo

ooooooooooooooooooooooo

III. The Law of Similarity: Congruous similar cognitive elements tend to be structured together (insofar as the elements are similar in that they are near one another, the law of proximity could be seen as a subcategory of the law of similarity); e.g. the following set of capital letters is perceived as vertical columns of the same letter rather than, say, horizontal sequences of mixed capital letters:

```
AIAIAIAIAIAIAIAIAIAI
AIAIAIAIAIAIAIAIAIAI
AIAIAIAIAIAIAIAIAIAI
AIAIAIAIAIAIAIAIAIAI
AIAIAIAIAIAIAIAIAIAI
AIAIAIAIAIAIAIAIAIAI
AIAIAIAIAIAIAIAIAIAI
AIAIAIAIAIAIAIAIAIAI
AIAIAIAIAIAIAIAIAIAI
AIAIAIAIAIAIAIAIAIAI
AIAIAIAIAIAIAIAIAIAI
AIAIAIAIAIAIAIAIAIAI
```

IV. The Law of Good Continuation: Congruous cognitive elements tend to be structured so as to minimise discontinuity or abrupt change; e.g. the following figure is perceived as the intersection of two lines, rather than four separate segments made of five to seven dots or a set of separate dots on a white field:

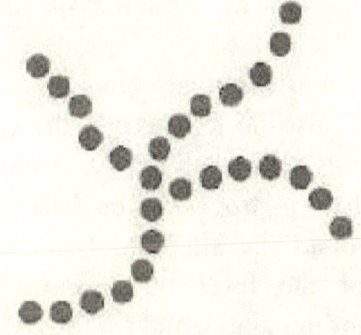

Fig. 1[737]

V. The Law of Symmetry: Congruous cognitive regions bound by symmetrical disposition tend to be apprehended as coherent structures; e.g. the following set of brackets is perceived as constituted by five pairs of symmetrical brackets rather than, say, ten individual brackets:

( )[ ]( )[ ]( )

VI. The Law of Simplicity: Complex, diverse, ambiguous or conflicting cognitive elements tend to be resolved in favour of the simplest; e.g. the image below is perceived as a series of rings rather than more complicated shapes:

Fig. 2[738]

Two Principal Ways in which the Gestalt *Principles Apply*

Few preliminary considerations are *de rigueur* in order to understand how it is possible to interpret the tropes of rhetoric in light of the *Gestalt* laws defined above. According to Barthes' 1970s seminal lectures on rhetoric, tropes can be distinguished between: (1) Those that pivot around the signified (i.e. Quintilian's *"res"* or "things"), namely at the level of meanings or concepts (i.e. Quintilian's "figures of thought"); and (2) those that pivot around the signifiers (i.e. Quintilian's *"verba"* or "words"), namely at the level of sounds or graphemes (i.e. Quintilian's "figures of speech", also known as "schemes").

Tackling the latter family of tropes first, it should be observed that all linguistic communication falls under the *Gestalt* laws at issue, to the point that confused talk, even sheer noise, can be re- or misinterpreted at times as intelligible. This is true of read words too, as missing or wrongly arranged letters are filled in or recombined in the correct order by the reader.[739]

Poorer hence cognitively more challenging sensorial or graphic circumstances, such as bad handwriting, erroneous typesetting or unergonomic design, may cause inexorable ambiguities and therefore serious failures in communication, precisely because they trespass the *Gestalt* laws at issue.[740] If they are to be successful, rhetorical tropes operating upon signifiers are likely to be cases of stringent adherence to the laws. Without any doubt, many tropes operate this way, e.g. Julius Caesar's immortal asyndeton *cum* alliteration, "*veni, vidi, vici*", which exploits both the proximity of the three verbal forms by elision of conjunctions and their similarity in initial sound/grapheme, length and tense.

Nevertheless, obscurity, ambiguities and partial communicative failures can be used too in order to force the listener/reader to listen/read more carefully, think more intently upon, and/or enjoy exposure to a given speech or text. Time-honoured figures of obscuring such as enigma, schematismus, noema or skotison constitute blatant examples of just such possible uses. Even apparent errors (e.g. barbarisms, solecisms) and most shocking communicative twists (e.g. cacozelia, soraismus) can be used in order to achieve the classical rhetorician's goal of persuasion. The same is true of the modern rhetorician's goal of "adherence"[741] or "consubstantiality" between the communicator and her audience, which persuasion presupposes.[742]

Rhetorically, what the communicator wants is for the audience to respond as she wishes, whether it is for the sake of experiencing their togetherness (i.e. sheer adherence or consubstantiality), laugh at her jokes (e.g. a stand-up comedian), reflect critically on their own prejudices (e.g. the Socratic method), or follow her advice (i.e.

persuasion and self-persuasion—the communicator and the audience being frequently one and the same).[743]

As long and insofar as it is effective, the communicator may seek striking deviation from the law, e.g. Shakespeare's (1564–1616) frequent apocope "oft" in lieu of "often". Moreover, the trespassed law is presupposed nonetheless by the striking deviation for the sake of the trope's effectiveness, insofar as a deviation that moves too far away from its relevant law is going to fail excessively in its communicative capacity and cease to be striking, e.g. by pushing further the apocope above and using the ambiguous and confusing "of" in lieu of "often". In short, the *Gestalt* laws of organisation can apply *via positiva* as well as *via negativa* (hence the markings "p" and "n" in the classification offered below).

As the former family of tropes is concerned, concepts or meanings can be manipulated rhetorically for the various ends individuated above, both ancient and modern. This too can be done *via positiva*, i.e. by seeking completeness, proximity, similarity, continuity, coherence or simplicity; or *via negativa*, i.e. by means of incompleteness, retraction, dissimilarity, discontinuity, incoherence or complexity.

Concerning the criteria that make such rhetorical manipulations forceful or notable, none is given in this chapter. In all things rhetorical, the proof is in the pudding. Whatever strikes a chord and brings the point home, that is forceful or notable enough. And although the most skilled rhetorician will do her best to predict and deploy what works, that cannot be determined *a priori* once and for all. Blunders await her too. Rhetoric is an art, not an algorithm. Consistently with the rhetorical notion of *kairos* or appropriateness to the circumstances, such forcefulness and notability are bound to change with the audience: fourth-grade school children are likely to respond to fairly basic and trite tropes, which sophisticated literati would promptly see through and dismiss instead as stuffy artifices.

How to Read the Classificatory Table

In *Gestalt* psychology, it is recognised that more than one law can operate at the same time, whether in a state of conflict (e.g. optical illusions) or cooperation (i.e. achieving *Prägnanz* or "good form"), and it may be sometimes difficult to determine which ones are at work, due to partial overlap between or amid the laws.[744]

For the sake of economy, the table offered below attributes to each rhetorical trope as few relevant *Gestalt* laws as possible, meaning one for most, two for some, and three for exceptional cases. Without forgetting that, following Tucker's lead on the subject, the figure/ground law applies to all tropes and therefore needs no inclusion in the table. As a result, differing interpretations could be plausible at times, e.g. tapinosis might fall under either similarity *via positiva* or good continuation *via negativa*, if not both. I do acknowledge such potential alternative interpretations and welcome any further studies in the classificatory endeavour deployed in this chapters.

Numerous and lengthy examples can be easily retrieved on the rich online archive *Silva Rhetoricae* of Dr Gideon Burton of Brigham Young University, which I myself have utilised extensively, especially as regards selecting denominations for the tropes. Often, given the great age of rhetoric as a reflexive organised discipline, many alternative names are available for the same linguistic phenomenon. In general, the oldest Greek names have been preferred here, if available, accompanied by one of their Latin equivalents (not all Latin terms are of classical origin; several were handed down to us by later rhetoricians, especially early modern ones).

Short examples are offered too, mostly in connection with lesser known, complex or obscure tropes. Also, some tropes are general and generic enough not to preclude the extensive use of other tropes within them (e.g. accumulation, exergasia, icon). In my classification, I limit their assessment to the likeliest laws making each a possibly effective, distinct trope.

In the classificatory table that follows the present text, four markings are used: "1" stands for figures of thought; "2" for figures of speech; "1/2" is used for figures that, depending on the operation performed, may then belong to either "1" or "2" (e.g. antiptosis); "p" stands for compliance with the law; "n" for deviation from the law; whilst the Roman numerals I–VI correspond to the definitions of the *Gestalt* laws provided above.

Tab.1

Name	Definition	Type	I	II	III	IV	V	VI
Abecedarian	An acrostic whose letters follow the order, more or less, of the alphabet, e.g. "active, bold, cunning, daring"	2	p			p		
Accismus	A feigned refusal of what is earnestly desired, e.g. "You are far too kind in talking about my accomplishments!"	1					n	
Accumulatio	Bringing the proofs together and presenting them again in a compact, climactic way leading to the desired conclusion	1	p	p		p		
Acoloutha	The substitution of reciprocal words, e.g. "shape" and "figure"	1			p			
Acrostic	When the first letters of successive lines are arranged in such a way as to spell a word	2	p					
Acyrologia, Improprietas	An incorrect, comedic use of words sounding alike but far in meaning, e.g. Malapropisms	2			p			
Acyron	The use of a word repugnant or contrary to what is meant, e.g. "crooks like you can offer this glory to us all"	1				n	n	
Adhortatio	A commandment, promise, or exhortation intended to move one's consent or desires, e.g. "yes, we can!"	1						p

Name	Definition	Type	I	II	III	IV	V	VI
Adianoeta	An expression that, in addition to an obvious meaning, carries a subtler meaning, e.g. "she does look fair"	1			p		p	
Adnominatio	Assigning to a proper name its literal or homophonic meaning, e.g. "As tall as a child, Mr. Short plays no basketball"	1/2			p		p	
Adynaton, Impossibilia	An open declaration of impossibility, e.g. "try as hard and long as you wish, but this cannot be done"	1						p
Aetiologia, Redditio causae	Attributing a cause for a statement or claim made, e.g. "I trust them, for they are wise"	1					p	
Aganactesis, Indignatio	An exclamation proceeding from deep indignation	1						p
Allegory, Allegoria	A sustained metaphor continued through whole sentences or a discourse	1			p			
Alliteration, Homeoprophoron	Repetition of the same letter or sound within nearby words; often, initial consonants, e.g. "let love live long"	2		p	p			
Amphibologia, Ambiguitas	Ambiguity, typically occasioned by mistaken punctuation, "let's all, eat grandpa"	1				n		
Ampliatio	Using the name of something or someone before it has obtained that name or after the reason for that name has ceased, e.g. "Leningrad" before 1924 or after 1991	1				p		
Anacephalaeosis, Enumeratio	A well-flowing final recapitulation of the relevant proofs to support the conclusion	1	p	p		p		
Anacoenosis, Communicacio	Asking the opinion or judgment of the judges or audience, usually implying agreement	1				n		

Name	Definition	Type	I	II	III	IV	V	VI
Anacoloutha	Substituting one word with another in a non-reciprocal fashion, e.g. "light" and "glory"	1			p			
Anacoluthon	Grammatical or logical interruption, e.g. "That man was a known gambler – so what?"	1				n		
Anadiplosis, Reduplicatio	Repeating the last word or phrase from the previous line, clause, or sentence at the beginning of the next	2		p	p			
Anamnesis, Recollectio	Citing a relevant past author from memory, e.g. "Dostoyevsky said that beauty will save us"	1				p		
Anangeon	Arguing on the basis of inevitability or necessity, e.g. "we must bail out Wall Street, there is no alternative"	1						p
Anaphora, Repetitio	Repetition of the same word or group of words at the beginning of successive clauses, sentences, or lines	2		p	p			
Anapodoton	A figure in which a main clause is suggested by the introduction of a subordinate clause, but that main clause never occurs, e.g. "If you think I am going to sit here quietly..."	1	n			n		
Anastrophe, Trajectio	Departure from normal word order for the sake of emphasis, e.g. "peace it is that I seek"	1				n		
Anemographia	Vivid description of the wind through sound and rhythm, e.g. "swift softer gushes of southern Zephyr whirl suddenly"	2			p			
Anesis, Abating	Adding a concluding sentence that diminishes the effect of what has just been said	1				n		
Antanaclasis, Refractio	Repeating a word or phrase whose meaning changes in the second instance, "I fast, but won't be fast"	2		p	p			

Name	Definition	Type	I	II	III	IV	V	VI
Antanagoge, Compensatio	Putting a positive spin on something that is acknowledged to be negative or difficult	1				n		
Anthimeria	Substitution of one part of speech for another, such as a verb used as a noun, "have a good sing!"	2			p			
Anthropopatheia, Condescensio	Ascribing human attributes to God, e.g. "God's merciful hand lifted them from misery and despair"	1			p			
Anthypophora, Rogatio	Asking and then immediately answering one's own questions, or imaginary objections	1					p	
Anticategoria, Accusatio adversa	A retort in which one turns the accusation made by one's adversary back against him	1					p	
Antilogy	A contradiction either in terms or ideas, e.g. "we will bomb them all for the sake of peace and human rights"	1			n		p	
Antimetabole, Commutatio	Repetition of words in successive clauses in reverse grammatical order: "we love a deal and deal in love"	2		p	p		p	
Antimetathesis	Inversion of the members of an antithesis	1/2					p	
Antiphrasis, Dictio contrarium significans	Irony of one word, through patent contradiction, e.g. "here's the giant!" (about a very short person)	1					n	
Antiprosopopeia, Antipersonification	The representation of persons as inanimate objects, e.g. "that mountain walked in and terrified us all"	1			p			
Antiptosis, Casus pro casu	An enallage substituting one grammatical case for another, e.g. "little wee me did it", or "me es fecit" (instead of "mihi")	1/2			p			
Antirrhesis	Rejecting reprehensively the opinion or authority of someone, e.g. "Marxism is an obsolete, subversive doctrine!"	1						p

Name	Definition	Type	I	II	III	IV	V	VI
Antisagoge	Using hypotheses to illustrate antithetical alternative consequences, e.g. "if we do it we live, if not we die"	1					p	
Antistasis, Refractio	The repetition of a word in a contrary sense, e.g. Benjamin Franklin's "Your argument is sound, all sound"	2			p		p	
Antisthecon, Littera pro littera	Substitution of one sound, syllable, or letter for another within a word, e.g. puns	2	n		p			
Antithesis, Contrarium	Juxtaposition of contrasting ideas or words in parallel structure, e.g. "it's his right, but it feels so wrong"	1					p	
Antitheton, Compositium ex contrariis	A proof or composition constructed of contraries, e.g. "it may start well, but there is no glory in the end"	1					p	
Antonomasia, Pronominatio	Substituting a descriptive phrase for a proper name, e.g. "the man without the eye is Israel's new president"	1			p			
Apagoresis	A statement designed to inhibit someone from doing something, e.g. "don't you dare move an inch away!"	1						p
Aphaeresis, Ablatio	The omission of a syllable or letter at the beginning of a word "'mory" instead of "armory"	2	n					
Aphorismus	Calling into question the proper use of a word, e.g. "I am an MIT economist, who has just lost all her money"	1						n
Apocarteresis	Casting of all hope away from one thing and placing it on another source altogether	1						p
Apocope, Abcisio	Omitting a letter or syllable at the end of a word, e.g. "oft" instead of "often"	2	n					
Apodioxis, Rejectio	Rejecting of someone or something, such as the adversary's argument, as bad	1						p

Name	Definition	Type	I	II	III	IV	V	VI
Apodixis	Proving a statement by referring to common knowledge or general experience	1						p
Apologue	Presenting proofs through comparisons made in form of a fable that simplifies the matter being considered	1			p			p
Apophasis, Expeditio	The rejection of several reasons and affirming a single one, considered most valid	1						p
Apoplanesis	Promising to address the issue but effectively dodging it through a digression	1						n
Aporia, Addubitatio	Deliberating with oneself or the audience as though in doubt over some matter	1				n		
Aposiopesis, Praecisio	Breaking off suddenly, usually to portray being overcome with emotion, e.g. "Alas! I cannot continue!"	1				n		
Apostrophe, Aversio	Turning one's speech from one audience to another, e.g. "and you, history's wisdom, what can you teach us today?"	1				n		
Ara, Execracio	Cursing or expressing detest towards a person or thing	1						p
Aschematiston, Aschematismus	The use of plain, unadorned or unornamented language	1						p
Asphalia	Offering oneself as a guarantee, "they may falter, but I am ready to face the enemy and death, if needed"	1						p
Assonance	Repeating similar vowel sounds, preceded and followed by different consonants, in the stressed syllables of adjacent words, e.g. "I wanna try whatever gonna take to gotta do it"	2		p	p			
Assumption	The introduction of a different point to be considered, e.g. "though now consider the fate he suffered"	1				n		

Name	Definition	Type	I	II	III	IV	V	VI
Asteismus, Facetia	Throwing back a term used by the first speaker with an unexpected twist, e.g. "yes, vain, glory it is yours to attain"	2				n	p	
Astrothesia	A vivid description of stars	1				p		
Asyndeton, Dissolutio	The omission of conjunctions between clauses, resulting in force or hurried rhythm, e.g. "veni, vidi, vici"	2		p				
Auxesis, Incrementio	Arranging words or clauses in a sequence of increasing force	1		p		p		
Barbarism	The use of nonstandard or foreign speech	1/2				n		
Battologia	Overbearing, pointless repetition, e.g. "psychology is the scientific science of the mind by scientific means"	2			p			
Bdelygmia, Abominatio	Expressing vocal hatred and abhorrence of a person, word, or deed, e.g. "what a horrible person!"	1						p
Benedictio	A blessing, e.g. "God bless Iceland"	1						p
Bomphiologia, Verborum bombus	Self-aggrandising exaggeration, e.g. "I am the Jesus Christ of politics"	1			p	n		
Brachylogia, Articulus	The absence of conjunctions between single words, e.g. "Observe, learn, reflect, try, endure, fight, win"	2		p				
Cacemphaton, Turpiloquum	An expression that is deliberately foul or ill-sounding, e.g. "this play is shit compared to the rest"	1/2						p
Cacosyntheton, Male collocutum	The unpleasing order of words, e.g. "now though the fate consider that he suffered"	2				n		
Cacozelia	Use of bad taste to make the facts appear worse or disgust the auditors, e.g. "her putrid words you heard"	1						p
Catachresis, Abusio	The use of a word in a context that differs from its proper one, e.g. "the table's legs"	1			p			

Name	Definition	Type	I	II	III	IV	V	VI
Catacosmesis, Ordo	Ordering words from greatest to least in dignity, or in correct order of time, e.g. "breakfast, lunch, dinner"	1	p			p		
Cataphasis, Affirmatio	A paralipsis in which one explicitly affirms the negative qualities that one then passes over	1				n	p	
Cataplexis	Threatening or prophesying payback for ill doing, e.g. "God shall punish those that betray their partner"	1						p
Categoria, Accusatio	Breaking open the secret wickedness of one's adversary before her face	1						p
Characterismus	The description of a person's character	1				p		
Charientismus, Graciosa nugutio	Mollifying harsh words by answering them with a smooth and appeasing mock	1				n		
Chiasmus	Repetition of ideas or grammatical structures in inverted order, e.g. "trust he deserves to merit our faith"	1/2					p	
Chorographia	The description of a particular nation	1				p		
Chreia	Employing a relevant anecdote which relates a saying or deed of someone well known	1			p			
Chronographia	Vivid representation of a certain historical or recurring time (e.g. the seasons of the year)	1				p		
Circumlocution	Talking around something by supplying a longer alternative description	1			p			
Climax, Gradatio	The arrangement of words, phrases, or clauses in an order of increasing importance	1	p			p		
Coenotes	Repetition of two different phrases: one at the beginning and the other at the end of successive paragraphs.	2		p	p			

Name	Definition	Type	I	II	III	IV	V	VI
Colon, Membrum	Completing a sentence with a second clause, e.g. "he loves her truly, since the first moment they met"	1				p	p	
Communicatio	To include one's audience overtly in a discourse, e.g. "now, you all know that I have never lied to you"	1				n		
Comprobatio	Approving and commending a virtue, e.g. "courage is what our people need most of all"	1						p
Conceit	An extended metaphor exploring the metaphoric possibilities in the qualities associated with a subject	1			p			
Conduplicatio	Repetition of words in adjacent phrases or clauses, e.g. "to end this war, we must end her wicked rule"	2		p	p			
Congeries	Piling up words of differing meaning but leading all to a similar emotional effect	1		p		p		
Consonance	The repetition of consonants in words stressed in the same place but whose vowels differ	2		p	p			
Contempt, Exouthenismus	An expression of contempt	1						p
Correctio	The amending of a term or phrase just employed, e.g. "love is madness, namely a sickness of the soul"	1				n	p	
Deesis, Obsecratio	The vehement expression of desire, e.g. "I want to see our nation united, strong and respected!"	1						p
Dehortatio	Deliberate dissuasion, e.g. "you shouldn't try, you don't have the right physique"	1						p
Dendrographia	Vivid description of a tree	1				p		
Deprecatio	A heartfelt prayer for the removal of some evil, e.g. "libera nos a malo, Domine!"	1						p

Name	Definition	Type	I	II	III	IV	V	VI
Descriptio	An exposition of the consequences of an act, e.g. "if she shops any more, her children will starve to death"	1				p		
Diacope	Repetition of a word with one or more between, e.g. "Senseless! What a waste! Senseless!"	2		p	p			
Diaeresis, Partitio	Dividing one syllable into two, especially contiguous vowels, e.g. "it happened in medi-eval times"	1/2	p	p				
Dialogismus	Speaking as someone else, e.g. "'I thought it was a bit of innocent fun' she said to him, but it was not"	1				n		
Dialysis, Divisio	Spelling out alternatives or either-or arguments to conclude, e.g. "To avoid imbalance, either pull here or push there"	1	p				p	
Dianoea, Subjectio	The use of lively questions and answers, e.g. "Why me? Because I am honest! Why now? For you are too!""	1					p	
Diaphora	Repetition of a common name so as to perform two logical functions, e.g. "boys will be boys"	2		p	p			
Diaskeue	Graphic description of circumstances to arouse emotions, e.g. "her peeling skin was covered with pus and red sores"	1				p		
Diastole, Ectasis	To lengthen a vowel or syllable beyond its typical length, e.g. end couplet "hit him hard, that great bastard!"	2			p	n		
Diasyrmus, Irrisio	Rejecting arguments via ridiculous comparison, e.g. "Smith's invisible hand is a child's imaginary friend"	1			p			
Diazeugma, Disjunctio	The figure whereby a single subject governs more verbs or verbal constructions, e.g. "he came, saw, won"	1						p

Name	Definition	Type	I	II	III	IV	V	VI
Dicaeologia	Admitting what's charged against one, but excusing it by necessity, e.g. "he did it, but couldn't avoid it"	1					p	
Digression, *Excursus*	A departure from logical progression in a speech	1				n		
Dilemma	Offering to an opponent a choice between two equally unfavorable alternatives, e.g. "pain or ridicule?"	1					p	
Dirimens copulatio	Balancing one statement with a contrary/qualifying statement, e.g. "love, though thought through by age"	1					p	
Distinctio	Eliminating ambiguity surrounding a word by explicitly specifying each of its distinct meanings	1			n			p
Distributio	Assigning roles among, or specifying the duties of, a list of people	1	p					
Ecphonesis, Exclamatio	Emotional exclamation, e.g. "For goodness' sake!"	1						p
Ecphrasis	Literary description of a work of art	1				p		
Ecthlipsis, Elisio	The omission or elision of letters or syllables for the sake of poetical meter	1	n					
Effictio, Blazon	A verbal depiction of someone's body	1				p		
Egersis, Excitatio	To excite an audience, especially out of a stupor or boredom	1				n		
Elenchus	A logical refutation or cross-examination (as in Socrates' irony or pars destruens)	1	p			p		
Elimination, *Expeditio*	After enumerating all possibilities by which something could have occurred, all but one are eliminated	1	p					
Ellipsis, *Defectus*	Omission of a word or short phrase easily understood in context	1	n					

Name	Definition	Type	I	II	III	IV	V	VI
Emphasis	Giving prominence to a quality or trait by conceiving it as constituting the very substance in which it inheres	1						p
Enallage	The substitution of grammatically different but semantically equivalent constructions	1			p			
Enantiosis, Contentio	Using opposing or contrary descriptions together, typically in a somewhat paradoxical manner	1					p	
Enargia, Descriptio, Representatio	Generic name for a group of figures aiming at vivid, lively description	1/2				p		
Encomium	Praising a person or thing, on a smaller scale than an entire speech	1						p
Energia	A general term referring to the "energy" or vigor of an expression	1/2						p
Enigma, Sermo obscurus	Obscuring one's meaning by presenting it within a riddle or by means that challenge the reader or hearer	1						n
Ennoia, Invitio	The purposeful holding back of information that nevertheless hints at what is meant	1				n	n	
Enthymeme, Conclusio	Truncated syllogisms typical of ordinary discourse, e.g. "trust him not, for he is a pagan"	1	n					
Epanalepsis, Resumptio	Repetition at the end of a line/phrase/clause of the words occurring at the beginning, e.g. "a lie begets a lie"	2		p	p			
Epanodos, Reditus as propositum	Repeating the main proofs or themes in the course of one' speech and/or providing additional detail	1				p	p	
Epanorthosis, Correctio	Amending a first thought by making it stronger or more vehement, e.g. "I'm so hungry today! I could eat you alive!"	1				.	n	p

Name	Definition	Type	I	II	III	IV	V	VI
Epenthesis, Interpositio	The addition of a letter, sound, or syllable to the middle of a word, e.g. "cursorary" in lieu of "cursory"	2	p		p			
Epergesis, Appositio	Interposing an apposition, often in order to clarify what has just been stated	1				n		
Epexegesis	Interpreting what one has just said, e.g. "it is the invisible brain, i.e. the irrationality of deregulated markets"	1					p	
Epicrisis, Adjudicatio	Quoting a relevant passage to comment upon it	1				p		
Epilogus, Conclusio	Providing an inference of what is likely to follow, e.g. "as shown in detail later on, these events are likely to bode well"	1	p			p		
Epimone, Commoratio	Persistent repetition of the same plea in much the same words, "Save him, bring him back, rescue him!"	1		p	p			
Epiphonema, Acclamatio	An epigrammatic summary which gathers into a pithy sentence what has preceded	1				p		p
Epiplexis, Increpacio	Asking questions in order to chide, to express grief, or to inveigh, e.g. "Why am I not dead?"	1				n		
Epistrophe, Conversio	Ending a series of lines, phrases, clauses, or sentences with the same word or words	2		p	p			
Episynaloephe, Conglutinatio	Blending two syllables together into one, the opposite of diaeresis	2	p					
Epitasis	The addition of a concluding sentence that merely emphasises what has already been stated	1						p
Epitheton, Appositio	Addition of an adjacent, coordinate, explanatory or descriptive element, "John Locke, known liberal thinker"	1		p				
Epitrochasmus, Percursio	To touch rapidly on one point and then another, e.g. "He loved Spain, she cheated her clients, we played snooker"	1		p				

Name	Definition	Type	I	II	III	IV	V	VI
Epitrope	Turning things over to one's hearers so as to suggest a proof of something without having to state it	1				n		
Epizeugma, Adjunctio	Placing the verb that holds together the entire sentence either at the very beginning or the very ending of that sentence, so as to emphasise it, e.g. "Bought are by Wall Street all congressmen, left and right"	1						p
Epizeuxis, Iteratio	Repetition of words with no others between, for vehemence or emphasis, e.g. "faith, faith alone will save us"	2		p	p			
Ethopoeia, Moralis confictio	The description and portrayal of a character	1				p		
Eucharistia	Giving thanks for a benefit received	1						p
Euche, Promissio	A vow to keep a promise	1						p
Eulogia	Pronouncing a blessing for the goodness in a person	1						p
Euphemism	Substituting a more favorable for a pejorative or socially delicate term, e.g. "soulless cocoon" for "corpse"	1			p			
Eustathia	Promising constancy in purpose and affection	1						p
Eutrepismus, Ordinatio	Numbering and ordering the parts under consideration, e.g. "First we open this, secondly that, third the eye"	1	p					
Example, Paradigma	Amplifying a point by providing a relevant, true or feigned example	1				p		
Exergasia, Expolitio	Repetition of the same idea, changing either its words, its delivery, or the general treatment it is given	1			p			
Geographia	Vivid representation of the earth	1				p		
Graecismus	Using Greek words, examples, or grammatical structures, so as to show superior knowledge	1				n		

Name	Definition	Type	I	II	III	IV	V	VI
Hendiadys, Endiadis	Expressing a single idea by two nouns instead of a noun and its qualifier, "the distinction and figure of him"	1			p			
Heterogenium	Avoiding an issue by changing the subject to something different	1				n		
Homeosis	Beautifying, enforcing and enlarging language through comparison by icons, parabolas or paradigms	1			p			
Homiologia, Sermo ubique sui similis	Inane repetition, e.g. "market forces unleash the market magic of market rewards and market miracles"	1/2		p	p			
Homoioptoton, Similiter cadens	The repetition of similar case endings in adjacent words or in words in parallel position	2		p	p		p	
Homoioteleuton, Similiter desinens	Similarity of endings of adjacent or parallel words	2		p	p		p	
Horismus, Definitio	Providing a clear, brief definition, e.g. "Truth is opinion supported by reason"	1						p
Hydrographia	Vivid description of water	1				p		
Hypallage, Submutatio	Shifting the application of words, e.g. "The eye of man hath not heard, the ear of man hath not seen"	1					p	
Hyperbaton, Transgressio	Adding a word or thought to a sentence that is semantically complete, thus emphasising the addition	1	p					p
Hyperbole, Superlatio	Rhetorical exaggeration, e.g. "you never listen to me!"	1			p			p
Hypozeugma	Placing last in a construction with several words or phrases of equal value the word(s) they all depend on	1						p
Hypozeuxis	Every clause has its own verb: the opposite of zeugma	1					p	
Hysterologia, Prepostera loquutio	Interposing a phrase between a preposition and its object, often a vice	1				n		

Name	Definition	Type	I	II	III	IV	V	VI
Hysteron proteron, Praeposteratio	Disorder of time or logical sequence, e.g. "Go to bed and brush your teeth"	1				n		
Icon	Painting, or comparing to another's, the likeness of a person	1			p	p		
Inopinatum	The expression of one's inability to believe or conceive of something, e.g. "It is unthinkable that..."	1						p
Insinuatio	Securing the audience's good will within the exordium with statements playing into their prejudice and expectations	1						p
Inter se pugnantia	Using direct address to reprove someone before an audience, e.g. "You the well-paid expert did not see it!"	1				p		p
Intimation	Hinting at a meaning but not stating it explicitly, e.g. "the alleged experts of our government state that..."	1					n	
Irony, Dissimulatio	Speaking in such a way as to imply the contrary of what one says	1					n	
Isocolon	A series of similarly structured elements having the same length, e.g. "out of jail, have a meal, come to sail"	1/2			p	p		
Litotes, Diminutio	Deliberate understatement, especially when mirroring a thought by denying its opposite	1					n	
Macrologia, Sedulitas superflua	Long-windedness	1				n		n
Martyria, Testatio	Confirming something by referring to one's own experience	1				p		p
Maxim, Proverb, Gnome, Adagium	Short, pithy sayings or traditional expressions of wisdom consistent with the point made	1				p		p
Medela	When you can't deny or defend friends' faults and seek to heal them with good words	1						p

Name	Definition	Type	I	II	III	IV	V	VI
Mempsis	Expressing complaint and seeking help	1						p
Merismus, Distributio	The dividing of a whole into its parts	1	p					
Mesarchia	The repetition of the same word or words at the beginning and middle of successive sentences	2		p	p			
Mesodiplosis, Mesophonia	Repetition of the same word or words in the middle of successive sentences	2		p	p			
Mesozeugma, Conjunctio	A zeugma in which one places a common verb for many subjects in the middle of a construction	1						p
Metabasis, Transitio	A transitional statement in which one explains what has been discussed until then and what will be said next	1				p	p	
Metalepsis, Transumptio	Reference to something by means of another thing that is indirectly related to it, e.g. "blazing love"	1			p			
Metallage, Materialis	A word or phrase is treated as an object within another expression, e.g. "they say 'reform' but mean 'poverty' by it"	1				n		
Metaphor, Translatio	A comparison made by referring to one thing as another, "King Richard is a lion"	1			p			
Metastasis, Transmotionem	Denying and turning back on your adversaries arguments used against you	1					p	
Metathesis, Transposicio	The transposition of letters within a word, e.g. "theatre" as "theater"	2	p		p			
Metonymy, Hypallage, Denominatio	Reference to something or someone by naming one of its attributes, e.g. "the pen is mightier than the sword"	1	n		p			
Mimesis, Imitatio	The imitation of another's gestures, pronunciation, or utterance	1/2			p			

Name	Definition	Type	I	II	III	IV	V	VI
Mycterismus, Subsannatio	A mock given with an accompanying gesture, such as a scornful countenance	1						p
Noema	An obscure and subtle speech	1						n
Oenismus, Optatio	Expressing a wish, often ardently	1						p
Ominatio	A prophecy of evil	1						p
Onedismus, Exprobatio	Reproaching someone for being impious or ungrateful	1						p
Onomatopoeia, Nominatio	Using or inventing a word whose sound imitates that which it names, e.g. "buzzing bees"	2			p			
Orcos	Swearing that a statement is true	1						p
Oxymoron	A compressed paradox, e.g. "pious orgy"	1		p			p	
Paenismus	Expressing joy for blessings obtained or an evil avoided	1						p
Parabola, Parabole	Drawing of a parallel between two essentially dissimilar things, especially with a moral or didactic purpose	1					p	
Paradiastole	Referring to a vice as a virtue, e.g. "greed is good"	1					p	
Paradiegesis	An introductory narrative used to open a speech	1				p		
Paradox	A statement that is self-contradictory on the surface, yet seems to evoke a truth nonetheless, e.g. "love is pain"	1					p	
Paraenesis, Admonitio	A warning of impending evil, e.g. "Beware the drums of war! Wars bring only death and despair!"	1						p
Paragoge, Preassumpcio	The addition of a letter or syllable to the end of a word, e.g. "fabulouso"	2	p					
Paralipsis, Praeteritio	Stating and drawing attention to something in the very act of pretending to pass it over	1					n	
Parallelism	Similarity of structure in a pair or series of related ideas, words, phrases, or clauses	1/2					p	

Name	Definition	Type	I	II	III	IV	V	VI
Paramythia, Consolatio	An expression of consolation and encouragement	1						p
Paregmenon	The repetition of a word or its cognates in a short sentence, e.g. "Social-democracy dies for the greed of the greedy"	2		p	p			
Parelcon	The use of redundant or superfluous terms, e.g. "the damaging blow caused much damage to his jaw"	2		p	p			
Parembole	An interruprion whose matter has a connection to the sentence subject	1				p	n	
Parenthesis, Interpositio	An interruprion whose matter has not a connection to the sentence subject	1					n	
Pareuresis, Excusatio	To put forward a convincing excuse	1						p
Paroemion	Alliteration taken to an extreme where nearly every word in a sentence begins with the same consonant	2		p	p			
Paromoiosis	Parallelism of sound between the words of adjacent clauses whose lengths are equal or almost equal	2					p	
Paromologia, Concessio	Admitting a weaker point in order to make a stronger one, "I have no PhD, but the experiment is irrefutable"	1					p	
Paronomasia, Allusio	Using words that sound alike but that differ in meaning, e.g. puns	2			p			
Parrhesia, Licentia	Either to speak candidly or to ask forgiveness for so speaking	1						p
Pathopoeia, Exuscitatio	Stirring others by one's own vehement feeling	1						p
Perclusio	A threat against someone, or something	1						p
Period, Circumductum	Whole periodic sentence characterised by the suspension of the completion of sense until its end (cf. German and Latin)	1	n					

Name	Definition	Type	I	II	III	IV	V	VI
Periphrasis	The substitution of a descriptive word or phrase for a proper name or, conversely, the use of a proper name as a shorthand to stand for qualities associated with it, e.g. "he is a Borgia in marketing strategies"	1			p			
Peristasis, Circumstantiae descriptio	A description of attendant circumstances	1				p		
Philophronesis	The pacification of an adversary by use of mild speech or promises	1						p
Pleonasm, Superabundantia	Use of more words in a sentence than is necessary semantically, typically a vice	1	p			n		
Ploce, Conduplicatio	General term for the repetition of a single word for rhetorical emphasis, e.g. "public banks mean wealth for the public"	2			p			
Polyptoton, Adnominatio	Using a cognate of another word in close proximity, e.g. "the courageous priest is brave in uniting zeal and humility"	1		p	p			
Polysindeton, Acervatio	Employing many conjunctions between clauses, often slowing the tempo or rhythm, i.e. "and... and... and... and..."	2		p	p			
Pragmatographia	The description of an action	1				p		
Procatalepsis, Praeoccupatio	Refuting anticipated objections	1				p	p	
Proclees	Challenging one's adversary	1						p
Prodiorthosis	A statement intended to prepare one's audience for something shocking or offensive that will follow	1				p		p
Proechtesis, Expositio	When, in conclusion of a series of observations, a justifying reason is provided	1	p			p		
Prolepsis, Anticipation	Speaking of something future as already done or existing, e.g. "in Paradise, I alternate rest and music"	1						p

Name	Definition	Type	I	II	III	IV	V	VI
Prosapodosis	Providing a reason for each division of a statement in parallel fashion	1					p	
Proslepsis, Circumductio	Paralipsis taken to its extreme, i.e. offering details of something in the very act of pretending to pass it over	1					p	
Prosopographia	Vivid description of someone's face	1				p		
Prosopopeia, Personification	Personification, e.g. "the Market tells governments what to do, not the voters"	1			p			
Protherapeia	Preparing one's audience for what one is about to say through conciliating words	1						p
Prothesis	The addition of a letter or syllable to the beginning of a word, "Amuch we ate"	2	p					
Protrope, Adhortatio	A call to action, often by using threats or promises	1						p
Prozeugma, Praeiunctio	A series of clauses in which the verb employed in the first is ellided and thus implied in the others	1					n	
Pysma, Quaesitio	The asking of multiple questions one after another	1		p				
Ratiocinatio	Reasoning by asking questions at regular intervals	1					p	
Repetitio	Repeating the same word variously throughout a sentence or discourse	2		p	p			
Repotia	The repetition of a phrase in the same discourse with differences in style, diction, tone, etc.	2		p	n			
Restrictio	Making an exception to a previously made statement, e.g. "seeking profit is fine, except when it is the sole aim of man"	1					p	
Rhetorical question, Erotema	To affirm or deny a point strongly by asking it as a question, i.e. a standard rhetorical question	1					n	p

Name	Definition	Type	I	II	III	IV	V	VI
Sarcasm, Amara irrisio	Use of mockery, verbal taunts, or bitter jokes, e.g. "he is so religious, so pious, so devoted, that he worships money"	1						p
Scesis onomaton	A series of successive, synonymous expressions, e.g. "we were overwhelmed by their force, their power, their strength"	1		p	p			
Schematismus	Concealing a meaning by using figurative language, e.g. "the great frog of Portugal shall leap into the forest and thrive"	1						n
Sermocinatio, Dialogue	Speaking dramatically in the first person for someone else, using appropriate language for that person	1				p		
Simile, Similitudo	An explicit comparison using "like" or "as"	1			p			
Skotison	Purposeful obscurity	1/2						n
Solecism	An element of speech or writing that is blatantly incorrect grammatically or otherwise	1/2				n		
Soraismus, Cumulatio	To mingle different languages affectedly to show erudition, though often a vice	2				n		
Sorites	A chain of enthymemes	1				p		
Syllepsis, Conglutinata conceptio	A single word governs two or more others and has different meanings, e.g. "holding hands and breath"	1		p	n			
Syllogismus	The use of a remark or an image which calls upon the audience to draw an obvious yet unstated conclusion	1	n					p
Symperasma, Athroesmus	A conclusion that includes a brief summary of the foregoing	1				p		
Symploce, Circulo rhetorica	The combination of anaphora and epistrophe	2		p	p			

Name	Definition	Type	I	II	III	IV	V	VI
Synaeresis	When two syllables are contracted into one, e.g. "New Orleans" pronounced "Nawlins"	2	n	p				
Synaloepha, Deletio	Omitting one of two vowels occurring at the end of one word and the beginning of another, e.g. "th'eternal"	2	n	p				
Synchysis, Confusio	The confused arrangement of words in a sentence, usually a vice	1						n
Syncope, Consicio	Cutting letters or syllables from the middle of a word, e.g. "defin'ly" instead of "definitely"	2	n					
Syncrisis	Comparison and contrast in parallel clauses, e.g. "we praise justice; they decry the penalty"	1					p	
Synecdoche, Intellectio	A whole is represented by naming one of its parts or vice versa, e.g. "the police came to my door"	1	n		p			
Synoeciosis, Contrapositum	A coupling of contraries yet not contrasted, e.g. "the day's light excites us, the night's darkness inspires us"	1					p	
Synonymia, Nominis communio	In general, the use of several synonyms together to amplify or explain a given subject or term	1			p			
Synthesis, Compositio	An apt arrangement of a composition regarding the sounds of adjoining syllables and words	2		p				
Syntheton, Combinatio	When by convention two words are joined by a conjunction for emphasis, e.g. "bride and groom"	1		p				
Systole, Contractio	To make short a naturally long vowel, e.g. end couplet "live for the thrill, try this new reel"	2			p	n		
Systrophe	The listing of qualities or descriptions of someone or something, without providing an explicit definition	1				p		

Name	Definition	Type	I	II	III	IV	V	VI
Tapinosis, Humiliatio	Giving X a name that diminishes it in importance, e.g. emperor Caligula as "little boots"	1				n		
Tasis, Extensio	Sustaining the pronunciation of a word or phrase because of its pleasant sound, e.g. "doctor love"	2						p
Tautologia, Inutilis repetitio eiusdem	The unnecessary repetition of the same idea in different words	1			p			
Thaumasmus	To marvel at something rather than to state it in a matter of fact way	1						p
Tmesis, Dissectio	Interjecting a word or phrase between syllables or parts of a word, e.g. "where love ever may lead us"	2				n		
Topographia	Description of a place	1				p		
Topothesia	The description of an imaginary place	1				p		
Tricolon	Three parallel equivalent elements in a concise series, e.g. "taste, trust, force – that's a gentleman in a nutshell"	2		p	p		p	

Continuities with Older Classifications

The reader who has a broader knowledge of rhetorical tropes is likely to note certain lines of continuity with traditional classifications:

- Figures of summary such as accumulation, anacephalaeosis, epanodos, epiphonema and symperasma rely *in primis* upon the law of good continuation, insofar as they combine relevant proofs together in view of the final point that the orator/writer wishes to make and, *a fortiori*, interruptions or distractions must be avoided.
- An analogous focus upon good continuation is to be found in the many forms of enargia, i.e. figures of description, recorded by

rhetoricians, such as anemographia (of wind), astrotesia (of stars), characterismus (of personality), chorographia (of nations), chronographia (of time), dendrographia (of trees), etc. Consistency of descriptive elements is necessary to obtain the desired result.

- Similarly, albeit *via negativa,* the law of good continuity explains the force of the figures of interruption (e.g. anacoluthon, aposiopesis, parenthesis) as well as of various forms of paralipsis (e.g. cataphasis, ennoia) and erotema (i.e. rhetorical questions), all of which operate by breaking the flow of the speech or text.
- Changes of tone, theme, as well as any other artful deviation from common usage and understanding may land the orator/writer into trouble though, as with the vices of hysteriologia. hysteron proteron and heterogenium, insofar as audiences can respond negatively to an excessive departure from the commonplace expectation of continuity.
- The success of the figures of order (e.g. chiasmus, hypallage, isocolon, parallelism) is attributed here chiefly to the law of symmetry, which is exemplified *via positiva* by many rhetorical tropes employing balanced juxtapositions of cause and effect (e.g. aetiologia, dialysis), precedent and consequent (e.g. antisagoge), question and answer (e.g. anthypophora, dianoea, ratiocinatio), accusation and defence (e.g. anticategoria, procatalepsis), affirmation and negation (e.g. antilogy, asteismus), not-to-be-stated and actually stated (i.e. paralipsis in its various forms), or statement and qualification (e.g. colon, correctio, dicaeologia, dirimens copulatio, epanorthosis, epexegesis, restrictio).
- Contraries (e.g. irony and related forms such as accismus and acyron), operate in an analogous fashion, albeit *via negativa,* for they rely upon the hearer's/reader's mental association between what is stated and its opposite, so that what is not being said by the orator/writer is itself present, if not paramount, in their mind. Needless to say, such operations are complex and generally more likely to fail than those done *via positiva,* as the ordinary

experiences of misfiring jokes and overly clever paradoxes exemplify.
- Persuasive appeals conducted primarily by means of figures of *pathos* and *ethos* (e.g. adhortatio, ecphonesis, eustathia) are primarily instantiations of the law of simplicity, for they seek to lead the audience into sharing a basic, clear and common emotional disposition, whether it is loyalty, sadness or trust.
- These appeals are mirrored *via negativa* in the figures of obscuring (e.g. aphorismus, apoplanesis, enigma noema, schematismus), which try to unsettle the audience and cast them in a state of doubt and uncertainty that should serve nevertheless the orator's/writer's ends.
- Many figures of substitution (e.g. anthimeria, antonomasia, circumlocution, periphrasis) rely upon the law of similarity, since the introduction of too remotely related a term for another would simply fail in making the meaning clear, which is a nearly absolute precondition for being rhetorically. This is particularly important in connection with the queen of tropes, metaphor, and her dependent figures (allegory prosopopeia, antiprosopopeia, bomphiologia, catachresis, conceit, simile, etc.), which work by exploiting an implicit similarity in key-traits or elements of the terms of comparison or, more rarely, by establishing some that had not been commonly noticed or conceived of until then (e.g. Jesus' taking love as a law or Marx's identification of history with class struggle).[745]
- Similarity, combined with proximity, is of crucial importance in explaining how the figures of repetition operate (e.g. alliteration, anadiplosis, conduplicatio, consonance, polyptoton, etc.). With these figures, similar or identical sounds, words, ideas or phrases are presented once, twice or more times within clauses, periods or paragraphs, and gain force by virtue not only of their similarity, but also of their being close enough not to be received and considered in reciprocal independence.
- Proximity itself plays a crucial role in figures of omission such as asyndeton and brachyologia, which reduce the interposed

grammatical elements, increase the mutual closeness of the key-terms and create a hurried, forceful rhythm.
- The law of closure explains those figures that set in place a structured continuity according to a known pattern serving as a whole, which can be as diverse as the alphabet (abecedarian), a single word (e.g. acrostic, diaeresis, ecthlipsis, epenthesis epitasis, metathesis, paragoge, prosthesis), a sentence or period (e.g. ellipsis, hyperbaton, period, pleonasm), an articulated reasoning or truncated syllogism (e.g. dialysis, elenchus, elimination, enthymeme, epilogue, syllogismus), a list (distribution) or a hierarchy (catacosmesis, eutrepismus, climax), and even as a speech or text taken into its entirety (accumulation, anacephalaeosis).
- The same can be said of those figures that imply a structured continuity according to a known pattern serving as a whole, whether they operate by omission or substitution (e.g. antisthecon, synaeresis synaloepha, syncope). Two of the major tropes, metonymy and synecdoche, rely themselves on the implicit grasp of the whole, as they refer, respectively, to an attribute or an element of it.

Concluding Remarks

In light of the comprehensive table above, it would be interesting to speculate about the patterns of correspondence discussed in the "Continuities with Older Classifications". Perhaps, the fact that *Gestalt* principles can be matched fairly regularly with the received categories of classification of rhetorical tropes indicates that ancient rhetoricians had already grasped the cognitive structures or schemata by which linguistic efficacious communication takes place. If one is honest and willing enough to note and appreciate the many analogies in the midst of obvious methodological and conceptual differences, a number of theories and studies of modern science do find precursors in ancient wisdom, including atomism (e.g. Democritus) and evolution by natural selection (e.g. Lucretius).

Still, this line of analysis would remain sheer speculation, as fascinating as it may be. Given the data at our disposal, I can see no way to establish such a point in any definitive way, unless we were to retrieve currently unknown ancient documents anticipating much more explicitly the insights and the studies of Wertheimer and his fellow *Gestalt* psychologists. At the present stage, I know of no such new ancient documents.

Rather, what the table above offers to us today is a substantial corroboration of Wertheimer's original claim that the laws or principles of organisation sought by *Gestalt* psychology do not deal with perception alone and that *Gestalt* psychology does actually work *qua* descriptive science of humankind's cognitive phenomena at large or, at least, of rhetorical tropes. Such tropes populate most, if not all, of linguistic communication, given at least the inherent metaphorical character of all verbal utterances, which associate by established convention objects of either internal or external perception with repeated sound patterns.

That the substantial corroboration offered above may be shown to possess a striking similarity to received classificatory categories of scholarship in the field of rhetoric does suggest that, perhaps inevitably, *Gestalt* principles have been tacitly at work in making certain types of tropes possible and effective and, *a fortiori*, in the way in which these types of tropes have been catalogued throughout the long life of rhetoric as a reflexive organised inquiry in the nature, articulation and ends of human communication.

PART III – Talking Rhetoric

Chapter 13: Heideggerian Aphorisms [746]

Beauty lives hidden in ordinariness

The world is not evil. It is the evil people's world

They call justice and integrity "utopias"—tell them utopias are the world's horizon
Unrealistic is to live in reality without dreams

Blindness to one's health is the first step towards sickness

Do not fear death: fear loss of life
Do not fear rules: fear their breaking
Defy your weakness: it's weak

Happiness means not to wish for more, contentedness not to need anything else

He who cares for clothes has no body
He who has personality follows himself; he who has none follows fashion

He who is a worm cannot conceive of humanity
He who is empty inside is flashy outside
He who is satisfied did not expect much
He who lacks focus gets buried by details
He who lives for money does not live but computes
He who lives to make money is inhumane; no man was ever born a bank
He who wants all stumbles onto something

The less you crave, the more you have

Nearly everything, in life, is luxury
Money is a servant dressed like a god

Honour life and you shall live honourably

Human mediocrity does not excuse one's own
If you play, play seriously
Imbeciles are flags

To be "in"—a cage

Your care for appearance, not your appearance as such, reveals your moral worth
Publicity feeds on dissatisfaction
Long-bearded fanaticism is the twin-brother of long-tied cynicism

Freedom is the narrow gap between character and circumstances

No man is an island, we all are oceans

You shall travel the world to discover your home
Inhabit the world like you inhabit yourself
Find your vocation and follow it—it has always been you

Respect what respects you

You cannot choose your starting point, but what you do with it
You cannot mature and face life but face life and mature
Nothing comes without effort—not even excrement

Pain is a noisy enemy, boredom a silent one
Pain is a place in the world. Be a tourist
Respect pain. Never love it

Everybody else looks horrible: you are sick

Everybody else sounds mistaken: you are so
Everything, no matter how luminous, casts a shadow

Reason is no reason to itself

Science knows how, not why
You need time to understand—and even longer to understand time
The perception of time changes with time

Silence is golden: be the ignorant silent
Silence is golden: disturb little and be little disturbed
Silence is golden: eloquence is platinum
Silence is golden: learn to be deaf to the world's noisy marketplace
Silence is golden: the idiot fills his pockets with voice

We all are ripples in the ocean of history; look at the previous ripples to understand yourself
We all are unique, also as repetitions of characters and generations
We all are bound to suffer; suffering is the measure of life's worth

Chapter 14: What Is Value? A Meditation on Inflation and the Meaning of Life

What is value? We thought that the banknotes in our wallets were valuable, and many amongst us wanted more and more of them, if not the shiny cars and the fancy TV screens showing how much money we had. Now, however, it seems that those banknotes would be more useful as insulation material or stuffing for our sofas, whilst shiny cars and fancy TV screens cannot be bought any longer. What were we thinking of? Probably, along the way, we forgot something very important, and not only here in Europe.

For the past thirty years, a worldwide mantra has recited that the value of anything at all is determined by its money value. A long string of American presidents, the IMF, and a heap of influential people and media have been very adamant about this equation at every level of existence, from public sector expenditures ("cost-benefit") to society's achievement of wellbeing ("GDP"). In essence, they all believe that if more money is gained at the end of any time sequence, then more value is created ("added value"); whereas if money is lost, then less value follows, even if many are healthier and better educated.

Almost everything has been used to create more value thus understood: cigarettes, water and waterfalls, arable land, the world's currencies, higher education, people's labour, their pensions, their fears and their hopes. This is the engine that has been moving individual and collective action around us: the citizen investing in shares yielding higher returns than treasury bonds, the banks expanding their operations abroad, the companies cutting costs by making use of cheaper manpower, the State squeezing more labour from its employees for the same pay or cutting off "unprofitable" branches.

Those who disagreed with this bounty-promising value-logic were marginalised, ridiculed, or dubbed "out of touch" with reality, incompetent "loony lefties" or even unruly subjects deserving a good thrashing by the market's "discipline". Nonetheless, the result of this bounty-promising value-logic is strangely grim: a 1929-style global financial meltdown and the ecological collapse of our planet denounced, amidst others, by the United Nations themselves. In the meantime, governments that argued that no money was available for schools, hospitals and social programmes, or that environmental and health-and-safety protections were too costly, are now throwing trillions at the world's richest banks and financial institutions, thus revealing their blatant lies. What went amiss?

The IMF, our venerable leaders, and many of us seem to have neglected the notion that it is possible to know the price of everything and the value of nothing. Much is valuable without having necessarily a price on it that contributes to the growth of monetary sums: health, the air we breathe, free time, the beauty of a sunset, the sight of our children playing at kindergarten, a quiet old age, the depths of learning, the meaningfulness of a job that we have chosen as a life-mission.[747]

Whenever any such item is turned into a priced good, two major problems arise. First of all, these items, when priced, are no longer available to as many people as before, but only to those who can afford to pay for them. Secondly, these items, when priced, can easily push life goods out of the market to sell more at less money cost, as with food. This means that money value can trump life value at every turn. Thus, a child can buy junk food at the expense of his health; a childish adult can buy a noisy snow-bike at the expense of a glacier's majestic silence; a gang of profit-seeking firms can buy a nation's water and savings at the expense of a whole society's enduring wellbeing.

Perhaps, one day we will learn to evaluate the success of an economic system by the actual wellbeing that it creates across peoples and generations, securing means of life and opportunities to lead a meaningful existence, rather than by the volume of lifeless sums of money stated by the balance sheet.

Chapter 15: A Letter from Iceland

If men were capable of reproducing without the aid of women, then the Irish could claim that Iceland was colonised by them—around the 8th century—and not by the Vikings. Unfortunately, the Irish monks that had chosen such a vast, cold island in the north Atlantic as their hermitage were never able to sustain an actual population. In the 9th century, when they saw the sails of well-known and much-feared Norse longboats approaching Iceland's shores, they decided that it was time to choose another location. Nevertheless, Celtic blood has been running in the veins of Icelanders since the time of settlement, which official historiography dates as starting in 874 AD. Precisely, on their way to Iceland, the Vikings seized women—and other slave labour—in Celtic Ireland and northern Scotland. Evidently, they were roughly aware of how human beings should reproduce.

Contrary to the myths of certain pseudo-science, which led Nazi experts to regard the Icelanders as a pure Aryan breed, Iceland has been a less isolated country, and Icelanders a less in-bred community, than many have thought—including a good number of Icelanders. Iceland was never a major hub of European trade, nor was the Icelandic nation a major player in European affairs. Still, its inhabitants travelled far and often, at least until the late Middle Ages. They brought home goods, ideas and, sometimes, genes from as distant lands as Russia and the Byzantine Empire. Meanwhile, they settled in Greenland and, for a short period of time, in Newfoundland.

Analogous exchanges took place with German, English and Dutch merchants, who visited fairly regularly the Icelandic ports and people until 1602. In that fateful year, the Danish crown introduced a mercantilist trade monopoly that brought Icelanders' travelling and trading internationally to a halt. This economic policy had disastrous consequences for the near totality of the inhabitants of the country. As masterly evoked in Nobel-laureate Halldór Laxness' 1943 novel *Iceland's Bell*, havoc, misery and destitution burdened the nation—

with the notable exception of the conservative élite comprising rich farmers and merchants with strong Danish connections.

Whereas Holland, Spain and the Genoese were enjoying their "golden century" and England its Renaissance, Iceland was beginning its true Dark Ages. Moreover, in the 18th century, volcanic eruptions, failing crops and recurrent famines prevented any recovery from taking place, even if the trade monopoly was eventually lifted. It is only in the 19th century that the benefits of free trade in fish and stock-fish were felt by the population at large, who then will start to think seriously about independence.

For a renewed, or even first golden age, Iceland shall have to wait for the late 20th century, when its substantial adoption of the Scandinavian development model allowed it to become one of the wealthiest (per capita) and happiest countries on the planet, at least according to all major international reports. It did not last long, though. In 2008, five years after the privatisation of the nation's largest banks, a massive financial crisis hit Iceland, whose government started accepting loans from the IMF and other international creditors in order to avoid sovereign default. Like many other countries on the planet since the early 1990s, Iceland has itself experienced a "meltdown". Perhaps, as a result of this experience, it will become clear that free trade in capital and currency is not the same thing as free trade in fish and stock-fish; or perhaps not.

During Iceland's history as one of the youngest countries in Europe, literature and religion, rather than philosophy, have played a major role in shaping the national culture. On the one hand, the fundamental sources of national pride and identity have been the medieval Sagas and the Icelandic language, the latter being de-internationalised during the Romantic age as most foreign terms and influences were thoroughly expunged. Ironically, the Sagas that Christian Icelanders wrote in the Middle Ages about their heathen past in order to show how much they had improved, were later taken as a glorious depiction of proud and rather murderous Viking ancestors. On the other hand, Christianity first and the Reformation later have provided an immaterial yet solid bridge to Continental

Europe and the Nordic countries, which has lasted until the present day.

If we set aside recent attempts by renowned educationalist and moral philosopher Kristján Kristjánsson (b.1959) to extrapolate a quasi-Aristotelian ethics from the Sagas, it is thanks to the latter player, i.e. religion, that philosophy was introduced and kept alive in Iceland. The adoption of Christianity, around the year 1000, and the establishment of two bishoprics and several monasteries allowed for intellectual exchanges with chief centres of learning, such as Paris and Rome. Books and clerics would sail over the Atlantic and the North Sea to enrich Iceland's cultural landscape. The Reformation severed many of these medieval ties, but promoted enough Lutheran theology not to cause philosophical erudition to perish completely.

As concerns the troubled two centuries that followed the 1500s, Icelanders were generally too worried about survival to have much time to spend on sophisticated intellectual activities. Out of necessity, most inhabitants became ancient cynics, if they were lucky enough to be able to satisfy their basic needs. Isolated cases such as Brynjólfur Sveinsson (1605–1675), Páll Björnsson (1621–1706) and Hannes Finnsson (1739–1796) show that a modicum of philosophical learning survived amongst the clergy, who could enjoy a slightly more leisurely lifestyle.

In the 19th century the situation improved a little, allowing more Icelanders to have access to literacy and schooling at higher levels. German idealism and, even more, Romantic ideals, swept across the Icelandic intelligentsia, turning Iceland's cruel mistress—its untamed nature—into another powerful positive symbol of national uniqueness. Poets and the Icelandic language, however, were the main vehicles for this process. Philosophy, despite the efforts made by clergymen Hannes Árnason (1812–1879) and Eiríkur Briem (1846–1929), remained marginal.

Under this perspective, significant is the fact that the first Icelandic department of philosophical studies was established at the University of Iceland only in 1972, long after the university itself had been founded in Reykjavík in 1911. Some philosophy had been taught there since its inception and, in the 1920s, it became an essential component of *philosophicum*, i.e. a basic curriculum in psychology and philosophy that all students had to take. Psychologist Guðmundur Finnbogason (1873–1944) and educationalist Símon Jóhannes Ágústsson (1904–1976) wrote extensively about philosophical matters, but it was not enough to start an actual programme in philosophy.

New universities were later established in Akureyri (1987), Bifröst (1988) and Reykjavík (1998), which have employed philosophers in various degree programmes, from the social sciences to law. Still, no new department of philosophy has seen the light yet. First of all, there has been no adequate 'critical mass' amongst the student population to justify such a move. Secondly, due to the sheer size of the Icelandic population, philosophers have been 'jacks of all trades' capable of contributing to the country's intellectual life at several different levels, which has included taking part in research and teaching within other disciplinary pigeonholes.

As regards the initiators of the one and only department of philosophy in Iceland, they were an interesting and creative blend of diverse philosophical currents, who brought together methodologies and themes originating in Edinburgh, Cambridge, Harvard, Brandeis and Louvain. Of crucial importance with regard to the establishment of the philosophy department were polymath Þorsteinn Gylfason (1942–2005) and the philosopher of culture and later rector of the University of Iceland Páll Skúlason (1945–2015). Among the founders was also US-born and US-trained Mikael M. Karlsson (b. 1943; Michael Marlies before Icelandic naturalisation), who embodies the often-underplayed openness of Iceland to foreign blood or, as in this case, brains. Almost single-handedly, he enabled the creation of a stable and extensive network of academic ties between Iceland and the rest of the world, which is still growing today.

In the 20th century, Iceland has been able to produce, export— many talented Icelandic philosophers have worked abroad—and, occasionally, attract respected members of the international academic community. In addition to the thinkers mentioned above, cultural scholar Sigurður Jóhannesson Nordal (1884–1974), logician

Bjarni Jónsson (1920–2016), Hume specialist Páll S. Árdal (1924–2003) and bio-ethicist Vilhjálmur Árnason (b.1953) are possibly the best-known names.

Whether Iceland will turn in the 21st century to any of them, or to their colleagues, for new ideas *vis-à-vis* how to resolve the current economic crisis, thus bringing philosophy centre-stage for the very first time in the nation's life, history alone will tell.

Chapter 16: Explaining Life-value Onto-axiology to a Child

The second edition of John McMurtry's *Cancer Stage of Capitalism* is recommended to anyone alive with a functioning brain —and a heart. Why? Because this book is not normal in either an academic or a popular sense. This book is philosophy at its best, that is, it is devoid of ivory-tower self-referential talk and yet it goes deeply and in the most articulate manner to the very core of the matter, which is what matters most: the choice between life and death, individual as well as social, present as well as past and future.

Rather than attempting to offer a brief and inevitably superficial synopsis, allow me to share with you the way in which I tried to communicate the wisdom of this book to my elder son, who saw me reading it and started asking questions about it. I mean no disrespect to the reader. It is the best way I could concoct to be both concise and expressive. If you think it inadequate, please accept my apologies, skip my words, and read the book.

- "What are you reading, dad?" (I translate from the Italian, which is the language that I use with my children)
- "A great book"
- "Why is it great?"
- "Well, do you recall all the people on TV who keep talking about money and the stock exchange market going up and down?"
- "Yes, I do. Why do they talk so much about it? Is it important?"

McMurtry's wisdom kicks in at this point (I shift to indirect speech for the sake of convenience). Is the Dow Jones index as important as the media would like us to believe? Does money matter truly so much? Certainly, bread matters more than money. We cannot eat money. Happiness matters more too. Would you sell your mother to make a lot of money? Would that make you happy? Certainly not! Let the Dow Jones go wherever it likes! We have more important things to think about!

But there is more. As long as the money going around on the stock exchange market—which some great minds have described as nothing but a casino—is not the money of people that can't afford to buy bread, then it is superfluous money. It is the money of people who have much more than enough. Since they have so much, they can even play with it.

Now, if someone needs bread but cannot buy it, then the money for the bread should come from the superfluous wealth of those who have much more than enough. That is what we have been taught to do at Sunday school, after all. If you have more than you need, not to mention much more, then you share it with those who don't. Who would be so callous as to let someone else starve, so that she can keep gambling? Would you be so horrible? Only a sick person would do it. Someone who needs help with her addiction.

The money played in the casino has even more to do with bread and the inability of some to buy it. In actual fact, all sorts of actions have been taken to make sure that the gambles on the casino generate some gains for the people who have already much more than enough. And many of these actions have caused other, less fortunate people, to get less, worse, or even no bread at all!

For example, some of these less fortunate people have been fired and left unemployed to increase the value of the stock exchanged in the casino. The wheat needed to make bread has been speculated upon in the same casino and sometimes made too expensive for many poorer people to be able to buy it. These poorer people's old-age pension savings have been played with, and lost, in the same casino—sometimes on top of any other savings of theirs—without having been given a choice or asked permission. The people's own money is no longer printed or lent out cheaply to let them buy bread. Only very rich bankers get money of that kind, so that they can keep gambling, even if they have already lost a lot of money. Indeed, the gamblers print themselves special money that they alone can use to become richer, even if other, poorer people's wallets foot the bill when their gambles go to the dogs.

Meanwhile, more bread of lesser quality has been produced for the same price, so as to reduce costs and increase revenues, which make companies look good in the casino. Lobbying, bribing and bullying have been most common in order not to have health-and-safety inspections in these companies or tight laws requiring them. Trade agreements to get cheaper ingredients from countries with less or no effective regulations and lower wages have been signed and ratified too. Not to mention how free trade across borders has been promoted to force countries with better regulations and wages to lower them.

In short, for the sake of making more money for people who have already plenty of it, poorer people have been left with less and worse bread, if any.

My son thought that 'tis all mad, and I think he's right. McMurtry agrees, but he also explains it in the most nuanced, carefully referenced and eloquently argued manner. There would be no point in me trying to do something analogous here. Just read the book.

Chapter 17: On Modernism

The noted British historian Eric Hobsbawm (1917–2012) stated on one occasion that the Catholic Church had "held the nineteenth century at bay with surprising success".[748] Under many respects, Hobsbawm was correct. The Church of Rome, as far as her official doctrine is concerned,[749] did not fall prey of any of the many intellectual fashions darting through the 19th century and its *"magnifiche sorti e progressive"* ("magnificent and progressive destinies"), as the Italian poet Giacomo Leopardi (1798–1837) aptly described the prevalent *Zeitgeist*.[750]

The Catholic Church did not embrace Romantic sentimentalism and naturalism, philosophical and historical idealism, progressive yet conflict-prone liberalism and socialism, the economists' hedonistic ophelimity and the other social scientists' detached positivism, nor did she accept racial and eugenic social Darwinism, unlike some Protestant denominations.[751] She adhered neither to the new abstract ideas nor to the concrete action programmes for socio-political transformation, so popular in the 19th century, variously characterised as 'civilising missions', 'manifest destinies' or 'historical dialectics'. The doctrine of God's Providence, especially as outlined in Saint Paul (ca. 5–ca. 67 AD) and the Church Fathers, provided her already with rich enough a philosophy of history,[752] and her record for missionary work was far older and geographically wider than any modern analogue, and still expanding. In 1857–8, for example, a "North Pole Mission" was dispatched, whose aim was "to regain the Northern part of the Scandinavian countries, Iceland, Greenland, the Faroes and the Polar region of North America for the Catholic faith."[753]

The Catholic Church aimed at continuing her staunch opposition to the secular and at times ferociously anticlerical spirit of the French Revolution, as well as of its intellectual, political and legal offshoots. On the one hand, during the 19th century, vigorous liberal forces pushed forth thoroughly secular civil and penal legislations that, *inter alia,* abolished the medieval guilds, forbade new workers' associations in the name of freedom,[754] whilst also tearing down religious edifices in order to erect monumental train stations.[755] On the other hand, atheism started spreading among the working class as a novel socialist creed, largely of Jacobin origin, reaching uneducated masses that had traditionally been faithful to the Church.[756] European and, to a lesser extent, American societies were de-Christianising at both ends of their polarising new social hierarchy.

Whether by then a frail paper tiger or a resilient actual power in the world, the Catholic Church soldiered on in what she believed to be her own sacred mission, which officially is still "that of proclaiming and communicating the salvation wrought in Jesus Christ" to all human beings, whether bourgeois or proletarian.[757] Tackling primarily the liberal potentates of the age, she resisted the ongoing process of secularisation of societies, and therefore faced frequent accusations of, *inter alia*, 'Popery' and 'Papism' in the Anglophone countries, 'Jesuitism' in Scandinavia, 'Ultramontanism' and 'Romanism' in German-speaking countries, and 'clericalism' in the Latin ones.[758]

The Catholic Church perceived all these fleeting 19th-century intellectual fashions as sharing a fundamental error with an older adversary of hers, namely the Protestant Reformation initiated by Martin Luther. The error consisted in the exaggerated distinction between reason and faith, whose mutual integration and agreement was instead a central tenet of the Catholic doctrine as this had evolved during the Middle Ages, especially thanks to the work of Thomas Aquinas (1225–1274). As the renowned English novelist, and Catholic apologist, Gilbert Keith Chesterton (1874–1936) eloquently put it in his 1933 book about him:

> *Simply as one of the facts that bulk big in history, it is true to say that Thomas was a very great man who reconciled religion with reason, who expanded it towards experimental science, who insisted that the senses were the windows of the soul and that the reason had a divine right to feed upon facts, and that it was the business of the Faith to digest the strong meat of the toughest*

and most practical of pagan philosophies. [...] Those who, for other reasons, honestly accept the final effect of the Reformation will none the less face the fact, that it was the Schoolman who was the Reformer; and that the later Reformers were by comparison reactionaries. I use the word not as a reproach from my own stand-point, but as a fact from the ordinary modern progressive standpoint. For instance, they riveted the mind back to the literal sufficiency of the Hebrew Scriptures; when St. Thomas had already spoken of the Spirit giving grace to the Greek philosophies. He insisted on the social duty of works; they only on the spiritual duty of faith. It was the very life of the Thomist teaching that Reason can be trusted: it was the very life of Lutheran teaching that Reason is utterly untrustworthy.[759]

By keeping reason and faith separate, if not even opposed to each other, Protestantism in general and its 19th-century secular equivalents were deemed bound to produce a twofold, troubling misunderstanding of reality, as argued fastidiously in the encyclical *Pascendi Dominici Gregis* by Pope Pius X (born Giuseppe Melchiorre Sarto, 1835–1914), who calls "modernism" a variety of intellectual tendencies reproducing the fundamental errors of the much-older Protestantism.[760]

On the one hand, there emerges a rationalistic, allegedly scientific accounting of human affairs and human history devoid of any room for faith, religion and, above all, for the possibility of God's intervention precisely in such affairs and history, thus contradicting the Holy Scriptures and the pivotal element of Christianity itself, that is, the Incarnation of Jesus Christ. Faithless and irreligious rationalistic accounts can be produced about the faith and religion themselves, leaving out that *quid* which makes the faith important to the faithful and religious phenomena different from secular phenomena. As the Pope states: "in every religious fact, when you take away the divine reality and the experience of it which the believer possesses, everything else, and especially the religious formulas of it, belongs to the sphere of phenomena and therefore falls under the control of science."[761]

Unsurprisingly, the 19th century was replete with more or less scientific explanations of religious life *qua* something else, i.e. other than itself: the species' self-selection of individuals that should not generate any offspring; self-soothing neuroses and sexual psychoses; class-based false consciousness; a sophisticated means of tribal solidarity; slave morality; a non-logical derivative of deeply ingrained instinctual residues; a cultural tool for survival typical of our animal species; etc.

The encyclical offers a picture of positivist explanations of religion *qua* something else than itself that is curiously reminiscent of the process of self-alienation discussed by Ludwig Feuerbach (1804–1872) and Karl Marx in order to discredit religion. The Pope suggests that scientifically minded inquirers posit scientific categories, which were designed to study only some specific aspects of reality, and then reify them into the only aspects of reality that the inquirers can think of *qua* reality, i.e. all the actual universe that they are able and/or willing to acknowledge. What Pius X argues is both simple and deep. If religion is studied like and as a psychological phenomenon, what the psychologist grasps and investigates is not religion, but a psychological phenomenon; if a sociologist studies religion like and as a social mechanism of sorts, then she is not tackling religion, but a social mechanism of sorts; and so on.

In his encyclical, Pius X anticipates an argument made in the mid-20th century by the chemist and philosopher Michael Polanyi, according to whom: "Only a Christian who stands in the service of his faith can understand Christian theology and only he can enter into the religious meaning of the Bible."[762] It is only by embracing, studying and dwelling within the categories and emotions of religion that we can make any *sense* of the holy texts as holy. Religion and the sciences are *Gestalten*, i.e. forms or modes of experience, but as different *Gestalten*, they do not pursue the same enquiry, they do not seek the same aim, they do not lead to the same sort of experience, and they do not attain the same truths.[763] Positivists regularly forget this essential difference and reduce the realm of possible meaning to what can be built upon few measurable aspects of reality (cf. Galileo's *affezioni particolari*) that we have concocted and variously label "physics", "chemistry", etc. Agnostic *ab initio*, all these rationalistic accounts cannot fathom, and even less explain, divine things *qua* divine things, but only as non-divine. The leap into unbelief is built therein *ab imis*.

On the other hand, the same fundamental error is seen by Pius X as the cause of voluntarist and enthusiastic interpretations of both faith and religion, whereby the Christian belief becomes a subjective, blindly emotional matter of the heart, akin to any other. Christian life turns then into an essentially irrational and hopeful choice of the individual, who alone relates to the divine *via* the Bible, if not even *via* nature itself in novel forms of quasi-pagan immanent pantheism.

Traditional Catholic teaching had always claimed that emotions are an important part of any religious existence and experience, and so is nature *qua* divine Creation. The believer can obtain much through either channel. Yet, when exclusive, such interpretations of faith and religion cannot but diminish, if not even deny altogether, the value of the immense wealth of Christian scholarship, which started building up since at least the Apostles' letters. Under this perspective, liturgy and "the sacraments" themselves become, at best, "symbolic", rather than genuine conduits for God's grace instituted by the Father *via* the Son.[764]

Pius X's encyclical shows particular concern *vis-à-vis* the Church's authoritative tradition expressed by her dogmas and in the learned *fora* for discursive growth that Western Christianity had established over the centuries (e.g. the universities of the Middle Ages, starting with Bologna, where the canonist revival of Roman Law blossomed in the 12th and 13th century).[765] From the Church's perspective, the enthusiastic and voluntarist interpretations of modernism were nothing less than an assault on the painstaking labour of the Church Fathers, of countless generations of theologians, popes and clergymen, of numerous schools and councils, if not even of angelic doctors and revered saints, who had not only investigated the Holy Scriptures, but also the works and wisdom of ancient heathen philosophers.

Back to basics, no matter how philologically keen on the original Hebrew and Greek sacred texts they could be on some occasions, the universal priesthood promoted by the Protestants was perceived as throwing aside the Church's hard-won knowledge of the highest mysteries. Rejecting historically accumulated authoritative understanding of all things divine, it gave the Bible back to each believer and uttered onto her: "read it and make up your mind: we start afresh".[766] Seemingly democratic and progressive to us today —for, whether we like it or not, we are all children of the liberal age —the Catholic Church resisted this move by "Protestants and pseudo-mystics".[767] It was seen as a dangerous step towards self-imposed ignorance[768] and potentially pulverising anarchy, which the subsequent historical experience of bitterly factional and endlessly splitting Protestant communities seemed only to have confirmed, in the eyes of Pius X, to a tragic extent.[769]

The prevailing 19th-century intellectual trends called "modernism", insofar as they shared in the same erroneous conception of faith and reason, seemed no better. Indeed, Pius X went so far in his condemnation that he made "all clergy, pastors, confessors, preachers, religious superiors, and professors in philosophical-theological seminaries" take an oath against the twofold, troubling misunderstanding just described.[770] If this is what modernity had in store, the Church of Rome did not like it a bit.

Chapter 18: On Catholicism, Abortion, and Social Democracy: Lessons from Iceland

In a secular world, religion is an antidote to dogmatism. Like religious societies before them, today's secular societies take many things for granted. There are beliefs, even life-and-death ones, that hardly anybody challenges seriously or thinks through, if not even about. Such beliefs are secular dogmas.

In the Nordic countries, for example, abortion is as much a long-secured legal right as it is an obvious fact of life and daily practice for hospitals and their personnel. Academic debates on the ethical nature and status of abortion are, *nomen omen*, academic. Students do not get particularly excited about them, unlike what a philosophy teacher would experience in, say, North America or Great Britain. Still, as British liberals like John Stuart Mill (1806–1873) or Leonard Trelawny Hobhouse (1864–1929) would purport, unchallenged belief, even if true, is worse than challenged belief, for which one must retrieve and think through solid reasons. Let contrary belief, even false belief, be heard, so that the human mind may not acquiesce into shared habit, prejudice, or *de facto* dogma.

Roman Catholicism, with its insistence on equating the destruction of embryos to the destruction of human life, serves as a token of contrary belief. Whilst heathen religions demanded life sacrifices and allowed infanticide, Christianity, at least in its declared intentions, stopped them, to the surprise of peoples that had been exposing children since time immemorial—Christ's death on the cross being ideally the last human sacrifice to the heavens.

In the Nordic countries, whenever I voice my doubts about the comprehensive and commonsensical ethical legitimacy of abortion, I am called an "Italian Roman Catholic", as though that label could put an end to the issue. It does not, however. Generally, I am regarded on almost all issues as a die-hard leftist. Personally, I consider myself a feminist, or at least I have been happily married and co-working with one for many years. Whether I am a leftist, a feminist, an Italian Roman Catholic, an Icelandic one, a Greek Orthodox, Jew or Buddhist, my doubts must be countered first through proper critical analysis, not put aside without critical consideration by uttering some sort of disqualifying label that, in the mind of the utterer, means that the brain can be switched off in good conscience. If not a classic token of *ad hominem* attack, the standard reply that I receive in the Nordic countries is a case of fallacy of relevance. Let me articulate my doubts, then, and engage reason, not automated numbness.

First of all, whatever a fertilised egg may be—a person, a cluster of cells, a magmatic centre of biological energy, a monad—we can all be certain of one thing: all persons have been precisely *that* at some early stage of their biological development. One does not have to deploy the full force of Aristotelian or scholastic metaphysics to grasp the fact, even if the notions of "potency" and "actuality" may appeal to her. After all, they appeal to engineers and physicists when dealing with energy; or to sport coaches and teachers when gauging the likely achievements or failures of a young athlete or pupil. But they do not appeal to me. Infinite regress seems excessive for something as temporally confined as a person, whom we know all too well to have a beginning and an end. Besides, my doubts do not start with the reproductive cells taken independently, but with the fertilised egg. Plenty of sperm cells and, fairly regularly, of eggs, are disposed of without ever becoming a person. Far fewer fertilised eggs do not evolve into a foetus, which later becomes, often, a person. In any case, *no person has never been a fertilised egg*.

Could then a fertilised egg be a person? I do not know for sure. Though I do know that it *might*. Hence abortion *might* be prenatal infanticide. As such, on prudential grounds, I am strongly inclined to suggest that we should be cautious with regard to how we treat it, for it might be the case that we are dealing with a person, and I myself as well as all of my Nordic interlocutors (I have yet to meet an inveterate sceptic, social Darwinist or sadist outside philosophy books) wish to treat persons respectfully. Annihilating them from

Earth is, with rare and typically tragically painful exceptions, something that we do not wish to do.

Secondly, when I look back at my personal experiences, and especially at whether growing up in a largely Roman Catholic country did make any difference, I can clearly see two things. One: on the most counterfactual level imaginable, I would be most displeased if my parents or just my mother had decided to abort me. I would have been deprived of my existence and all the experiences, bad as well as good, that have made it worth living. Two: when debating the legalisation of abortion in Italy, one of the most frequently heard arguments from the pro-abortion side was that, as painful and possibly harmful as it could be, it would have saved nonetheless the lives of many women, who would have otherwise sought illegal abortions.

Like several advocates of legalised drugs or prostitution, many who favoured State-sanctioned and operated abortion suggested a choice in the face of empirical inevitability between two evils—one greater, another lesser—rather than between an evil and a good. Saving life, rather than contributing to destroying it, was a paramount aim to be attained by regulating abortions, even when it was found profoundly unappealing. Thus, the question arises: were we ever to find a way to save life to a higher extent, could we try to reduce the frequency of abortion, or establish conditions that could lead to the same result?

Please note that I have stated nothing so far about women's rights and liberties. I am not indifferent to them. Quite the reverse, they are so obviously paramount to me that I did not waste time debating them or their legitimacy. I do not wish to see them diminished. Rather, as with all cases of possible limitation of anyone's liberty and self-direction, such as penal law and traffic regulations, one can only intervene if some serious harm could be the case if no intervention takes place. Now, given that the ontological nature of the fertilised egg *might* be that of a person, or be so closely related to being a person as to entail some serious moral consideration, how could one ever intervene with all the authority, impersonality, clumsiness and yet inevitable necessity of State regulation in such an intimate sphere as a woman's control over herself, her body, her earthly existence?

Certainly, since I have not ascertained with much certainty that fertilised eggs are real persons and, at the same time, I do know that all reasonable human beings would avoid harming persons as far as plausibly possible, whilst granting them as much freedom as possible, I cannot allow the State, in principle as well as in practice, to be heavy-handed.

The solution that I propose is therefore a fairly indirect and, in the lack of certainty, prudential one, which is bound to prove dissatisfactory to many pro-life advocates. It is partly the result of the theoretical considerations spelled out above, as tentative and imperfect as they may be. And it is partly the result of personal and, if one wishes to be a little more 'scientific', socio-cultural observations occurred in different European countries.

These observations can be summarised fairly quickly: in Iceland, compared to the United Kingdom, there is at least as easy an access to lawful abortion, coupled with a high rate of unplanned pregnancies, especially amongst young women. Overall, however, more children are born from younger mothers, even in comparison with the other Nordic countries. Emblematically, while I never had young students with children when I was teaching in the England, that has been a most commonplace experience in my long professional life in Iceland. Why?

Several factors are at play, all of which are relevant, though I cannot say which ones carry more weight than the others. To begin with, the social stigma attached to unwanted and teenage pregnancies is almost non-existent. Secondly, Icelandic women can continue to study or work without fear of dismissal, for the existing legal provisions protect them, if not actually facilitate, the commencement of a young, double- or single-parent family *via* tax credits, free public childcare, maternity leaves and affordable education for children up to adult age. Also, many young Icelandic women seem to regard parenthood as a fundamental step in their personal growth, self-realisation and long-term well-being, whether there will be a father available or just the State *qua* surrogate parent.

Finally, families tend to be willing to help young parents and many generations come together to raise the new baby.

Given this sketchy but nevertheless useful picture of the situation, my suggestion is as follows: let the United Kingdom and any other nation on Earth be more like Iceland, for the welfare State is actually pro-life. While changing local cultures may be complicated, changing taxation, labour law, access to education and healthcare provision is a fairly common practice, at least as the history of the past hundred years or so has shown across the globe. Moreover, the resources are available, especially if one considers the amount of money that is siphoned every year into tax havens or that Central Banks have "injected" into the world's economies over recent years to keep failed private banks afloat.

If only a tiny fraction of that huge monetary mass were created to support family policies along Icelandic lines, then the worries about budgets could be easily overcome (I do not enter here the details of the funding process, for they would obscure the simple fact of the actual availability of funds, given a positive political will). If Iceland managed to achieve all this, despite being one of the poorest countries in Europe at the beginning of the 20th century, it is bizarre to think that at least all other high- and middle-income countries could not do the same. The Roman Catholic can thus conclude, in a spirit of hope: give us more Icelandic-style, or for that matter, Scandinavian social-democracy in family policies, love thy children and thy nation's children, and more births will occur. That, in turn, could translate into fewer abortions though, I must admit, it is no strict guarantee of it: after all, we do live in a secular world. Nonetheless, better conditions for life-enablement would be established, while it would still be up to personal liberty and conscience whether to make full use of them or not, consistently with existing constitutional human-rights provisions. The imperfect knowledge of imperfect humankind can only usher imperfect solutions.

Chapter 19: The Inequality of Political Correctness

Religious divides have been the source of many a bloody conflict. Even today, across the world, atrocities are committed by Hindus over Christians, Buddhists over Muslims, Jewish over Muslims, Hindus over Muslims, Muslims over Hindus, Muslims over Christians, Christians over Muslims, Sunni Muslims over Shia Muslims and, in a tiny corner of Europe, Protestant Christians over Catholic ones and *vice versa*.

Who benefits from all such division and tragedy?

Assuming here, at least for sheer argument's sake, that the traditional Marxist answer to that question is correct, then there is one class *cui bono* accrue all such division and tragedy: the bourgeoisie. Who are they? This term is a bit *passé* today, I must admit. "The 1%", "the corporate élite", "the job creators", or just "the rich", would be more popular expressions in contemporary parlance. The concept is not *passé*, however. The idea that the ruling class preserves its power by keeping the ruled ones internally divided by means of, *inter alia*, ideological decoys and distracting identities is as old as Philip II of Macedonia (382–336 BC), who lived long before Marx and Marxism and is said by ancient tradition to have uttered the momentous phrase "διαίρει καὶ βασίλευε" ("divide and rule").

In light of today's levels of skewed market power, *de facto* regressive taxation, immense wealth disparity reminiscent of the *Belle Époque*, fantastic unearned incomes by way of financial rent, mass unemployment, workers' precariousness, widespread de-unionisation, technological replacement of the workforce, growing underemployment of vainly trained young minds, substantive inequality before the law, and the concomitant absence of large-scale socio-political dissent, there seems to be no reason to believe that such a well-tested means of social control should not be at work in contemporary societies too. Therein, the class of billionaires and their corporate manifestations have been thriving unchecked, as proven repeatedly—and at the very least—by a plethora of unpunished financial and fiscal scandals of truly global proportions. Not to mention the credit lifelines and special bail-outs granted to gargantuan banks and their wealthy owners after the self-inflicted international collapse of 2008, while common people were crushed by austerity across continents in order to pay for such generous rescue missions.[771]

What is more, the very same billionaires have often taken direct control of the political game *qua* party leaders, government officials, cabinet ministers and populist trailblazers. Not even Marx could have expected them to become so shameless in their command of political institutions. At the same time, Marx's ghost, the ghost of communism *per* his 1848 *Manifesto*, not to mention the now mythical chimeras of internationalism and mass revolution, have all been eerily vacant from the world's stage.

When religion cannot do good enough a job, viable alternatives exist: race, nationality and region-, party- or even football-based affiliation can be often as effective. The New York City draft riots of 1863, pitting poor Irish immigrants against poor blacks while well-off Americans could avoid being sent to battle by paying a set fee, are just one historical example among many. Poor people that would be far better off by joining numbers, forces and concerted efforts against the tiny minority exploiting them waste instead their best energies and, at times, their livelihood and life, by fighting among themselves and against designated others most combative of all. Trouble is thus taken by the truly troubled to suppress the much-maligned "troublemakers", who are in fact the ones trying to find a solution.

About twenty years before *The Communist Manifesto*, the liberal and Catholic novelist Alessandro Manzoni (1785–1873) described the long-lived logic and common practice of *divide et impera* most vividly in a rustic allegory of his. He depicts Renzo, the poor, rural, male protagonist of Manzoni's most famous book, *I promessi sposi*, holding several living capons by their legs. That's the beginning; let me explain. Renzo is carrying these poor capons as his only means of payment to a well-off city lawyer, whom Renzo intends to hire in the attempt to redress the wrongs that he and his betrothed—the poor, rural, and female Lucia—have been suffering from a local nobleman that, to the young couple's great misfortune, fancies Lucia well beyond the boundaries of common decency and aristocratic gentlemanship. Manzoni notes that, had the capons been a little more intelligent, they would have started picking the hand that kept them captive and therefore regained their freedom. Instead, the capons bickered among themselves and ended up being delivered with great ease to their recipient. The lawyer enjoyed a few good meals out of the animals, but also failed to help Renzo in his human, far too human plight.

Renzo's capons, or "*i capponi di Renzo*", have become a proverbial admonition in Italian culture, though little followed its inherent wisdom may be in the nation's daily habits. Despite Manzoni's hefty novel being a mandatory reading in the nation's secondary schools, millions of Italians can still be kept internally divided in all sorts of ways, such as Northerners *versus* Southerners, natives *versus* immigrants, Catholic *versus* secular, progressive *versus* conservative, private-sector *versus* public-sector, and old *versus* young.

As concerns contemporary Western nations, gender is being used in the same manner. Men and women spend endless time and effort squabbling about the so-called "male privilege" and an alleged set of attendant disparities, rather than combining their efforts in order to pursue better wages, better working conditions, sensible monetary and fiscal policies by State authorities, true economic security and autonomy, a life-saving stop to the all-embracing profit-motive that is destroying the planet, as well as emancipatory self-ownership and democratic self-stewardship. Such squabbles split the front of the exploited many into two warring fronts: men *versus* women, women *versus* men or, in the shouting matches that frequently result thereof, radicals *versus* right-thinking persons, or feminists *versus* chauvinists, depending on the side one is on.

Curiously enough, the chauvinist camp includes some women that, apparently, don't realise that they have been duped by patriarchy and are not actually free, even when they do think that they are free or act without visible restraint, committing crimes against their gender such as wearing high heels, becoming Catholic nuns, or buying copies of *Fifty Shades of Grey*. Somehow, in the female camp, some women are more equal than others, and the former can tell the latter what is actually good for them to think, do, and be—like older sisters to younger ones, or patriarchs of old. As to those articulate women that openly complain about this peculiar state of affairs, such as Camille Paglia (b. 1947) in today's academia, they end up being reviled as "Nazi", akin to Rush Limbaugh (b. 1951) and, inexorably, "patriarchal".

Not that patriarchs, male prejudice and male privilege may have not existed at some point in history or may not exist somewhere on Earth today. Saudi Arabia has remained to the very present a hellish place for women, and so do several other oil-rich countries in the Middle East that have glorious business relations with the liberal West. Across the globe, there are indeed some nations where women are regularly beaten, have little access to healthcare, are not allowed to pursue any education worthy of note, and cannot walk in the street without male chaperons for fear of being assaulted. If I look at today's developed world, however, I see no real male privilege in, say, Sweden, Germany, France, Switzerland, Iceland or Canada.

It is not a matter of there being no inequality at any level; some inequality does exist but, as I shall argue, it cuts both ways, not just one. Let me be clear. Male privilege is a matter of there being—or not being—*blanket* better conditions for persons who were born male, similarly to the way in which a person would enjoy blanket better conditions by being born into an aristocratic family in 17th-century France, or in a 1% family today. Anyone who was born in the aristocracy back then, or in plutocratic families today, enjoyed and enjoys better food, longer lives, legal and muscled protection from physical harm, access to enterprising credit, top-level education, conspicuous leisure, better healthcare, and a thousand more life-enabling resources denied to others. The well-born person's benefit or advantage over the rest is notable and blatant. That's group privilege, in a nutshell.

Logic can be of some help here. One of the standard forms of reasoning identified since ancient times is the so-called "*modus tollens*", according to which if, from a certain condition A follows unescapably another condition B, and condition B is not the case, then it has to be concluded that A is not the case either. Formally, $A \rightarrow B, -B$, ergo $-A$. If I drink the hemlock like Socrates, then I feel ill and die shortly thereafter; I am alive and well; therefore, I have not drunk the hemlock. This much logic is not phallic. Contradicting it is, however, fallacious. Coming to our case, if there is male privilege, then there must be conspicuous benefit or blatant advantage for men; if such a conspicuous benefit or blatant advantage does not occur, then male privilege doesn't occur either.

In today's advanced societies, if someone is born male, he is more likely to die younger, to suffer from mental illness leading to suicide, to die in combat, to die in the workplace, to be the victim of violent crime, to be the perpetrator of violent crime, to serve time in prison and, in prison, to suffer rape. Living nastier, brutish and shorter lives is no conspicuous benefit or blatant advantage, whatever creatively postmodern way we may choose to look at it. There could be still some advantages at some level, but they would be neither blanket nor notable, insofar as men's longevity, physical integrity, mental health and law-abidingness signal losses compared to women's.

Let me be redundant. There may be some benefits that originate from being born a man. They may be small things, such as the likelihood of being allowed to play contact sports as children or swearing publicly with impunity. They may be 'bigger' ones, such as increased chances of becoming a top manager, smashing the glass ceiling, and belonging to the 1%—if that can be considered a good thing: I wonder what Marx would say about it. Still, even then there would be male privilege *as well as* female privilege, for being born female would still increase one's chances of wearing skirts as well as trousers as an adult, or of being addressed politely by strangers as a child—not to mention living the longer, healthier and more law-abiding lives just mentioned.

Gender roles, as debatable and mutable as we may wish them to be, imply in concrete reality several different gains, not just losses, for both sexes, and when essential dimensions of human wellbeing are considered, such as physical, mental and moral integrity, Western women are on the winning side. The suffragettes, the witches-that-returned, and the brave activists that fought for women's health and education in times of actual female segregation, have won big time. Their feisty descendants, today, as well-meaning as they may be, repeat slogans and employ concepts that are factually anachronistic. Meanwhile, the Luddites, Owenites, Marxists, revisionists, Trotskyists and middle-way Swedish social-democrats have seen their battles end up in humiliating defeats, to the point that in today's US no politician dares speak of the "working class" in public debates, for fear of being accused of "socialism". Only the "middle class" is allowed to exist, verbally. In Europe, these dangerous words are still audible, though a *non-working class* is actually the chief problem there, since Europe's working class has emigrated to China under the banner of "globalisation".

The enduring talk of "male privilege" is, at heart, a remnant of a by-gone past and a gross misrepresentation of a much more toxic reality, where the one and only true callous and outrageous privilege is that of a few rich family networks directing everyone else's life to maximise their take, irrespective of gender, to a massive extent. If life is a valley of tears, then both men and women are crying aplenty. Who, for example, can lead his or her life without spending much, if not most of it, working for someone else, who has the power to hire, fire, disenfranchise and impoverish them? Who, whether man or woman, can afford to be indifferent to the boom-bust hot-money cycles that financial moguls and their clients have been unleashing on the world's nations since the end of the Bretton Woods system? Who, after the crash of 2008, can say in good conscience to have been left untouched and undamaged by the gigantic waves of transnational speculation engulfing the global economy? Who, in constitutionally free and independent countries, has not heard the government justify their austere policies because of "the markets", "the creditors", "foreign direct investment", or "international competition"?

What is more, the notion of male privilege flies in the face of much theoretical and experimental literature, in which the negative consequences *for men* of traditional gender roles have been identified again and again. Stunted emotional development, personal unhappiness, limited self-expression, lack of empathy and other "maladies of the soul", as Julia Kristeva (b. 1941) would dub them, have been studied and catalogued in the accounts of what exactly standard assumptions and stereotypes about men do *to men themselves* from their early childhood to their deathbed, whether such assumptions and stereotypes are held by women or by other men.[772]

The persistence of traditional male gender roles, which are enforced also by women, is combined today with the growing hypocrisy and the double standards that the much-desired empowerment of women has made possible. As the ethicist John Kekes (b. 1936) has often remarked in his works, granting more freedom to more people—women included—means granting more opportunity for the evils of cruelty or, as Luce Irigaray (b. 1930) would word it, the evils of "possession", "appropriation" and "domination"—by the empowered women as well.[773] Truly, there is no such thing as a free lunch.

It all starts from an early age, by the way, as Mary Wollstonecraft (1759–1797) had rightfully lamented long ago. This time it works in reverse, though, as genders are concerned. The list is endless. Let me indulge in it below: it is somewhat amusing—though maybe not for the young men who grow up under such confusing premises or the older ones who get trapped by their paradoxes, especially in the Nordic countries that I know so well. Hopefully, my long and strange list will get someone thinking of the male teardrops drenching life's valley. Contrary to much popular belief, boys do cry; but more often than not they do it while hidden, behind doors. Doing so openly would cause them to be derided and dismissed by women —not just by men—as unmanly moaners, in yet another crippling instance of traditional gender roles and expectations, according to which boys don't cry unless they are sissies.

Girls with trousers are normal; boys wearing a skirt are laughed at, told better, or advised a sex change. Tomboys are cool; effeminate boys the butt of the joke. Boisterous girls are future adventurers in the making; boisterous boys an ill-educated nuisance. A girl squad is worth celebrating in pop songs; a group of teenage boys can't even be allowed into a shopping mall. Man-eating dancing queens and pussycat dolls can tease at will, break hearts with spears, lose them in the game, and do it again; boys are expected to endure it and be thankful, reminiscent of male mantises and male spiders. Crass humour about women is sexist; crass humour about men is universal. Young girls, often drunk, vomiting innuendos, or worse, at men in the middle of a busy street on a Saturday night are having a bit of fun; boys doing the same are intolerable pigs. The same goes for hiring male strippers on a hen night *versus* hiring female strippers on a stag night: stags are actually pigs, and pigs should not pursue such vile objectifications; hens are excused. An intolerable pig is also a man sleeping around, while a woman doing the same is exploring her sexuality or asserting her independence. Women making a pass are seen as a glorious sign of liberation; men making a pass as a threatening step towards harassment. Even alone, a man with a sex doll is a creepy pig that is better avoided; a woman with a dildo is a liberated person who does not need men for her self-realisation. Women who enjoy porn are emancipated, like the heroines of *Sex and the City*; men who do the same are, again, pigs. Women's menopausal crises deserve warmth and compassion; men's midlife crises are the fodder for TV comedies. Women can talk freely for both sexes—or more, given the alleged fluidity and plurality of genders of the human race; men, on their part, can never understand what it is like to be a woman, for they are not women. On the job, a man seeking sexual favours in exchange for professional advantages is deemed to be harassing another—"me too" think that; a woman offering sexual favours in exchange for professional advantages, though, is still deemed to be the victim of harassment. An older woman parading a much younger lover is cheered on: "Go Cathrine!", says the British historian Lucy Worsley (b. 1973) in her TV documentary, *The Empire of the Tsars*. No TV personality would dare utter "Go Donald!" or "Go Silvio!" on the same grounds. Oppression may be unseen, but eyes matter: men can create a hostile environment by merely looking at a woman. Words matter too: "cunt" and "bitch" are condemned as sexist, while "prick" and "dickhead" are used with liberality and much gusto. Women who work and see to domestic chores suffer from a double burden; men who do the same are emancipated, almost Swedish. A woman slapping a man in the face in public leads to amused or perplexed curiosity; a man slapping a woman in public leads to the cops being called onto the scene. A woman working as a childminder is the image of motherly love; a man doing the same is a potential pedophile whose identity and penal record must be triple-checked—these days, many men are quite simply terrified of talking to children in public. Female bisexuality is experimental and accepted as part of growing up; male bisexuality is unsettling and rejected as screwing up. A penniless woman hooked on antidepressant calls rightly for universal pity; a penniless man hooked on alcohol calls sinisterly for the epithet of "loser". A woman who kills a baby is the embodied tragedy of depression; a man who does the same a monster to be locked away or fried to a crisp. A woman who commits a crime deserves the attention of psychologists and social workers; a man who is found guilty of the same crime can simply be locked away and forgotten—though his prison rapists may notice him. Male-only priesthood in the Roman Church is condemned by unbelieving feminists, who celebrate the creed of Finland's SuperShe island for excluding men. Tearooms packed with women are an oasis of independence; bars packed with men a gateway to hell. Women who are afraid of men have only good reasons; men who are afraid of women have only bad problems. Women's access to the cohort of corporate multi-millionaires is a profound matter of equality to be fought for by all; the plight of poor mine workers, lorry drivers and bin men something that is habitually forgotten by the most vocal female activists—corporate executive glass ceilings trump common drone-work cellars.

One does not need to be Jordan Peterson (b. 1962) to abhor these more-and-more commonplace forms of misandry. It is enough to be an old-fashioned egalitarian. Whether then to err on the side of conservative prudence and uptight censorship, or on that of liberal freedom and loose pluralism, is not something that I can settle here. The reader is free to err as she wills. Who is infallible, after all? The inequality, however, is settled. Someone is certainly benefitting immensely from the *status quo*, but it is not men at large.

Endnotes

[1] Regarding the present endnotes, I make use of the Chicago Style Citation standard, i.e. the most common among Anglophone academic philosophers, though purged of some of its quixotic aspects.
[2] Giambattista Vico, *The New Science*, 3rd ed., Ithaca: Cornell University Press, 1988, §§ 63 & 149 (originally published in 1744).
[3] Cf. Donald A. Norman, *The Psychology of Everyday Things*, New York: Basic Books, 1988 (republished in later editions as *The Design of Everyday Things*).
[4] Cf. Konrad Lorenz, *Civilized Man's Eight Deadly Sins*, New York: Harcourt & Brace, 1974.
[5] Cf. Christopher DiCarlo, *How to Become a Really Good Pain in the Ass*, London: Prometheus Books, 2011.
[6] Cf. Plato, *Apology*, in *The Last Days of Socrates*, London: Penguin Classics, 1993, 29–68.
[7] Gilles Deleuze, *Difference and Repetition*, New York: Columbia University Press, 1994, 7 (originally published in 1968).
[8] Cf. Michael Polanyi, *The Tacit Dimension. With a New Foreword by Amartya Sen*, Chicago: The University of Chicago Press, 2009 (originally published in 1966).
[9] Sergi Avaliani, "Philosophy of the Pseudoabsolute", *Philosophical Investigations*, V, 2001, 21–32. Avaliani's English-language book-length treatment of the same subject was issued in September 2018 by Nova Science Publishers under the title *The Philosophy of Pseudoabsolute*.
[10] Ibid., 24–5.
[11] Ibid., 21.
[12] Ibid., 23.
[13] Ibid.
[14] Ibid., 21.
[15] Ibid., 24.
[16] Cf. Michael Polanyi, *Personal Knowledge*, London: Routledge, 2002 (originally published in 1958).
[17] Sergi Avaliani, "Philosophy of the Pseudoabsolute", 24.
[18] Ibid., 21.
[19] Ibid., 22.
[20] Ibid.
[21] Ibid.
[22] Ibid., 24.
[23] Ibid.
[24] Ibid.
[25] Cf. Immanuel Kant, *Critique of Pure Reason*, 2nd ed., London: MacMillan, 1922 (originally published in 1787).
[26] Ibid.

²⁷ Cf. Georg W.F. Hegel, *Phenomenology of Spirit*, Oxford: Oxford University Press, 1979 (originally published in 1807).
²⁸ Cf. Galileo Galilei, *Il saggiatore*, 1623, as cited in Edwin Arthur Burtt, *The Metaphysical Foundations of Modern Science* (Mineola: Dover, 2003), 75.
²⁹ Sergi Avaliani, "Philosophy of the Pseudoabsolute", 27.
³⁰ Ibid., 22.
³¹ Cf. Gilles Deleuze and Félix Guattari, *A Thousand Plateaus. Capitalism and Schizophrenia volume 2*, Minneapolis: University of Minnesota Press, 1987 (originally published in 1980).
³² Ibid., 40.
³³ Ibid.
³⁴ Ibid., 40–3.
³⁵ Ibid.
³⁶ Ibid., 40.
³⁷ Ibid., 63–4.
³⁸ Ibid., 50.
³⁹ Ibid., 69.
⁴⁰ Sergi Avaliani, "Philosophy of the Pseudoabsolute", 22–3.
⁴¹ Richard P. Feynman, *QED, The Strange Theory of Light and Matter*, London: Penguin Books, 1990, 9.
⁴² As cited in Peter Coveney and Roger Highfield, *The Arrow of Time* (London: Flamingo, 1991), 67.
⁴³ Charles Darwin, *The Origin of Species,* London: John Murray, 1859, 1. Admittedly, Darwin did believe that the eye was too the result of natural selection and stated: "When it was first said that the sun stood still and the world turned round, the common sense of mankind declared the doctrine false; but the old saying of Vox populi, vox Dei, as every philosopher knows, cannot be trusted in science. Reason tells me, that if numerous gradations from a simple and imperfect eye to one complex and perfect can be shown to exist, each grade being useful to its possessor, as is certainly the case; if further, the eye ever varies and the variations be inherited, as is likewise certainly the case and if such variations should be useful to any animal under changing conditions of life, then the difficulty of believing that a perfect and complex eye could be formed by natural selection, though insuperable by our imagination, should not be considered as subversive of the theory."
⁴⁴ Ludwig Boltzmann, *Theoretical Physics and Philosophical Problems,* Dordrecht: Reidel, 1974, 64.
⁴⁵ Richard Rorty, *Contingency, Irony, and Solidarity*, Cambridge, Mass.: Cambridge University Press, 1989, 5–7.
⁴⁶ Ibid., 16.
⁴⁷ Cf. Michael Polanyi, *Personal Knowledge.*
⁴⁸ As cited in James Reston, *Galileo, A Life* (New York: HarperCollins, 1994), 461.
⁴⁹ Richard Rorty, *Contingency, Irony, and Solidarity*, 16.
⁵⁰ Ibid., 8.
⁵¹ Ibid., 59 (emphasis in the original).
⁵² Ibid., 9.
⁵³ Ibid., 165.
⁵⁴ Richard Rorty, *Philosophy and the Mirror of Nature*, Princeton: Princeton University Press, 1979, 378.

⁵⁵ Cf. Steffen Mau, Heike Brabandt, Lena Laube and Christof Roos (eds.), *Liberal States and the Freedom of Movement. Selective Borders, Unequal Mobility* (Houndmills: Palgrave-Macmillan, 2012) and Pieter Bevelander and Bo Petersson (eds.), *Crisis and Migration. Implications of the Eurozone Crisis for Perceptions, Politics, and Policies on Migration* (Lund: Nordic Academic Press, 2014).
⁵⁶ Jürgen Habermas, "Citizenship and National Identity", *Theorizing Citizenship*, edited by R. Beiner, Albany: State University of New York Press, 1995, 262.
⁵⁷ R. Beiner, "Why Citizenship Constitutes a Theoretical Problem in the Last Decade of the Twentieth Century", *Theorizing Citizenship*, 3.
⁵⁸ Jürgen Habermas, "Citizenship and National Identity", 260.
⁵⁹ R. Beiner, "Why Citizenship Constitutes a Theoretical Problem in the Last Decade of the Twentieth Century", 2.
⁶⁰ Ibid., 7.
⁶¹ Jürgen Habermas, "Citizenship and National Identity", 260.
⁶² Ibid., 264.
⁶³ Michael Walzer as cited in R. Beiner, "Why Citizenship Constitutes a Theoretical Problem in the Last Decade of the Twentieth Century", 5.
⁶⁴ J. L. Hudson, "The Philosophy of Immigration", *The Journal of Libertarian Studies*, 8(1), 1986, 51–2.
⁶⁵ Cf. *Theorizing Citizenship*, edited by R. Beiner.
⁶⁶ Cf. Ludwig Wittgenstein, *Philosophical Investigations*, London: MacMillan, 1953.
⁶⁷ Cf. Giorgio Baruchello, "Richard Rorty - Una filosofia tra conversazione e politica" (an interview with Richard Rorty), *Iride: Filosofia e discussione pubblica*, 25, 1998 (translation mine).
⁶⁸ Cf. John McMurtry, *The Cancer Stage of Capitalism*, London: Pluto Press, 1999 (2nd ed. 2013). I discuss extensively life-value onto-axiology in my third and fourth volumes for Northwest Passage Books. In this fifth volume, instead, I limit its treatment to two mere brief introductions, i.e. chapters 3 and 16.
⁶⁹ Ibid., 20.
⁷⁰ A notable, though late exception to this dismal trend can be found in the proponents of "ecosocialism" listed in Richard Westra, *Socialism in the 21st Century* (New York: Nova Science Publishers, 2018).
⁷¹ John McMurtry, *Unequal Freedoms*, Toronto: Garamond Press, 1998, 325.
⁷² John McMurtry, *The Cancer Stage of Capitalism*, 308.
⁷³ This assessment is echoed in much literature of our time, within as well as outside the sole discipline of economics, e.g. Andrew Glyn's 2006 *Capitalism Unleashed* (Oxford: Oxford University Press), Nick Hewlett's 2007 *Badiou, Balibar, Rancière. Re-thinking Emancipation* (New York: Continuum) and Jacques Rancière's 2010 *Chronicles of Consensual Times* (New York: Continuum).
⁷⁴ John McMurtry, *The Cancer Stage of Capitalism*, 92 & 143.
⁷⁵ Ibid., 161 & 163.
⁷⁶ Ibid., 151.
⁷⁷ Ibid., 152.
⁷⁸ Ibid., 153.
⁷⁹ Ibid., 188 & 257.
⁸⁰ Ibid., 214.
⁸¹ Ibid., 190.
⁸² Ibid., 204.

[83] Ibid.
[84] Cf. ibid., 206–7.
[85] Ibid., 218.
[86] Ibid., 231.
[87] Analogous conclusions have been reached by the US leading K. Polanyi scholar, Fred L. Block, in his 2018 book *Capitalism. The Future of an Illusion* (Oakland: University of California Press).
[88] Ian Hacking, *The Social Construction of What?*, Cambridge: Cambridge University Press, 1999, 6–7, 22–5 & 83–4. Cf. also Richard Rorty, "Phony Science Wars", *The Atlantic Monthly*, November 1999, 120–2.
[89] Ian Hacking, *The Social Construction of What?*, 83–4.
[90] Richard Rorty, *Objectivity, Relativism, and Truth. Philosophical papers I*, Cambridge: Cambridge University Press, 1991, 1–2 & 5.
[91] Ian Hacking, *The Social Construction of What?*, 83–4.
[92] Cf. ibid, 3–5.
[93] Ibid., 170–2.
[94] Cf. ibid.
[95] Ibid., 104.
[96] Ibid., 114.
[97] Ibid., 68, 80 & 84.
[98] Ibid., 68.
[99] Ibid.
[100] Ibid.
[101] Ibid., 67.
[102] Cf. ibid., 83–4 & 233–4, especially note 23.
[103] Ibid., 33.
[104] Ibid., 104–8.
[105] Ibid., 167.
[106] Ibid., 41–2.
[107] Ibid., 120.
[108] Ibid., 21.
[109] Ibid., 232 note 14.
[110] Ibid., 22; cf. also 80 & 233–4.
[111] Ibid., 123.
[112] Ibid., 29.
[113] Ibid., 232–3 note 16 & 236–7 note 2.
[114] Ibid., 234 note 23.
[115] Ibid., 237 note 2 (emphasis added).
[116] Ibid., 4, 232–3 note 16 & 236–7 note 2.
[117] Richard Rorty, *Objectivity, Relativism, and Truth*, 21.
[118] Ibid., 61.
[119] Ibid., 22 & 55.
[120] Cf. David Lewis, *Papers in Metaphysics and Epistemology*, Cambridge: Cambridge University Press, 1999.

[121] The first six papers of the collection deal with properties and universals (1. "New work for a theory of universals", 2. "Putnam's paradox", 3. "Against structural universals", 4. "A comment on Armstrong and Forrest", 5. "Extrinsic properties", 6. "Defining 'intrinsic'"). The following four papers deal with the issue of ontological commitment (7. "Finkish dispositions", 8. "Noneism or allism?", 9. "Many, but almost one", 10. "Casati and Varzi on holes"). The subsequent five papers deal with possibility, causality and chance (11. "Rearrangement of particles: Reply to Lowe", 12. "Armstrong on combinatorial possibility", 13. "A world of truthmakers?", 14. "Maudlin and modal mystery", 15. "Humean supervenience debugged"). Then, four others are devoted to the analysis of the mind-body problem and the issue of *qualia* (16. "Psychophysical and theoretical identifications", 17. "What experience teaches", 18. "Reduction of mind", 19. "Should a materialist believe in qualia?"). Three papers tackle the metaphysics of colour and visual experience (20. "Naming the colours", 21. "Percepts and colour mosaics in visual experience", 22. "Individuation by acquaintance and by stipulation"). The final three papers face questions about rational belief and other aspects of contemporary theory of knowledge (23. "Why conditionalize?" 24. "What puzzling Pierre does not believe", 25. "Elusive knowledge").
[122] Ibid., 33–4.
[123] Ibid., 34.
[124] Ibid., 37.
[125] Ibid., 67.
[126] Ibid., 291.
[127] Ibid., 34.
[128] Ibid., 5.
[129] Ibid., 248.
[130] Ibid., 34.
[131] Ibid., 292.
[132] Ibid., 35.
[133] Ibid., cf. also note 9.
[134] Ibid.
[135] Ibid.
[136] Ibid., 9.
[137] Ibid., 400–1.
[138] Ibid., 401.
[139] Ibid., 423.
[140] Ibid., 123.
[141] Ibid., 291.
[142] Ibid., 292–3. It should be noted that supervenience or emergence state that phenomena and qualities irreducible to underlying ontological preconditions arise thereof, e.g. conscious thought from the neurons' chemical composition, but do not explain either how or why emergence occurs.
[143] Cf. ibid., essays 16–9.
[144] Cf. ibid.
[145] Ibid., 187–8.
[146] Ibid., 332.
[147] Ibid.
[148] Ibid., 333.

[149] Ibid., 357.
[150] Ibid., 320.
[151] Ibid., 179–80.
[152] Ibid., 49.
[153] Michele Marsonet, *Science, Reality, and Language*, Albany: SUNY Press, 1995, 31.
[154] Ibid., 100.
[155] Ibid., 101.
[156] Donald Davidson, *Essays on Actions and Events*, Oxford: Clarendon Press, 1980.
[157] Donald Davidson et al., *Truth and Interpretation. Perspectives on the Philosophy of Donald Davidson*, edited by E. LePore, Oxford: Blackwell, 1986.
[158] Edmund Husserl, "Phenomenology", *Husserl's Shorter Works*, edited by P. McCormick and F.A. Elliston, Notre Dame: University of Notre Dame Press, 1981, 21–35 (originally published in *Encyclopaedia Britannica*, 1927; reprinted in the *Journal of the British Society for Phenomenology*, 2, 1971, 77–90).
[159] Ibid., 21.
[160] Ibid., 21–2.
[161] In the 1870s, while studying astronomy, Husserl had attended Wundt's lectures at the University of Leipzig, where the latter worked *qua* professor of philosophy (cf. Christian Beyer, "Edmund Husserl", *The Stanford Encyclopedia of Philosophy*, 2016, <https://plato.stanford.edu/archives/win2016/entries/husserl/>).
[162] My interpretation of phenomenology may sound very Kantian. This is neither an unaware assumption of mine nor an unwarranted exegesis. My reading of Husserl's "Phenomenology" has led me to reconcile, rather than to contrast, Kant's and Husserl's positions, in spite of their divergences on other aspects of human cognition. As far as my comparison between Donald Davidson and Edmund Husserl is concerned, it is not important to consider, say, that the constitution of the object by the subject within an intentional relation happens not only in the form of judgement, or that time and space are not only those of the Newtonian physics, or that logic can be different from the Aristotelian one. What counts for my purposes here is that Kant opened the door to phenomenological research. He discovered the active role played by the cognising subject, thus describing knowledge, from lower perceptions to higher judgments, neither as a mere gathering of sense data (e.g. empiricism, externalism), nor as an archaeology of truths located inside the mind itself (e.g. rationalism, internalism).
[163] Edmund Husserl, "Phenomenology", 24.
[164] Donald Davidson, *Essays on Actions and Events*, 4.
[165] Ibid., 63–82 & 207–24.
[166] Ibid., 163–80 & 181–8.
[167] Cf. Donald Davidson et al., *Truth and Interpretation*, 307–19.
[168] Donald Davidson, *Essays on Actions and Events*, 5.
[169] Ibid., 10.
[170] Edmund Husserl, "Phenomenology", 23.
[171] Donald Davidson, *Essays on Actions and Events*, 211.
[172] Ibid.
[173] Cf. Donald Davidson et al., *Truth and Interpretation*, 308–11.
[174] Edmund Husserl, "Phenomenology", 24.
[175] Cf. Donald Davidson, *Essays on Actions and Events*, 164.

[176] Ibid., 3–20.
[177] Cf. ibid.
[178] Ibid., 111.
[179] Ibid., 186.
[180] Ibid., 3–20 & 43–62.
[181] Ibid., 83–102.
[182] Ibid., 21–42 & 83–102.
[183] Cf. ibid., 3–20.
[184] Edmund Husserl, "Phenomenology", 23.
[185] Donald Davidson, *Essays on Actions and Events*, 3–20.
[186] Ibid., 163–80 & 181–8.
[187] Ibid., 165.
[188] Donald Davidson et al., *Truth and Interpretation*, 310.
[189] Edmund Husserl, "Phenomenology", 23.
[190] Often the meaning of "formalised language" is confused with that of "symbolised language", insofar as formalisation and symbolisation tend to occur together.
[191] Edmund Husserl, "Phenomenology", 25.
[192] Ibid.
[193] These cases are nevertheless cases of extremely limited sharing of public standards, not of actual non-sharing of public standards. As concerns both the pre-linguistic human being (the infant) and the non-linguistic one (the madman), the process of interpretation of their behaviour would seem to imply the attribution of a minimal consistent pattern of beliefs, attitudes and behaviour, which allow us to recognise them as similar to us and, upon that basis, as different from most of us too.
[194] Cf. Donald Davidson et al., *Truth and Interpretation*, 316–9.
[195] Edmund Husserl, "Phenomenology", 24.
[196] Cf. Donald Davidson, *Essays on Actions and Events*, 210–1.
[197] Donald Davidson et al., *Truth and Interpretation*, 331.
[198] Ibid.
[199] E.g. Donald Davidson, *Essays on Actions and Events*, 3–20.
[200] E.g. ibid., 163–80 & 181–8.
[201] Cf. Donald Davidson et al., *Truth and Interpretation*, 319.
[202] Ibid., 307.
[203] Edmund Husserl, "Phenomenology", 26.
[204] Cf. Donald Davidson et al., *Truth and Interpretation*, 316–9.
[205] Edmund Husserl, "Phenomenology", 29.
[206] Ibid., 31.
[207] Ibid., 26.
[208] Cf. Donald Davidson, *Essays on Actions and Events*, 3–20 & 43–62.
[209] Cf. ibid., 83–102.
[210] Cf. ibid., 207–24, 229–38 & 245–60.
[211] Edmund Husserl, "Phenomenology", 26.
[212] Cf. Donald Davidson, *Essays on Actions and Events*, 163–80 & 181–8.
[213] Edmund Husserl, "Phenomenology", 26.

²¹⁴ Donald Davidson, *Essays on Actions and Events*, 207–24, 229–38 & 245–60. If there is anything else to be understood as the *Wesendeskription* of the *Gesamtgestalt*, this is not clear to me, since I cannot figure out any further essential feature of the stream of consciousness than its being relational and global.
²¹⁵ Edmund Husserl, "Phenomenology", 26.
²¹⁶ Gilles Deleuze, *The Logic of Sense*, New York: Columbia University Press, 1990, 134 (originally published in 1969).
²¹⁷ Ibid.
²¹⁸ Cf. ibid., chapter 1.
²¹⁹ Ibid.
²²⁰ Ibid.
²²¹ Gilles Deleuze and Félix Guattari, *A Thousand Plateaus*, 75–7.
²²² Gilles Deleuze, *Difference and Repetition*, 260; cf. also the reference to Foucault's "silent order of things" in Gilles Deleuze and Félix Guattari, *A Thousand Plateaus*, 87.
²²³ Ibid., 117.
²²⁴ Cf. Gilles Deleuze *Foucault*, London: The Athlone Press, 1988, 55–7 (originally published in 1986).
²²⁵ Gilles Deleuze and Félix Guattari, *A Thousand Plateaus*, 87.
²²⁶ Ibid., 108.
²²⁷ Ibid., 85–91 & 107–8.
²²⁸ Ibid., 87.
²²⁹ Gilles Deleuze, *Difference and Repetition*, 207–14; cf. also chapter 2.
²³⁰ Lucian Blaga, "From *Philosophical self-presentation* (1938): A lecture delivered at the University of Cluj", *Selected Philosophical Extracts*, edited by A. Botez, R.T. Allen and H.A. Serban, Wilmington: Vernon Press, 2018, 27–35.
²³¹ Gilles Deleuze, *The Logic of Sense*, 135.
²³² For reasons of synthesis I have been using conceptual categories of understanding and linguistic ones as co-extensive, henceforth both 19th-century transcendental and absolute idealism and 20th-century linguistic idealism are regarded here as "idealism" without any additional distinction.
²³³ Gilles Deleuze, *The Logic of Sense*, 135. I use "non-sense" to refer to the surface of events from which sense arises and "nonsense" for witty absurd statements (e.g. British understatements, Yiddish jokes).
²³⁴ Gilles Deleuze, "Coldness and Cruelty", *Masochism*, New York: Zone Book, 1989, 16.
²³⁵ Cf. also Donald Davidson, *Truth and Interpretation*, 307–32.
²³⁶ Gilles Deleuze, *Difference and Repetition*, 75; cf. also Gilles Deleuze and Félix Guattari, *A Thousand Plateaus*, 69.
²³⁷ Cf. Gilles Deleuze, *Difference and Repetition*, 77 on fatigue, 138–41 on encounter, 151–2 on cruelty, 232–5 & 237–8 on explication of intensity.
²³⁸ Ibid., 143.
²³⁹ Ibid., 143–5.
²⁴⁰ Ibid.
²⁴¹ Gilles Deleuze, *The Logic of Sense*, 137.
²⁴² Ibid., 136.
²⁴³ Ibid., 135.
²⁴⁴ Ibid., 136.

[245] Ibid., 139.
[246] Gilles Deleuze, *Difference and Repetition*, 5.
[247] Ibid., 245.
[248] Ibid., 5.
[249] Gilles Deleuze, "Coldness and Cruelty", 88–9.
[250] Gilles Deleuze, *Foucault*, 110–1.
[251] Ibid.
[252] Gilles Deleuze, *Difference and Repetition*, 5.
[253] Ibid., 7.
[254] Ibid., 11.
[255] Ibid., 63.
[256] Ibid., 68 & 182.
[257] Cf. Gilles Deleuze, "Coldness and Cruelty", 86–7.
[258] Gilles Deleuze, *The Logic of Sense*, 8–9.
[259] Ibid., 139–41.
[260] Gilles Deleuze, "Coldness and Cruelty", 86–7.
[261] Ibid., 89.
[262] Ibid., 124.
[263] Paradoxes, puns and nonsense, are the examples of humour given by Deleuze in the "19th Series of Humor", *The Logic of Sense*, 134–41 (cf. also notes 34, 39, 41–4, 49–50, 52 & 61).
[264] Gilles Deleuze, *Difference and Repetition*, 224–7.
[265] Cf. ibid. & Gilles Deleuze and Félix Guattari, *A Thousand Plateaus*.
[266] Cf. Gilles Deleuze, *The Logic of Sense*, 67–70 on the "Carroll-Chrysippus' effect" & 74–7 on the function of paradoxes.
[267] I am using here Heidegger's terminology for the sake of analogy, although I am aware that Deleuze's technical use of "being", "encounter" and "disclosure" differs from Heidegger's.
[268] Gilles Deleuze, *Kafka. Pour une litterature mineure*, Paris : Les Editions de Minuit, 1975, 75.
[269] Cf. ibid. note 59 & the defense of Carroll's mastering of surfaces from Artaud's criticism in Gilles Deleuze, *The Logic of Sense*, 84–93.
[270] Gilles Deleuze, *Difference and Repetition*, 202–3.
[271] Cf. ibid., notes 52–3.
[272] Cf. Gilles Deleuze, *Nietzsche and Philosophy*, New York: Columbia University Press, 1983, 186–94.
[273] Friedrich Nietzsche, *The Gay Science*, Vintage Books, New York, 1974, 125 (originally published in 1882). The full passage, in English translation, recites: "God is dead. God remains dead. And we have killed him. How shall we comfort ourselves, the murderers of all murderers? What was holiest and mightiest of all that the world has yet owned has bled to death under our knives: who will wipe this blood off us? What water is there for us to clean ourselves? What festivals of atonement, what sacred games shall we have to invent? Is not the greatness of this deed too great for us? Must we ourselves not become gods simply to appear worthy of it?"
[274] Gilles Deleuze, *Cinema 1. The Movement-image*, University of Minnesota Press, Minneapolis-London, 1986, 170–1 (originally published in 1983; emphasis added).
[275] Ibid., 171–2 (emphasis added).

[276] Luigi Pirandello, *On Humor*, Chapel Hill: University of North Carolina Press, 1974, 113 (originally published in 1908).
[277] Ibid.
[278] Ibid., 107.
[279] Ibid., 112.
[280] Ibid.
[281] Ibid., 113.
[282] Ibid.
[283] Cf. ibid., notes 64–7.
[284] Cf. ibid., 59–60.
[285] Cf. ibid., 61–2.
[286] Ibid., 137.
[287] Ibid., 141 & 144.
[288] Ibid., 142.
[289] Deleuze himself stresses this point in order to defend Carroll from Artaud's criticisms. Cf. Deleuze' series on Carroll in Gilles Deleuze, *The Logic of Sense*.
[290] Cf. F.C.T. Moore, *Bergson. Thinking Backwards*, Cambridge: Cambridge University Press, 1996.
[291] Gilles Deleuze, *Difference and Repetition*, 203.
[292] The quotes in this chapter come from the English translation of the second edition of Gadamer's *Warheit und Methode* (1965).
[293] Gadamer's misreading of Vico might be retrieved already in the alleged shift that he perceives between Vico's *De nostri temporis* and his later works. I believe Vico's thinking to have been substantially linear in its historical development and, above all, in his overall judgment on the cognitive powers of human rationality. However, this is an issue that I do not address in this chapter.
[294] Hans-Georg Gadamer, *Truth and Method*, 2nd ed., New York: Crossroads, 1985, 10.
[295] Ibid., 253.
[296] Ibid., 242.
[297] Ibid., 278.
[298] *Inter alia*, Vico acknowledged also the epistemic and human importance of the fine arts (cf. Malcolm Bull, *Inventing Falsehood, Making Truth: Vico and Neapolitan Painting,* Princeton: Princeton University Press, 2013).
[299] Giambattista Vico, *On the Study Methods of Our Times* (with a translation of *The Academies and the Relation between Philosophy and Eloquence*), Ithaca: Cornell University Press, 1990, 12 (originally published in 1709).
[300] Giambattista Vico, *On the Most Ancient Wisdom of the Italians*, Ithaca: Cornell University Press, 1988, 45 (originally published in 1710).
[301] Vico believed mathematics to be construed by men through mental operations. In this sense, mathematics belongs to the realm of fully intelligible human disciplines. Yet, his interpretation of Descartes remains as negative as that of any preacher of scientism. This because Descartes was a methodological monist, because his analytics wanted to replace Euclidean geometry with a more abstract form of geometry, and, above all, because he claimed such analytics to be natural and not constructed.
[302] Cf. Giambattista Vico, *On the Study Methods of Our Times*, xxxi–xxxiii.

[303] The two terms cristallising in the early Middle Ages with Boethius (475–526), the gradualistic conception of the *trivium* and *quadrivium* can be attributed to Varro (116–27 BC) and Martianus Capella (5th century AD).
[304] Christian Jermann, "La recezione di Vico in Gadamer", *Bollettino del Centro di Studi Vichiani*, 22–3, 1993, 325–43.
[305] J.D. Schaeffer, "*Sensus Communis* in Vico and Gadamer", *New Vico Studies*, 5, 1987, 117–30; and *Sensus Communis. Vico, Rhetoric, and the Limits of Relativism*, Durham: Duke University Press, 1990.
[306] Needless to say, I agree with their conclusions. Quite limitedly, I disagree with Schaeffer's interpretation of Vico as an anti-Platonist thinker. On the contrary, I would be ready to claim that Plato is one of Vico's inspirational points of reference, indeed "the prince of philosophers", as Vico wrote in his *Scienza nuova*.
[307] Hans-Georg Gadamer, *Truth and Method*, 27.
[308] Cf. J.D. Schaeffer, "*Sensus Communis* in Vico and Gadamer", 101–4 & 107–11.
[309] Giambattista Vico, *The New Science*, § 142.
[310] Hans-Georg Gadamer, *Truth and Method*, 27.
[311] Giambattista Vico, *The New Science*, § 145.
[312] The violent horrors following Luther's schism are particularly dramatic when read against the background of older, largely forgotten, successful examples of religious tolerance within Christian Europe and around the multi-confessional Mediterranean area (cf. Cary J. Nederman, *Worlds of Difference. European Discourses of Toleration, c.1100 – c.1550*, University Park: The Pennsylvania State University Press, 2000).
[313] Hans-Georg Gadamer, *Truth and Method*, 27–9.
[314] Ibid., 24.
[315] Cf. Friedrich Christoph Oetinger, *Inquisitio in sensum communem et rationem, mit einer Einleitung von Hans-Georg Gadamer*, Stuttgart: Friedrich Fromann, 1964 (originally published in 1753), chapter III, § 58.
[316] Ibid., chapter I, § 2.
[317] Cf. ibid., chapter I, § 7.
[318] Ibid., chapter II, § 22.
[319] Cf. ibid., chapter II, § 9.
[320] Ibid., chapter II, § 11.
[321] Cf. ibid., chapter II, § 17.
[322] Ibid., chapter II, § 14.
[323] Ibid., chapter II, §§ 12 & 17.
[324] Ibid., chapter II, § 18.
[325] Ibid.
[326] Ibid., chapter IV, § 93.
[327] Ibid., chapter II, § 18.
[328] Ibid., chapter V, *Epilogus*.
[329] Ibid., i–ii.
[330] Cf. L.W. Beck, *Early German Philosophy. Kant and His Predecessors*, Cambridge: Belknap, 1969.

[331] Cf. G. Cacciatore and G. Cantillo, "Studi vichiani in Germania", *Bollettino del Centro di Studi Vichiani*, 22–3, 1993, 7–39; A.M. Jacobelli-Isoldi, "I limiti della fortuna di Vico nel pensiero contemporaneo", *Bollettino del Centro di Studi Vichiani*, 22–3, 1993, 377–84; P. Olivier, "Le tricentenaire de Vico en France", *Rivista di Studi Crociani*, 7, 1970, 187–95; and P. Rossi, "Chi sono i contemporanei di Vico?", *Rivista di Filosofia*, 72, 1981, 51–82.

[332] Hans-Georg Gadamer, "Vi racconto questo secolo aggrappato al Titanic", interview by A. Gnoli and F. Volpi, 2001, <http://sol.falco.mi.it/db900/inter...zioni/Questo_secolo_aggrappato.htm> (translation mine).

[333] Cf. Hans-Georg Gadamer, *Kleine Schriften II–IV. Interpretationen*, Tuebingen: J.C.B. Mohr, 1967–77.

[334] Cf. J.M. Aguirre-Oraa, "Raison critique ou raison hermenetique?", *Revue Philosophique de Louvain*, 91, 1993, 409–40; and "Pensar con Gadamer y Habermas", *Revista Portuguesa de Filosofia*, 56(3–4), 2000, 489–507.

[335] The most thorough analysis of Pareto's understanding of linguistic communication has been put forward in Italian by Francesco Aqueci in *Le funzioni del linguaggio secondo Pareto* (Bern: Peter Lang, 1991). Insightful remarks have been formulated also in French by Alban Bouvier in "Une anthropologie sociologique des topoï: La théorie des dérivations de Pareto" (*Lieux communs, topoï, stéréotypes, clichés*, edited by C. Plantin, Paris: Edition Kimé, 1993, 182–92) and *Naturalisme et actionnisme chez Pareto. Pareto aujourd'hui* (Paris: Presses Universitaires Françaises, 1999, cf. 273–92). Bouvier interprets Pareto's derivations as rhetorical commonplaces serving social utility. As regards Aqueci's work, instead, his book does not tackle rhetoric *per se*, yet it sheds light on exquisitely rhetorical notions such as the emotional appeal of reasoning (§ 5.1.2), the argumentative effectiveness of moral injunctions and other logico-experimentally unwarranted linguistic expressions (§§ 5.3 & 5.5), and the ideal orator (§ 6.5).

[336] Bouvier argues that the study of why certain arguments are persuasive and others are not remains an underdeveloped area of investigation in the social sciences and communication studies, especially as far as rational choice theory is concerned (cf. his 2002 article "An Epistemological Plea for Methodological Individualism and Rational Choice Theory in Cognitive Rhetoric", *Philosophy of the Social Sciences*, 32(1), 51–70).

[337] Plato, *Gorgias*, in *Complete Works*, edited by J.M. Cooper, Indianapolis: Hackett, 1997, 791–869, 465b–c (written originally around 380 BC).

[338] Interestingly, Whidden observes how Socrates, in Plato's *Gorgias*, fails to persuade his third and last interlocutor, Callicles, despite the former's superior knowledge and higher moral ground (cf. his 2005 article "True Statesmanship as True Rhetoric in Plato's 'Gorgias'", *Polis*, 22(2), 206–29).

[339] Aristotle, *Rhetoric* (aka *Ars Rhetorica*), in *The Basic Works of Aristotle*, edited by R. McKeon. New York: Random House, 1325–454, 1941, I, 1, 1355a, 25.

[340] Vilfredo Pareto, *The Mind and Society*, New York: Harcourt, Brace & Company, 1935, § 28 (emphases in the original; originally published in 1916).

[341] Ibid., § 275 note 1. By and large, Pareto manifests a preference for "Aristotle, the naturalist" who "gets closer to realities... than does Plato, the metaphysicist" (§ 2553 II–γ).

[342] "The main thing in metaphysical theories" being "sentiments... not the arguments" (ibid., § 598).

³⁴³ Ibid., § 1922 note 8.
³⁴⁴ Ibid., § 2349.
³⁴⁵ Ibid., § 2463 note 1.
³⁴⁶ Ibid., § 2573.
³⁴⁷ Ibid., § 1576.
³⁴⁸ Ibid., § 625.
³⁴⁹ Vilfredo Pareto, "The New Theories of Economics", *The Journal of Political Economy*, 5(4), 1897, 485.
³⁵⁰ Vilfredo Pareto, *The Mind and Society*, § 29.
³⁵¹ Ibid., § 42.
³⁵² Ibid., § 468.
³⁵³ Ibid., § 384 (emphasis added).
³⁵⁴ Ibid., § 1476.
³⁵⁵ Ibid., § 1458, II–γ.
³⁵⁶ Ibid., § 1614.
³⁵⁷ Ibid., § 1610.
³⁵⁸ Ibid., § 1930.
³⁵⁹ Cf. Joseph Femia, *Pareto and Political Theory*, London: Routledge, 2006, 36.
³⁶⁰ Vilfredo Pareto, *The Mind and Society*, § 870.
³⁶¹ Ibid., § 888.
³⁶² Ibid., § 2007.
³⁶³ Ibid., §§ 887–8.
³⁶⁴ Ibid., §§ 889–1396.
³⁶⁵ Ibid., § 1690.
³⁶⁶ Ibid., § 883. Pareto was always cautious *vis-à-vis* making any claim of actual knowledge; after all, inasmuch as knowledge can only be possessed by living persons, "all human knowledge is subjective." (§ 149) We may stipulate a distinction, as Pareto himself does for explanatory reasons, between "subjective" and "objective", which is warranted "in view of the greater or lesser fund of factual knowledge that we ourselves have" (ibid.). Nevertheless, all that we know is ultimately what we individually claim to know at a given point in time, due to the many experiences and careful observations tested until then, all of which are logically revisable, including those established in the most glorious realms of our "logical actions" i.e. humankind's "arts and sciences... political economy... military, political, legal, and similar activities." (§§ 151–2) Prudently, when presenting his most innovative sociological accomplishment, i.e. his theories of residues and derivations, Pareto suggests that the origin of residues can be hypothesised rather than ascertained, since only social phenomena "observable today" are available to the social scientist, plus mere "traces... in documents of the past." (§ 887)
³⁶⁷ Ibid., § 1400.

³⁶⁸ Scholars disagree on the extent to which sentiments and instincts can be distinguished from appetites, tastes, inclinations and interests, and all of these from one another (cf. also Vilfredo Pareto, *Sociological Writings*, Oxford: Basil Blackwell, 1966, 41–4). Given what Pareto asserts about the fuzzy, *post-factum* and stipulative character of our knowledge of human instincts, I believe such disagreements to be impossible to resolve (cf. Vilfredo Pareto, *The Mind and Society*, § 870). Still, it must be noticed that he does treat interests as noteworthy insofar as they lead often to logical action and play a crucial role in determining the social equilibrium by inspiring economic activities (e.g. § 1207).
³⁶⁹ Ibid., § 1690.
³⁷⁰ Ibid., § 975.
³⁷¹ Ibid., § 868.
³⁷² Ibid., §§ 1420–1686.
³⁷³ Ibid. The physical activities underpinning linguistic communication (e.g. the bodily articulation of sound, our utterances) and accompanying it (e.g. gazing, smiling, blushing, heart-throbbing) are dubbed "manifestations" in an example discussed by Pareto in a letter to G. H. Bousquet (*Oeuvres complètes*, Geneva: Droz, 1964, vol. XIX, 1092). Pareto's *Trattato* treats "manifestation" as meaning either "derivative" (e.g. §§ 868, 1688, 1826 & 1830) or the end that certain derivations pursue, as distinguished from the actual derivations (e.g. §§ 1413–4, 1688, 1832 & 1877). The interpretation offered in his 23 August 1922 letter to Bousquet is successive to Pareto's 1916 *Trattato* and is conceptually easier to accommodate within Pareto's overall understanding of social phenomena, hence I opt for it here.
³⁷⁴ Cf. P. Aspers, "Crossing the Boundary of Economics and Sociology", *American Journal of Economics and Sociology*, 60(2), 2001, 519–45.
³⁷⁵ Vilfredo Pareto, *The Mind and Society*, § 150.
³⁷⁶ Ibid., § 154.
³⁷⁷ Ibid., § 149.
³⁷⁸ Ibid., § 154.
³⁷⁹ Ibid., § 160.
³⁸⁰ Ibid., § 159.
³⁸¹ Ibid., § 154.
³⁸² Ibid., § 1404.
³⁸³ Ibid.
³⁸⁴ Ibid., § 1405.
³⁸⁵ Pareto's *Trattato* does not address one important aspect that Aristotle highlights in connection with rhetorical arguments, i.e. that they start from probable premises upon which the audience is likely to agree, rather than from apodictically true scientific premises.
³⁸⁶ Ibid., § 1406.
³⁸⁷ Ibid.
³⁸⁸ Ibid., § 1407.
³⁸⁹ Ibid., § 1408.
³⁹⁰ Ibid., §§ 1407–8.
³⁹¹ Ibid.
³⁹² Ibid., § 1421. In Pareto's classification of derivations, assertions constitute type number one (§ 1420).
³⁹³ Ibid., § 1407.

[394] Ibid., § 958.
[395] Ibid., § 1407.
[396] Ibid., § 1115.
[397] Ibid., § 1113.
[398] Ibid., § 1932.
[399] Ibid., § 1409.
[400] Ibid., § 480.
[401] Ibid., § 636.
[402] Ibid., § 854.
[403] Ibid., § 1892.
[404] Ibid., § 445.
[405] Ibid., § 1411.
[406] I.e. ibid., § 1411.
[407] Aristotle, *Rhetoric*, I, 1, 1355a, 14–5.
[408] Cf. ibid., II, 24, 1400b–1402a.
[409] Cf. ibid, I, 1, 1355b, 15–20.
[410] The *Organon* comprises Aristotle's most important works on logic, language and hermeneutics.
[411] Aristotle, *Rhetoric*, I, 1, 1355a, 30–34.
[412] Ibid., I, 1, 1355b, 4–9.
[413] Ibid., I, 1, 1355b, 1–3.
[414] Jennifer Richards calls this discipline in her 2008 book *Rhetoric* "the new critical idiom" (London: Routledge), which can spot true and apparent instances of reasoning because of its emphasis upon arguing both sides of a question, as Aristotle himself instructed.
[415] Vilfredo Pareto, *The Mind and Society*, § 42.
[416] Ibid., § 76.
[417] Ibid.
[418] Ibid.
[419] Ibid., § 113.
[420] Ibid., § 1455.
[421] Ibid., § 817.
[422] Ibid.
[423] Cf. Aristotle, *Rhetoric*, most of book II.
[424] Roland Barthes, "The Old Rhetoric: An Aide-mémoire", *The Semiotic Challenge*, New York: Hill and Wang, 1988, § B.1.29.
[425] Cf. Aristotle, *Rhetoric*, II, 1, 1378a, 6–19.
[426] Bouvier builds upon two short quotes (i.e. §§ 1397 & 1418) in Pareto's *Trattato* suggesting that rational arguments may, marginally and rarely, persuade their recipients, on top of the emotions that they stir (*Naturalisme et actionnisme chez Pareto*, 279). Perhaps Pareto would have not dissented entirely from Aristotle, on such *exceptional* cases.
[427] "For all advice to do things or not to do them is concerned with happiness and with the things that make for or against it; whatever creates or increases happiness or some part of happiness, we ought to do." (Aristotle *Rhetoric*, I, 5, 1360b, 10–12)
[428] Vilfredo Pareto, *The Mind and Society*, § 1399.
[429] Ibid.

[430] Ibid. This is no small problem, insofar as Pareto ascribes to "social utilities" the very success of modern science or, as he dubs it, of those "[e]xperimental researches" that, even if capable of "shaking the foundations of the social order" as dramatically as some daring "ethical researches", have not been contrasted as fiercely "by public opinion ... and ... public authority." (§ 2002)

[431] Ibid., §§ 1893–5. Pareto's half-spoken notion of the good translates as life-enhancing "material well-being" (§ 1930) and the continuation in time of society (e.g. § 1206). Though partial, under-theorised and cautiously underplayed not to contradict Pareto's scepticism *vis-à-vis* any strong notion of cardinal utility (cf. L. Bruni and F. Guala, "Vilfredo Pareto and the Epistemological Foundations of Choice Theory", *History of Political Economy*, 33(1), 2001, 21–49), this is consistent with Aristotle's own notion of happiness, which he variously defines (e.g. "prosperity ... independence of life ... pleasure ... good condition of property and body"; *Rhetoric*, I, 4, 1360b, 14–7), *never* objecting to a modicum of material comforts and to harmonious social coexistence.

[432] Vilfredo Pareto, *The Mind and Society*, §§ 1929–30. Pareto goes as far as to claim that "every device of ingenious sophistry" has been employed "to eliminate very obtrusive contradictions between solutions and experience", so as to please our pseudo-logical cravings and, at the same time, preserve that which is "beneficial socially" even if "false experimentally" (§ 1931).

[433] Ibid., § 1206.

[434] E.g. Francisco de Vitoria OP (1483–1546), who in his first 1532 *Relectio* on the American Indians (*De Indis*, §3 [second proposition following the summary of the Third Section], concluding remarks), in a typical scholastic fashion, mixes heathen and Christian sources in order to assert: "And, as is said in Dig., 1, 1, 3, 'Nature has established a bond of relationship between all men,' and so it is contrary to natural law for one man to dissociate himself from another without good reason. 'Man,' says Ovid, 'is not a wolf to his fellow man, but a man.'" (translation by John Pawley Bate; <http://www.constitution.org/victoria/victoria_.htm>)

[435] Cf. Fiorenzo Mornati, *Una biografia intellettuale di Vilfredo Pareto: II. Illusioni e delusioni della libertà (1891–1898)*, Rome: Edizioni Storia e Letteratura, 2017, 158 & 208 (translation mine). Pareto's paradoxical predicament affects today Peter Singer's (b. 1946) attempt at combining utilitarianism and egalitarianism (cf. *A Darwinian Left: Politics, Evolution and Cooperation*, New Haven: Yale University Press, 2000).

[436] Vilfredo Pareto, *The Mind and Society*, § 286 note 1.

[437] Aristotle's *endoxa*, i.e. the received wisdom of the community within which the rhetorician operates, embody the experience and observations of generations. *Via* the precepts of religion and morality, they lead people towards that generic happiness, which is similar to Pareto's equally generic "social utility" (ibid., §§ 1897–8).

[438] Cf. R. Collins, R. and M. Makowsky, *The Discovery of Society*, 6th ed., Boston, MA: McGraw-Hill, 1998, 211. This book's being an undergraduate textbook cannot but highlight how *commonplace* the objection has been.

[439] Cf. Roland Barthes, "The Old Rhetoric: An Aide-mémoire".

[440] Ibid.

[441] As my ensuing remarks on diagrams imply, choices of 'airs' involve stylistic choices: *inventio* begets *elocutio*.

[442] Vilfredo Pareto, *The Mind and Society*, §§ 84–5.

[443] E.g. ibid., § 1206.
[444] Cf. ibid., § 1999.
[445] E.g. ibid., §§ 6, 19–21, 46–7, 83, 86 & 941.
[446] Ibid., § 1431.
[447] Ibid., § 1434.
[448] Ibid., § 1430.
[449] I endorse Hirschman's assessment of Pareto and I refer the reader to his intriguing *Rhetoric of Reaction* for relevant quotations from Pareto's works (*The Rhetoric of Reaction*, Cambridge, MA: Belknap Press, 1991).
[450] Ibid., 55, 71 & 78.
[451] Ibid., 55–6.
[452] Ibid., 77–9.
[453] Ibid., 58–9.
[454] Cf. Aristotle, *Rhetoric*, III, 13, 1414a–20b.
[455] Ibid., 1414a, 30–35.
[456] Cf. Donald/Deirdre McCloskey, *The Rhetoric of Economics*, 2nd ed., Madison, WI: University of Wisconsin Press, 1998; and Alan G. Gross, *The Rhetoric of Science*, Cambridge, MA: Harvard University Press, 1990. The present book chapter is itself organised according to classical rhetorical standards: *captatio benevolentiae*, *partitio*, *narratio*, etc.
[457] Cf. Aristotle, *Rhetoric*, III, 1, 1403b.
[458] Cf. Quintilian, *Institutes of Oratory*, 2006, <http://penelope.uchicago.edu/Thayer/E/Roman/Texts/Quintilian/Institutio_Oratoria/home.html> (originally published around the year 95 AD). 20th-century linguists similarly distinguish between *signified* and *signifiers* (cf. Roland Barthes, "The Old Rhetoric: An Aide-mémoire").
[459] Crick argues that thought experiments, commonly used in evolutionary theory and other branches of modern science where empirical substantiation is limited or impossible, are actually enthymemes (cf. N. Crick, "Conquering Our Imagination", *Philosophy and Rhetoric*, 37(1), 2004, 21–41).
[460] Alan G. Gross, *The Rhetoric of Science*, 10.
[461] Ibid.
[462] Ibid.
[463] Ibid., 11.
[464] Vilfredo Pareto, *The Mind and Society*, § 6.
[465] Ibid., §§ 6 & 8. Implicit, but never truly spelled out, is the realisation that a positive, scientific sociology would have very little to say about the ends of social life, its existential meaning, or the fundamental values that should inform and guide it. Science, in other words, may well produce an accurate depiction of select aspects of reality, but is not equipped to tell us what to do with and within such a reality.
[466] As regards the fifth canon of rhetoric, tropes possess a mnemonic function too i.e. they allow for the swifter and more durable acquisition of concepts, as with the standard brachylogy of tables of contents, titles and headings, and with vivid metaphors such as Pareto's own comparison of "the circulation of elites" to a "river" experiencing occasional floods (§ 2056), or the political typology of "lions" and "foxes" (§ 2178), which A.J. Marshall even employs as fundamental categories of political psychology (cf. his 2007 book, *Vilfredo Pareto's Sociology*, Aldershot: Ashgate).

[467] Vilfredo Pareto, *The Mind and Society*, § 302.
[468] Ibid., § 21.
[469] Ibid., § 20.
[470] Ibid., § 503 note 6.
[471] Ibid., § 2.
[472] Ibid., § 62.
[473] Ibid., § 46.
[474] Ibid., § 35.
[475] Ibid., § 63. Both Hirschman and Gross make use of notions belonging to classical, not modern, rhetoric.
[476] Vilfredo Pareto, *The Mind and Society*, § 1552 (emphasis removed).
[477] Ibid., § 275.
[478] Ibid., § 273.
[479] Ibid., § 468.
[480] Pareto disagrees with Aristotle and, for that matter, with Plato, upon the notion that we may be able to steer consciously and by logical means the deep-seated sentiments causing non-logical action. Their hope that "inclinations" may be moulded and "virtue" be taught is one that Pareto does not share in the least (ibid., §§ 280–1). Also, the *vir bonus peritus dicendi* implied by Aristotle's notion of the well-meaning rhetorician and idealised by Roman rhetoricians, to whom Pareto makes a fleeting remark (§ 1397 note 2), is very much analogous to the politician mocked by Pareto, as "[he] comes eventually to believe that his real interest is the welfare of others", rather than the deep-seated, unvarying and quintessential "ambition to obtain money, power, distinctions" from which all politicians start off, whether consciously or not (§ 854).
[481] Perelman and Olbrechts-Tyteca argue that theory of argumentation, which includes rhetoric, is prior and irreducible to scientific investigation, insofar as scientific investigation relies inevitably upon argumentation in order to operate at any level of complexity (cf. Chaïm Perelman and Lucie Olbrechts-Tyteca, *The New Rhetoric. A Treatise on Argumentation*, Notre Dame: University of Notre Dame Press, 1969; originally published in 1958).
[482] Cf. Kenneth Burke, *A Rhetoric of Motives*, Berkeley, CA: University of California Press, 1969; Chaïm Perelman and Lucie Olbrechts-Tyteca, *The New Rhetoric*; and Alain Bouvier, *L'argumentation philosophique*, Paris: Presses Universitaires Françaises, 1995. Indeed, I would argue that each and every living author writes also to persuade herself to go on writing. Were she to write in a style utterly devoid of beauty, wit, depth, or any other aesthetically fulfilling character, then the likelihood that she may complete her task would diminish considerably.
[483] Vilfredo Pareto, *The Mind and Society*, §§ 42 & 76.
[484] Ibid., § 1712. Cf. Friedrich Nietzsche, "Lecture Notes on Rhetoric", *Philosophy and Rhetoric*, 16(2), 1983, 94–129 (originally published in 1874); and Paul De Man, *Blindness and Insight*, London: Routledge, 1983.
[485] Vilfredo Pareto, *The Mind and Society*, § 108. Pareto was aware of how "the more advanced sciences" had developed languages that gave "senses very different ... from ... everyday usage" to ordinary terms such as "water", "light" and "velocity" (§ 115).

[486] The classical technical notion of "kairos" refers precisely to the rhetorician's awareness of, and responsiveness to, the particular setting in which her speech is delivered and, supremely, the audience to whom the speech is delivered (cf. Roland Barthes, "The Old Rhetoric: An Aide-mémoire").

[487] Although rhetoric had been discussed and implicitly defended by Nietzsche, whose 1870s lecture notes had been circulating in German since 1922, and by I.A. Richards in the 1930s, the positivistic *Zeitgeist* of much of the late 19th century and its fairly commonplace dismissal of rhetoric continued well into the 20th century (cf. I.A. Richards, *The Philosophy of Rhetoric*, Oxford: Oxford University Press, 1936). It is only in the late 1950s that rhetoric began a process of intellectual revival, which has persisted in philosophical circles up to this day.

[488] John McMurtry, "Human Rights versus Corporate Rights: Life Value, the Civil Commons and Social Justice", *Studies in Social Justice*, 5(1), 2011, 17.

[489] All references in this chapter are by fragment number as they appear in the latest complete English translation of the 1976 Sellier edition of the so-called "Copy B" of Pascal's thoughts, that is, the second copy prepared for his sister and least likely of having undergone third-person reordering (*Pensées*, edited by Roger Ariew, Indianapolis/Cambridge: Hackett, 2005). I have also made use of the original French and related Italian translation of Pascal's thoughts by Adriano Bausola contained in *Pensieri* (Milan: Rusconi, 1993).

[490] Cf. "the machine", 680.

[491] A valuable and possibly unique recent exception is constituted by: William D. Wood's 2009 article "Axiology, Self-deception, and Moral Wrongdoing in Blaise Pascal's Pensées" (*Journal of Religious Ethics*, 37(2), 355–84). The first footnote in Wood's essay contains a laconically brief account of the negligible record of Pascal studies in modern Anglophone ethics. The main difference with regard to Wood's own commendable 2009 attempt is my further avoidance of strictly epistemological and theological considerations, to either of which Pascal's moral philosophy is regularly reduced. Also, I attempt hereby to provide more numerous references to relevant fragments in Pascal's *Pensées*.

[492] Blaise Pascal, *Thoughts*, 12.

[493] Ibid., 339.

[494] Cf. ibid., 41.

[495] Cf. also ibid., 804 from the Manuscript Guerrier (*not* Copy B).

[496] Ibid., 450.

[497] Ibid., 142. Pascal's emphasis upon intuition *vis-à-vis* first principles is analogous to Aristotle's *epagoge* in connection with the fundamental laws of thought that cannot be obtained through any set of syllogisms but that underpin them all nonetheless (*Anal. Post.* II, 99b–100b; *Meta.* 980a–981a).

[498] Blaise Pascal, *The Art of Persuasion*, Harvard: Harvard Classics, 2013. Pascal's distinction is not to be confused with Descartes' distinction between empirical and innate knowledge. Rather, Pascal wishes to separate knowledge that we can reach through explicit reasoning processes of demonstration, whether deductive or inductive, and the indemonstrable fundamental principles that make them possible.

[499] Blaise Pascal, *Thoughts*, 598. Given Pascal's regular use of "wisdom" rather than "knowledge" in his *Pensées*, I would venture to argue that this different study object is one of the reasons why "ethics" is said to be a "special" science.

[500] Cf. ibid., 157–9 & 527.

⁵⁰¹ Customs, for Pascal, are very powerful, to the point of establishing causality itself (661), though they are neither absolute (e.g. 527) nor certain (e.g. 94–6).
⁵⁰² Cf. ibid., 97–8, 132 & 171.
⁵⁰³ Ibid., 116.
⁵⁰⁴ Ibid., 142.
⁵⁰⁵ Ibid., 412; cf. also 443, 448, 450, 646 & 717.
⁵⁰⁶ Ibid., 580.
⁵⁰⁷ Ibid., 2 & 5.
⁵⁰⁸ Ibid., 680.
⁵⁰⁹ Ibid., 360 (emphasis in the original).
⁵¹⁰ Ibid., 287.
⁵¹¹ Ibid., 662.
⁵¹² Ibid., 1.
⁵¹³ Ibid., 680 (emphasis added).
⁵¹⁴ Ibid., 46.
⁵¹⁵ Ibid., 232; cf. also 106 & 117.
⁵¹⁶ Ibid., 187. On repeated occasions (e.g. *Gesammelte Werke*, Bern: Francke Verlag, 1971–97, volume V, 104) did Max Scheler praise Pascal and his spiritual mentor Augustine for attempting to overcome Western thought's long-standing prejudice that grants epistemic objectivity and evidential value to rational proofs alone, ignoring sentiment and religious revelation or, worse, condemning them as subjective and dangerously irrational.
⁵¹⁷ Cf. Blaise Pascal, *Thoughts*, 455.
⁵¹⁸ Ibid., 214.
⁵¹⁹ Cf. ibid., 25.
⁵²⁰ Cf. ibid.
⁵²¹ Cf. ibid.
⁵²² Cf. ibid., 75 & 601.
⁵²³ Cf. ibid., 645.
⁵²⁴ Cf. especially ibid., 145–67, 230–4, 690 & 707–8; cf. also 753 from the Manuscript Périer (*not* Copy B).
⁵²⁵ E.g. ibid., 736; cf. also 749 & 771 from the Manuscript Périer (*not* Copy B). Pascal seems to allow for cases of commendable moral virtue in non-Catholic and non-Christian settings, e.g. "the Jewish religion" (276; cf. 692–6 & 715), but not of salvation altogether.
⁵²⁶ "I believe in order to understand"; as cited in Perry Cahall, "The Value of St Augustine's Use/Enjoyment Distinction to Conjugal Love", *Logos* (8)1, 2005, 117. Under this perspective, Pascal's heart can be seen as opening a hermeneutical horizon, which embraces much more than just the knowledge that can be rationally demonstrated. (Augustine's original formulation was "*crede, ut intelligas*", but Saint Anselm's reformulation of it is the one that has become canonical and is commonly referred to Augustine himself.)
⁵²⁷ Cf. Blaise Pascal, *Thoughts*, 142.
⁵²⁸ E.g. ibid., 287.
⁵²⁹ E.g. ibid., 662.
⁵³⁰ Ibid., 462.
⁵³¹ Ibid., 566.
⁵³² Cf. ibid., 57.

[533] Ibid., 329. This is another notion that Pascal derives from Augustine, i.e. the "order of love" [*ordo amoris*], whereby the heart, accompanied by reason and the correct Christian tradition, loves to different degrees worthy realities upon their actual, differing merit.
[534] Cf. ibid., 13.
[535] Ibid., 339.
[536] Ibid., 92.
[537] Ibid., 669.
[538] Ibid., 182, 536 & 681–2; cf. also 544 in which "the will" is said to be the human faculty that "loves".
[539] Ibid., 210.
[540] E.g. ibid., 309, 311, 378 & 504; cf. also 707.
[541] Ibid., 29; cf. also 144, 164, 203, 414, 503 & 514.
[542] Ibid., 445.
[543] E.g. ibid., 498; cf. also 770 from the Manuscript Périer (*not* Copy B) & 800 from the Recueil Original (*not* copy B).
[544] Ibid., 680.
[545] Cf. ibid., 87 & 544.
[546] Ibid., 680.
[547] Cf. ibid., 531; needless to say, Pascal's conception of the two kinds of esprit anticipates Michael Polanyi's reflections on explicit and tacit knowledge.
[548] Ibid., 622.
[549] Ibid.
[550] Cf. Richard Rorty, *Objectivity, Relativism, and Truth*.
[551] Blaise Pascal, *Thoughts*, 661.
[552] Ibid., 662.
[553] Ibid., 78.
[554] Ibid.
[555] Cf. ibid., 689.
[556] E.g. ibid., 195–8 & 686.
[557] Ibid., 494; cf. also 509–10.
[558] Ibid., 743.
[559] Ibid., 455–6 & 576.
[560] Cf. "Cleopatra's nose", ibid., 31–2 & 228.
[561] Ibid., 201; cf. also 203–13.
[562] Cf. "Luther: everything outside the truth.", 791 from the Recueil Original (*not* Copy B).
[563] Ibid., 258.
[564] Ibid., 709–10.
[565] Ibid., 408.
[566] Ibid., 458.
[567] Ibid., 500; cf. also 759 from the Manuscript Périer (*not* Copy B).
[568] Ibid., 457.
[569] Ibid., 739.
[570] Ibid., 451.
[571] Ibid., 447–8.
[572] Ibid., 469; cf. also 753 from the Manuscript Périer (*not* Copy B).
[573] Ibid., 558.
[574] Ibid., 658.

[575] Ibid., 27; cf. also 16 & 714.
[576] Ibid., 568.
[577] E.g. ibid., 699; cf. also 744 from the Manuscript Périer (*not* Copy B).
[578] E.g. ibid., 25, 62, 90–1, 165–6 & 180–1.
[579] Ibid., 335.
[580] Richard Rorty, *Contingency, Irony and Solidarity*.
[581] Blaise Pascal, *Thoughts*, 329; cf. also 496 & 702.
[582] E.g. J. Haidt, "The Emotional Dog and its Rational Tail", *Psychological Review*, 108(8), 2001, 14–34.
[583] E.g. Blaise Pascal, *Thoughts*, 570.
[584] Cf. Hans Jonas, *The Imperative Responsibility*, Chicago: University of Chicago Press, 1984 (originally published in 1979).
[585] Herbert W. Simons, *The Rhetorical Turn: Invention and Persuasion in the Conduct of Inquiry*, Chicago: Chicago University Press, 1990, vii.
[586] Cf. Paul Trembath, "The Rhetoric of Philosophical 'Writing': Emphatic Metaphors in Derrida and Rorty", *Journal of Aesthetics and Art Criticism*, 47(2), 1989: 169–73; Áine Kelly, "The Provocative Polemics of Richard Rorty", *Minerva*, 12, 2008, 78–101.
[587] Cf. Janet S. Horne, "Rorty's Circumvention of Argument: Redescribing Rhetoric", *Southern Communication Journal* 58(3), 1993, 169–81.
[588] Péter Csato, "Antipodean Conversations: Rhetorical Strategies of Discursive Authority in Richard Rorty's Metaphilosophy and Political Thought", 2009, <http://unideb.academia.edu/PeterCsato/Papers>.
[589] Cf. Mario Moussa, "Misunderstanding the Democratic 'We': Richard Rorty's Liberalism and the Radical Urge for a Philosophical Foundation", *Philosophy and Social Criticism*, 17, 1991, 297; and Christopher M. Duncan, "A Question to Richard Rorty", *The Review of Politics*, 66(3), 2004, 387 note 5.
[590] Cf. Rebecca Comay, "Interrupting the Conversation", *Telos* 69, 1986, 119–30.
[591] Cf. Michael Billig, "Nationalism and Richard Rorty: The Text as a Flag for Pax Americana", *New Left Review*, 202(1), 1993, 69–83.
[592] Cf. Lynn A. Baker, "'Just Do It': Pragmatism and Progressive Social Change", *Virginia Law Review*, 78(3), 1992, 697–718.
[593] Richard J. Bernstein, "One Step Forward, Two Steps Backward: Richard Rorty on Liberal Democracy and Philosophy", *Political Theory*, 15(4), 1987, 554.
[594] Cf. Mark Kingwell, *A Civil Tongue. Justice, Dialogue and the Politics of Pluralism*, University Park, PA: Pennsylvania University Press, 1995, 36–41.
[595] Cf. Susan Haack, *Manifesto of a Passionate Moderate*, Chicago: University of Chicago Press, 1998, 31–47.
[596] Jonathan Rée, "Strenuous Unbelief", *London Review of Books*, 20(22), 1998, 8.
[597] Jenny Teichman, "The Philosophy of We", *The New Criterion*, 17, 1998, 60.
[598] Cf. Daniel Conway, "Irony, State and Utopia: Rorty's 'We' and the Problem of Transitional Praxis", *Richard Rorty: Critical Dialogues*, edited by Matthew Festenstein and Simon Thompson, Malden, MA: Polity Press, 2001, 55–88; and Manuel Moussa, "Misunderstanding the Democratic 'We'", 307.
[599] E.g. John D. Caputo, *More Radical Hermeneutics. On Not Knowing Who We Are*, Bloomington: Indiana University Press, 2000.
[600] Anthony Gottlieb, "The Most Talked-About Philosopher", *The New York Times*, 2 June 1998, <http://www.nytimes.com/1991/06/02/books/the-most-talked-about-philosopher.html?pagewanted=all&src=pm>.

[601] Jean Bethke Elshtain, "Don't Be Cruel: Reflections on Rortyan Liberalism", *Richard Rorty*, edited by Charles Guignon and David R. Hiley, Cambridge: Cambridge University Press, 2003, 139.
[602] David Rondel, "Liberalism, Ethnocentrism, and Solidarity: Reflections on Rorty", 2009, <http://www.davidrondel.com/David_Rondel/Papers_files/Reflections%20on%20Rorty.pdf>, 16 note 4.
[603] Richard Rorty, "Response to Bernstein", *Rorty and Pragmatism: The Philosopher Responds to His Critics*, edited by Herman J. Saatkamp Jr, London: Vanderbilt University Press, 1995, 69.
[604] Richard Rorty, *Take Care of Freedom and Truth Will Take Care of Itself: Interviews with Richard Rorty*, edited by Eduardo Mendieta, Stanford: Stanford University Press, 2006, 32.
[605] Richard Rorty, *Contingency, Irony, and Solidarity*, 59.
[606] Steven A. Miller, "Richard Rorty's Sellarsian Uptake", *Pragmatism Today*, 2(1), 2011, 101.
[607] Cf. Tom Hilde, comment posted on "Peter Levine: A Blog for Civic Renewal", 1st March 2006, <http://www.peterlevine.ws/mt/archives/000805.html>.
[608] E.g. Asger Sørensen's assessment of the effectiveness of the vague expression "cultural Marxism" in contemporary politics (*Capitalism, Alienation and Critique*, Aarhus: Nordic Summer University Press, 2016).
[609] Cf. Roland Barthes, "L'ancienne rhétorique". Barthes argues that rhetoric is not only a technique (i.e., the democratic art of persuasion) but also a system of instruction (i.e., the standard education of the affluent youth in ancient Greece and Rome), a science evolved over 2,500 years (i.e., the observation, classification and explanation of a vast array of linguistic phenomena), an ethic (i.e., rules for proper speech and writing), a social practice (i.e., the public demonstration of the affluent class's ownership of cultured language), and a ludic practice (i.e., the poor's reversal of the affluent's ethic and social practice by rhetoric-rich humour).
[610] Cf. ibid.
[611] Vilfredo Pareto, *The Mind and Society*, §§ 1430–1 & 1434.
[612] Cf. Deirdre McCloskey, *The Rhetoric of Economics*; and Alan G. Gross, *The Rhetoric of Science*.
[613] Cf. Quintilian, *Institutes of Oratory*, edited by Lee Honeycutt, <http://rhetoric.eserver.org/quintilian/>, 95.
[614] Cf. Friedrich Nietzsche, "Rhetorik", *Gesammelte Werke*, vol. 5, Lectures 1872–76, Munich: Musarion Verlag, 1922, 287–319. In this connection, rhetoric is nothing but a technique organising and exploiting the inherent rhetorical character of human language, also known as "rhetoricality" among scholars (e.g., John Bender and David E. Wellbery, "Rhetoricality: On the Modernist Return to Rhetoric", *The Ends of Rhetoric*, Stanford: Stanford University Press, 1990, 3–41).
[615] Vilfredo Pareto, *The Mind and Society*, §§ 1407 & 1932.
[616] Cf. William Van Orman Quine, "Two Dogmas of Empiricism", *The Philosophical Review*, 60, 1951, 20–43.
[617] Cf. Jenny Teichman, "The Philosophy of We".
[618] Chaïm Perelman and Lucie Olbrechts-Tyteca, *The New Rhetoric*, 19.
[619] Ibid., 51.
[620] Ibid.
[621] Ibid., 62.
[622] Kenneth Burke, *A Rhetoric of Motives*, 20.

[623] Ibid., 172.
[624] Ibid., 41 & 43 (emphasis in the original).
[625] Ibid., 21 (emphasis in the original).
[626] Ibid., 178.
[627] Richard Rorty, "Postmodernist Bourgeois Liberalism", *Objectivity, Relativism, and Truth*, 200.
[628] Chantal Mouffe, *On the Political*, Abingdon, UK: Routledge, 2005, 18.
[629] Taking into account rhetoric, "they" may even mean "we", as when Rorty refers to "historicist philosophers like Ortega [y Gasset]" and writes that "they think" and "but Ortega would reply" while it is obvious that Rorty thinks and would reply in the very same way (Richard Rorty, "Philosophy-envy", *Daedalus*, 133(4), 2004, 23).
[630] Richard Rorty, "Who Are We? Moral Universalism and Economic Triage", *Diogenes*, 173, 1996, 5.
[631] John Tambornino, "Philosophy as the Mirror of Liberalism: The Politics of Richard Rorty", *Polity*, 30(1), 1997, 67.
[632] Christopher M. Duncan, "A Question to Richard Rorty", 412–3.
[633] Keith Topper, "Richard Rorty, Liberalism and the Politics of Redescription", *American Political Science Review*, 89(4), 1995, 961.
[634] Cf. Chantal Mouffe, "Deconstruction, Pragmatism and the Politics of Difference", *Deconstruction and Pragmatism*, edited by Chantal Mouffe, London: Routledge, 1996, 9.
[635] Cf. John Tambornino, "Philosophy as the Mirror of Liberalism", 78.
[636] Cf. Simon Critchley, "Deconstruction and Pragmatism: Is Derrida a Private Ironist or a Public Liberal?", *Deconstruction and Pragmatism*, 25; and Graeme Garrard, "The Curious Enlightenment of Professor Rorty", *Critical Review*, 14(4), 2000, 428.
[637] Ernesto Laclau, *Emancipation(s)*, London: Verso, 1996, 120.
[638] Richard Rorty, "Remarks on Deconstruction and Pragmatism", *Deconstruction and Pragmatism*, 17.
[639] Richard Rorty, "Response to Simon Critchley", *Deconstruction and Pragmatism*, 45.
[640] Cf. Ian Shapiro, *Political Criticism*, Berkeley: University of California Press, 1990, 37.
[641] Cornel West, *The American Evasion of Philosophy: A Genealogy of Pragmatism*, Madison: The University of Wisconsin Press, 1989, 207.
[642] Chantal Mouffe, *On the Political*, 87.
[643] Gayatri Chakravorty Spivak, *A Critique of Postcolonial Reason: Toward a History of the Vanishing Present*, Cambridge, MA: Harvard University Press, 1999, 354 note 59.
[644] Keith Topper, "Richard Rorty, Liberalism and the Politics of Redescription", 954.
[645] Christopher Voparil, "Rortyan Cultural Politics and the Problem of Speaking for Others", *Contemporary Pragmatism*, 8(1), 2011, 125.
[646] Cf. Keith Topper, "Richard Rorty, Liberalism and the Politics of Redescription", 963.
[647] Cf. Urs Marti, "Die Fallen des Paternalismus. Eine Kritik an Richard Rortys politischer Philosophie", *Deutsche Zeitschrift für Philosophie*, 44(2), 1996, 268.

[648] Clifford Geertz, "The Uses of Diversity", *Michigan Quarterly Review*, 25(1), 1986, 113.
[649] Cf. Richard Rorty, "On Ethnocentrism: A Reply to Clifford Geertz", *Michigan Quarterly Review*, 25(3), 1986, 526.
[650] E.g. Marianne Janack, "Rorty on Ethnocentrism and Exclusion", *The Journal of Speculative Philosophy*, 12(3), 1998, 214.
[651] Cf. Seyla Benhabib, *The Claims of Culture: Equality and Diversity in the Global Era*, Princeton: Princeton University Press, 2002, 33.
[652] Richard Rorty, "Method, Social Science, and Social Hope", *Consequences of Pragmatism*, Minneapolis: University of Minnesota, 1982, 210 note 16.
[653] Cf. Gayatri Chakravorty Spivak, *A Critique of Postcolonial Reason*, 354 note 59; and Urs Marti, "Die Fallen des Paternalismus", 269.
[654] Richard J. Bernstein, "One Step Forward, Two Steps Backward", 541 & 556; cf. also Cornel West, *The American Evasion of Philosophy*, 207; Simon Critchley, "Deconstruction and Pragmatism", 24; and Farid Abdel-Nour, "Liberalism and Ethnocentrism", *The Journal of Political Philosophy*, 8(2), 2000, 224.
[655] Cf. Ian Shapiro, *Political Criticism*, 37.
[656] Richard J. Bernstein, "One Step Forward, Two Steps Backward", 545 & 547.
[657] Robert Burch, "Conloquium Interruptum: Stopping to Think", *Anti-Foundationalism and Practical Reasoning*, edited by Evan Simpson, Edmonton, Canada: Academic, 1987, 102.
[658] Bernhard Waldenfels, *Verfremdung der Moderne: Phänomenologische Grenzgänge*, Göttingen: Wallstein, 2001, 74.
[659] Richard Rorty, "Response to Udo Tietz", *Hinter den Spiegeln: Beiträge zur Philosophie Richard Rortys*, edited by Thomas Schäfer, Udo Tietz and Rüdiger Zill, Frankfurt on Main: Suhrkamp, 2001, 110 (English draft available at Richard Rorty born digital files, 1988–2003, University of California, Irvine: MS-C017-FD029).
[660] Richard Rorty, "Solidarity or Objectivity?", *Objectivity, Relativism, and Truth*, 21–34.
[661] Richard Rorty, "Pragmatism, Relativism, and Irrationalism", *Consequences of Pragmatism*, 173.
[662] Richard Rorty, "The Priority of Democracy to Philosophy", *Objectivity, Relativism, and Truth*, 177.
[663] Richard Rorty, "On Ethnocentrism", 530.
[664] Richard Rorty, *Contingency, Irony, and Solidarity*, 191.
[665] Richard Rorty, "Response to Udo Tietz", 108.
[666] David A. Hollinger, "How Wide the Circle of the 'We'? American Intellectuals and the Problem of the Ethnos since World War II", *The American Historical Review*, 98(2), 1993, 328.
[667] For such a question-begging attempt, cf. Seyla Benhabib, *The Claims of Culture*, 193 note 5.
[668] Cf. Ethan J. Leib, "Rorty's New School of American Pride: The Constellation of Contestation and Consensus", *Polity*, 36(2), 2004, 178.
[669] Richard Rorty, "Introduction: Antirepresentationalism, Ethnocentrism and Liberalism", *Objectivity, Relativism, and Truth*, 15.
[670] Cf. David A. Hollinger, "How Wide the Circle of the 'We'?", 328.
[671] Cf. Richard J. Bernstein, *The Pragmatic Turn*, Cambridge: Polity Press, 2010, 211.

[672] Richard Rorty, "Letter 4: Richard Rorty to Anindita Balslev", *Cultural Otherness: A Correspondence with Richard Rorty*, edited by Anindita Niyogi Balslev, 2nd ed., Atlanta: Scholars Press, 1999, 70.
[673] Richard Rorty, "On Ethnocentrism", 526; cf. also Pablo Quintanilla, "Truth, Justification, and Ethnocentrism", *Pragmatism Today*, 3(1), 2012, 112.
[674] Cf. Richard Rorty, "Response to Udo Tietz", 111.
[675] Richard Rorty, "Introduction: Antirepresentationalism, Ethnocentrism and Liberalism", 15.
[676] Richard Rorty, "Postmodernist Bourgeois Liberalism", 200–1.
[677] Richard Rorty, "Justice as a Larger Loyalty", *Ethical Perspectives*, 4(2), 1997, 145.
[678] Cf. Richard Rorty, *Contingency, Irony, and Solidarity*, 191.
[679] Richard Rorty, "Justice as a Larger Loyalty", 145.
[680] Richard Rorty, "Response to Thomas Schaefer", *Hinter den Spiegeln*, 198 (English draft available at Richard Rorty born digital files, 1988–2003, University of California, Irvine: MS-C017-FD029).
[681] Richard Rorty, "Response to Udo Tietz", 109.
[682] Udo Tietz, "Das 'principle of charity' und die ethnozentristische Unterbestimmung der hermeneutischen Vernunft", *Hinter den Spiegeln*, 102.
[683] Richard Rorty, "Response to Udo Tietz", 112.
[684] Richard Rorty, *Contingency, Irony, and Solidarity*, 189.
[685] Richard Rorty, "Habermas and Lyotard on Post-Modernity", *Essays on Heidegger and Others: Philosophical Papers II*, Cambridge: Cambridge University Press, 1991, 172.
[686] Michel Foucault, "Polemics, Politics, and Problematizations: An Interview with Michel Foucault", *The Foucault Reader*, edited by Paul Rabinow, New York: Pantheon Books, 1984, 385.
[687] Cf. Richard Rorty, "Response to Thomas Schaefer", 198.
[688] Richard Rorty, "The Demonization of Multiculturalism", *Journal of Blacks in Higher Education*, 7, 1995, 74.
[689] Richard Rorty, "Habermas and Lyotard on Post-Modernity", 167.
[690] Richard Rorty, "Solidarity or Objectivity?", 30.
[691] Richard Rorty, "Introduction: Antirepresentationalism, Ethnocentrism and Liberalism", 13.
[692] Richard Rorty, "Putnam and the Relativist Menace", *Journal of Philosophy*, 90(9), 1993, 452.
[693] Richard Rorty, "Who Are We?", 8.
[694] Richard Rorty, "Introduction: Antirepresentationalism, Ethnocentrism and Liberalism", 15.
[695] Ernesto Laclau, *Emancipation(s)*, 112.
[696] Richard Rorty, "Response to Simon Critchley", 45.
[697] Richard Rorty, "Introduction: Antirepresentationalism, Ethnocentrism and Liberalism", 13–4.
[698] Ibid., 15 note 29.
[699] Richard Rorty, "Cosmopolitanism without Emancipation: A Response to Jean-François Lyotard", *Objectivity, Relativism, and Truth: Philosophical Papers I*, 214.
[700] Ethan J. Leib, "Rorty's New School of American Pride", 191.
[701] David A. Hollinger, "How Wide the Circle of the 'We'?", 328–9.

[702] Ibid.
[703] Cf. Richard Rorty, "A Pragmatist View of Rationality and Cultural Differences", *Philosophy East and West*, 42(4), 1992, 589.
[704] Marcus T. Cicero, *Brutus*, 1776, <http://onlinebooks.library.upenn.edu/webbin/gutbook/lookup?num=9776> (originally published in 46 BC).
[705] Cf. Roland Barthes, "L'ancienne rhétorique".
[706] E.g. D. Shen, *Style and Rhetoric of Short Narrative Fiction: Covert Progressions Behind Overt Plots*, London: Routledge, 2013.
[707] E.g. R. Andrews, *A Theory of Contemporary Rhetoric*, London: Routledge, 2013.
[708] E.g. G.O. Hutchinson, *Greek to Latin: Frameworks and Contexts for Intertextuality*, Oxford: Oxford University Press, 2013.
[709] E.g. C. Hale, *Sin and Syntax: How to Craft Wicked Good Prose*, New York: Three Rivers Press, 2013.
[710] E.g. I. Martin, *Rich People's Movements: Grassroots Campaigns to Untax the One Percent*, New York: Oxford University Press USA, 2013.
[711] E.g. S.B. and J.C. Kaufman, *The Psychology of Creative Writing*, Cambridge: Cambridge University Press, 2009.
[712] E.g. A. Barker, *Improving Your Communication Skills: Creating Success*, Philadelphia: Kogan, 2013.
[713] E.g. G. Rossolatos, *//rhetor.dixit// Understanding and Texts' Rhetorical Structure for Differential Figurative Advantage*, (npa) Create Space, 2013.
[714] E.g. W.D. Hoyer, D.J. MacInnis and R. Pieters, *Consumer Behaviour*, Boston: Cengage Learning, 2012.
[715] E.g. D. Dabner, S. Calvert and A. Casey, *The New Graphic Design School: A Foundation Course in Principles and Practice*, New York: Wiley, 2009.
[716] E.g. C. Killian, *Writing for the Web*, Bellingham: Self-Counsel Press, 2013.
[717] E.g. N. Spiller, *Drawing Architecture AD*, New York: Wiley, 2013.
[718] E.g. S.J. Dobrin and S. Moray, *Ecosee: Image, Rhetoric, Nature*, New York: State University of New York Press, 2009.
[719] E.g. D. Bate, *Photography: The Key Concepts*, London: Bloomsbury Academic, 2009.
[720] Cf. M. Castells, *Communication Power*, New York: Oxford University Press USA, 2013; C.A. Hill and M. Helmers, *Defining Visual Rhetorics*, London: Routledge, 2004; and L.C. Olson, C.A. Finnegan and D.S. Hope, (eds.), *Visual Rhetoric*, Los Angeles: Sage, 2008.
[721] E.g. G. Hart, "Technical Communications Primer: Gestalt Theory and Visual Design", *TechWhirl*, 12th March 2012, <http://techwhirl.com/technical-communications-primer-gestalt-theory-and-visual-design/>; P.M. Lester, *Visual Communication: Images with Messages*, Boston: Cengage Learning, 2013; and J. van den Broek, W. Koetsenruijter, J. de Jong and L. Smit, *Visual Language*, The Hague: Eleven International, 2012.
[722] Cf. R. Luccio, "Gestalt Psychology and Cognitive Psychology", *Humana Mente*, 17, 2011, 95–128.
[723] E.g. E.S. Spelke, K. Breinlinger, K. Jacobson and A. Phillips, "Gestalt Relations and Object Perception: A developmental study", *Perception*, 22, 1993, 1483–501.

[724] E.g. B. Pinna, "New Gestalt Principles of Perceptual Organization: An extension from grouping to shape and meaning", *Gestalt Theory - An International Multidisciplinary Journal*, 32, 2009, 11–78.
[725] Cf. R. McKerrow, "Research in Rhetoric: A Glance at Our Past, Present, and Potential Future", *Review of Communication*, July 2010, 197–210.
[726] Cf. D. Rail, "The Metaphor-gestalt Synergy Underlying the Self-organisation of Perception as a Semiotic Process", *Nonlinear Dynamics, Psychology and Life Sciences*, 17(2), 2013, 205–21; and B. Tuller, P. Case, M. Ding and J.A.S. Kelso, "The Nonlinear Dynamics of Speech Categorization", *Journal of Experimental Psychology, Human Perception and Performance*, 20, 1994, 3–16.
[727] Cf. R.E. Tucker, "Figure, Ground and Presence: A Phenomenology of Meaning in Rhetoric", *Quarterly Journal of Speech*, 87(4), 2001, 396–414.
[728] Cf. L. Talmy, "The Relation of Grammar to Cognition", *Topics in Cognitive Linguistics*, edited by B. Rudzka-Ostyn, Amsterdam: John Benjamins, 1988, 165–205.
[729] Cf. P. Koch, "Frame and Contiguity: On the cognitive basis of metonymy and certain types of word formation", *Metonymy in Language and Thought*, edited by K.U. Panther and G., Radden, Amsterdam: John Benjamins, 1999, 139–69.
[730] D. Rail, "A Model of Language Development Based on Self-Organisation of Gestalts and Metaphor", *Dynamical Psychology*, 2010–1, <http://goertzel.org/dynapsyc/a_model_of_language_development.htm>, §3.
[731] Cf. Max Wertheimer, "Gestalt Theory", *A Source Book of Gestalt Psychology*, edited by W.D. Ellis, New York: Humanities Press, 1938, 1–11 (originally published in 1924).
[732] E.g. B. Hampe and J.E. Grady, *From Perception to Meaning: Image Schemas in Cognitive Linguistics*, Berlin: de Gruyter, 2005.
[733] E.g. M. Barrett, L. Heracleous and G. Walsham, "A Rhetorical Approach to IT Diffusion: Reconceptualizing the Ideology-Framing Relationship in Computerization Movements", *MIS Quarterly*, 37(1), 2013, 201–20.
[734] E.g. J. Aritz and R.C. Walker, (eds.), *Discourse Perspectives on Organizational Communication*, Lanham: Fairleigh Dickinson University Press, 2012.
[735] Cf. G. Burton, *Silva Rhetoricae*, 1997–2007, <http://rhetoric.byu.edu/>.
[736] Cf. Thomas S. Kuhn, *The Structure of Scientific Revolutions*, Chicago: Chicago University Press, 1962.
[737] E. Wickelgren, *CSUS Personal Web Page*, nda, <http://www.csus.edu/indiv/w/wickelgren/>.
[738] N. Hieter, S. Sien, K. Goulet and J. Galea, "Exercise Three: Strategies for Conveying Information", blog entry on *OCAD Introduction to experience design*, 18th January 2009, 16:13, <http://ocad-ited-w09-s1.blogspot.com/2009/01/exercise-three-strategies-for-conveying.html>.
[739] E.g. N. Wolchover, "Breaking the Code: Why Your Barin Can Raed Tihs", *Livescience*, 9th February 2012, <http://www.livescience.com/18392-reading-jumbled-words.html>.
[740] E.g. P. Moore and C. Fitz, "Using Gestalt Theory to Teach Document Design and Graphics", *Technical Communication Quarterly*, 2(4), 1993, 389–410.
[741] Cf. Chaïm Perelman and Lucie Olbrechts-Tyteca, *The New Rhetoric*.
[742] Cf. Kenneth Burke, *A Rhetoric of Motives*.
[743] Cf. J. Nienkamp, *Internal Rhetorics: Towards a History and Theory of Self-Persuasion*, Carbondale: Southern Illinois University Press, 2001.

[744] Cf. L. Albertazzi (ed.), *The Form of Shapes*. New York: Kluwer, 2011.

[745] Cf. Richard Rorty, *Contingency, Irony, and Solidarity*.

[746] Upon the birth of my first son, Kieran Logi Baruchello, I wrote several aphorisms in his honour. They were meant to be a private divertissement, a probable gift, and an attempt to crystallise the practical wisdom of philosophers that I admire. Amidst my aphorisms some drew inspiration from Heidegger's thought, which is pregnant with existential insight, although notoriously abstract and oracular. The aphorisms presented here were translated from Italian—the language in which they were written—into English in view of publication, following an invitation from Professor Gabor Ferge, chief editor of *Existentia*. As such, they are likely to have less lyrical value, if they ever had any, but they might be still an example of how inspirational Heidegger's thought can be, despite Heidegger's fully deserved bad name *qua* proud Nazi and the intricacies of his thought.

[747] The ecological, moral and aesthetic wisdom of the "stationary state" of growth advocated by liberal icon John Stuart Mill is regularly forgotten by today's self-proclaimed heralds of the liberal order (cf. *Principles of Political Economy*, book IV, chapter VI, section 2; 7th ed. ,1871)

[748] Eric J. Hobsbawm, "Should the Poor Organize?", a review of *Poor People's Movements: Why They Succeed, How They Fail*, by Frances Fox Piven and Richard A. Cloward (New York: Pantheon, 1977), *The New York Review of Books*, 25, 23rd March 1978, 44–9.

[749] Because of its hierarchical structure, it is possible to speak of "the Catholic Church" as a clearly unified body or corporation, for it possesses a supreme head, i.e. the Pope, who exercises final authority and issues binding official statements, notably encyclicals (circular letters) on doctrine.

[750] Giacomo Leopardi, "La ginestra", *I canti*, 1835, v.51, <http://www.leopardi.it/canti34.php> (translation mine). I adhere hereby to the long-established convention of referring to the Catholic Church as a "she", given its Biblical role as "the Bride of Christ" (*Ephesians* 5:27) and the feminine gender of the Greek noun ἐκκλησία, which is used in the New Testament.

[751] Cf. John K. Galbraith, *The Age of Uncertainty* (London: BBC, 1977) for an effective presentation of some of the aims and effects of the late-19th-century marriage between scientific racial theories (especially Herbert Spencer's social Darwinism) and US Protestantism. Compare this with G.K. Chesterton, *What I Saw in America* (New York: Dodd, Mead & Co., 1922), for an early Catholic critique of it.

[752] Cf. *The Catholic Encyclopedia*, edited by Charles G. Herbermann, Edward A. Pace, Conde B. Fallen, Thomas J. Shahan and John J. Wynne (New York: Robert Appleton, 1907–12), s.v. "Divine Providence".

[753] Birgir Guðmundsson and Markus Meckl, "The North Pole Mission in Iceland. 1857 – 1858", *Þjóðarspegillinn: Ráðstefna í félagsvísindum XV*, edited by Helga Ólafs and Thamar M. Heijstra, Reykjavík: University of Iceland Press, 2014, 1.

[754] Cf. Paul Misner, "The Predecessors of *Rerum Novarum* within Catholicism", *Review of Social Economy*, 49, 4, 1991, 444–64.

⁷⁵⁵ Cf. *Cathopedia*, 20th June 2016, s.v. "Chiese scomparse di Forlì", for a representative list of churches and monasteries that disappeared in the town of Forlì alone, mostly during the French occupation and then after the birth of the Kingdom of Italy (<http://it.cathopedia.org/wiki/Chiese_scomparse_di_Forl%C3%AC>). Whilst the Reformation had already caused the looting and destruction of many religious edifices in Britain, central and northern Europe, France and Italy witnessed analogous phenomena primarily in the very late 18th century and throughout the 19th century. However beneficial or justified such trends might have ever been, they were not even the most patent signs of conflict between the Church of Rome and the liberal powers of the age. The captivity of two popes under Napoleon Bonaparte (1769–1821) and the military conquest of Rome by the Kingdom of Italy in 1870 are plausibly stronger signs of this friction.

⁷⁵⁶ Socialism, like liberalism, has many fathers and many faces, but the role of the French Revolution and of Jacobinism in both its birth and its growth was noteworthy, cf. G.D.H. Cole, *Socialist Thought: The Forerunners, 1789-1850, Vol. I* (London: MacMillan, 1953) and George Lichtheim, *The Origins of Socialism* (New York: Weidenfeld & Nicolson, 1969).

⁷⁵⁷ Pontifical Council for Justice and Peace, *Compendium of the Social Doctrine of the Church*, 2004, § 49, <http://www.vatican.va/roman_curia/pontifical_councils/justpeace/documents/rc_pc_justpeace_doc_20060526_compendio-dott-soc_en.html#The Church, sign and defender of the transcendence of the human person>.

⁷⁵⁸ For examples of 19th-century liberal and socialist anticlericalism, cf. *European Anti-Catholicism in a Comparative and Transnational* Perspective, edited by Yvonne M. Werner and Jonas Harvard, Leiden: Brill, 2013.

⁷⁵⁹ Gilbert Keith Chesterton, *St. Thomas Aquinas*, 1933, chapter 1 "On Two Friars", <http://gutenberg.net.au/ebooks01/0100331.txt>.

⁷⁶⁰ Pius X, *Pascendi Dominici Gregis*, 8th September 1907, §§ 9–10 & 14–7, <http://w2.vatican.va/content/pius-x/en/encyclicals/documents/hf_p-x_enc_19070908_pascendi-dominici-gregis.html>.

⁷⁶¹ Ibid., § 17.

⁷⁶² Michael Polanyi, *Personal Knowledge*, 281.

⁷⁶³ Michael Oakeshott makes an analogous point in his 1933 book *Experience and Its Modes* (Cambridge: Cambridge University Press, 1986): different disciplined discover different truths about reality because of their defining standpoint of observation and study. The natural sciences approach it *sub specie quantitatis*; politics, economics, ethics and jurisprudence *sub specie voluntatis*; history *sub specie praeteritorum*; and philosophy or metaphysics *sub specie aeternitatis*.

⁷⁶⁴ Pius X, *Pascendi Dominici Gregis*, § 19.

[765] Cf. Brian Edwin Ferme, *Introduction to the History and Sources of Canon Law: The Ancient Law up to the* Decretum *of Gratian*, Montreal: Wilson & Lafleur, 2007; and Wilfrid Hartmann and Kenneth Pennington (eds.), *The History of Medieval Canon Law in the Classical Period, 1140-1234: From Gratian to the Decretals of Pope Gregory IX*, Washington: The Catholic University of America Press, 2008. Famous Catholic historian Brian Tierney observes also that in the age of revival of Roman and canon law, i.e. the 12th and 13th centuries, constitutional conceptions, documents and institutions became more and more common (e.g. "Scandinavia... Spain... England... Hungary"), to the point of "trying to replace papal monarchy [itself] with conciliar government" ("Medieval Canon Law and Western Constitutionalism", *The Catholic Historical Review*, 52(1), April 1966, 6).

[766] Protestant confessions and conceptions are now too many and too diverse to be characterised in any straightforward manner on this point.

[767] Pius X, *Pascendi Dominici Gregis*, § 14.

[768] The reader may wish to compare the Protestant's abandonment of established interpretative tradition to the decision of today's school boards or ministries to drop subjects such as music, art history, geography or higher maths in primary and/or secondary schools. Gaps, if not sheer black holes, are thus formed in the pupils' education, such that, later on in life, they are not only unable to recover the losses, but also of grasping the value of those disciplines, hence reinforcing the novel form of ignorance that was generated by the original bureaucratic and pedagogical decision.

[769] E.g. Hogweard, "Churches of Scotland timeline.png", *Wikipedia*, 22nd September 2014, <https://en.wikipedia.org/wiki/Church_of_Scotland#/media/File:Churches_of_Scotland_timeline.svg>:

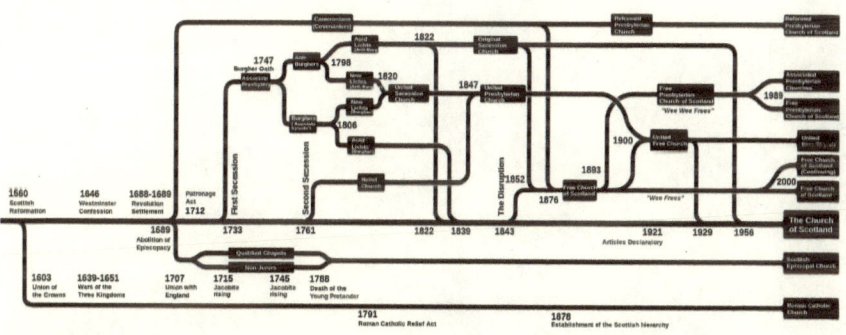

[770] Pius X, "The Oath Against Modernism", 1st September 1910, <http://www.papalencyclicals.net/Pius10/p10moath.htm>. Tradition, i.e. holding fast to the valuable legacy of the past, is granted importance over innovation, i.e. the quest for novel, 'modern' things. Over the course of the 20th century, however, Pius X's emphasis on tradition and abhorrence of modernity were gradually diluted.

[771] The case of 21st-century Greece is particularly telling of these troubling trends and striking contradictions (cf. Yannis Varoufakis, *Adults in the Room. My Battle with Europe's Deep Establishment*, London: Bodley Head, 2017).

[772] Julia Kristeva, *Les nouvelles maladies de l'âme*, Paris: Fayard, 1993.

[773] Luce Irigaray, *Sharing the World*, London: Continuum, 2000, 134–5.

www.ingramcontent.com/pod-product-compliance
Lightning Source LLC
Chambersburg PA
CBHW021849230426
43671CB00006B/318